Democracy in Crisis
Around the World

Democracy in Crisis Around the World

Edited by
Saliba Sarsar and Rekha Datta

LEXINGTON BOOKS
Lanham • Boulder • New York • London

Published by Lexington Books
An imprint of The Rowman & Littlefield Publishing Group, Inc.
4501 Forbes Boulevard, Suite 200, Lanham, Maryland 20706
www.rowman.com

6 Tinworth Street, London SE11 5AL, United Kingdom

British Library Cataloguing in Publication Information Available

Library of Congress Cataloging-in-Publication Data

Names: Sarsar, Saliba G., 1955- editor. | Datta, Rekha, editor.
Title: Democracy in crisis around the world / edited by Saliba Sarsar and Rekha Datta.
Description: Lanham, Maryland : Lexington Books, 2020. | Includes bibliographical references. | Summary: "Democracies across the globe are in crisis as authoritarian regimes rise and populist leaders emerge worldwide. Democracy in Crisis across the World weaves threads of history and politics in two parts to analyze how long this trend may last and what the future may bring"—Provided by publisher.
Identifiers: LCCN 2020033154 (print) | LCCN 2020033155 (ebook) | ISBN 9781793601667 (cloth) | ISBN 9781793601674 (epub) ISBN 9781793601681 (pbk)
Subjects: LCSH: Democracy—Case studies. | Democratization—Case studies. | Comparative government—Case studies. | World politics—21st century—Case studies.
Classification: LCC JC423 .D381318 2020 (print) | LCC JC423 (ebook) | DDC 321.8—dc23
LC record available at https://lccn.loc.gov/2020033154
LC ebook record available at https://lccn.loc.gov/2020033155

To Our Students and Students Around the World.
Our Democracies Need you

Contents

PART II: COUNTRY CASE STUDIES 143

Acknowledgments

This book, *Democracy in Crisis around the World*, is important as it examines a vital issue facing humanity. Different world regions and key countries are experiencing difficulties maintaining the strength of some of their basic democratic institutions and sustaining the core of their enduring political principles and values. Increasingly, authoritarian regimes are flexing their muscles and populist leaders with authoritarian tendencies are asserting themselves. How long will this trend last? What will the future bring? Ultimately, much depends on citizens—all of us—working together, and through proper elected leaders, to address needs and ensure democracy's responsiveness and viability.

When the idea of writing about democracy in crisis was shared with colleagues at Monmouth University, the response was immediate and enthusiastic. With research and teaching interests in international relations, area studies, American politics, history, criminal justice, and pedagogical analyses, they proceeded to author or co-author individual chapters on five world regions (i.e., Sub-Saharan Africa, Eastern Europe, Western Europe, Latin America, and the Middle East and North Africa), and four major countries (i.e., India, China, Russia, and the United States). It is to them that we express our deep gratitude: Julius O. Adekunle, Kenneth L. Campbell, Stephen J. Chapman, Kevin L. Dooley, Justin M. Liu, Peter W. Liu, Samuel Maynard, Kenneth Mitchell, Joseph Patten, and Thomas S. Pearson. Similarly, when the book proposal was submitted for consideration to Lexington Books, Joseph Parry, the acquisitions editor, was most receptive. It is to him and to Alison Keefner, assistant editor at Lexington Books, that we extend our heartfelt thanks for their guidance and assistance. This work was supported, in part, by a Creativity and Research Grant from Monmouth University. It is gratefully acknowledged.

Saliba Sarsar and Rekha Datta

Introduction

Saliba Sarsar and Rekha Datta

Dreams of freedom and waves of democracy have captured the imagination and aspirations of people around the world for centuries. Scholars and practitioners have prolonged debated about the Western and non-Western origins as well as the virtues and vicissitudes of democracy. Winston S. Churchill once acknowledged the flaws of this ideal form of government when he said, "Indeed, it has been said that democracy is the worst form of Government except for all those other forms that have been tried from time to time."[1]

As we move toward the third decade of the twenty-first century, democracy seems to be at a crossroads worldwide. The wave of democracy that swept through most of the world in the twentieth century was followed by the Arab Spring movement in the second decade of the twenty-first century that brought democratic hopes of many in the Middle East to the attention of their rulers and others. In recent years, the world has been witnessing the rise of populist leaders with authoritarian tendencies in established as well as in fledgling democracies. The question, therefore, arises whether we are facing a crisis of democracy and what the underlying causes and impact of such a trend would mean for the values of liberty and equality.

Freedom House, "an [American] independent watchdog organization dedicated to the expansion of freedom and democracy around the world,"[2] has been a leading voice in reporting and promoting political rights and civil liberties globally. In its 2017 overview essay, "Populists and Autocrats: The Dual Threat to Global Democracy," it is argued that freedom in the world is facing major challenges. Out of the 195 countries assessed, 87 (45%) are rated Free, 59 (30%) Partly Free, and 49 (25%) Not Free. Even countries rated Free had major setbacks in freedom compared with prior annual scores. These include Brazil, the Czech Republic, Denmark, France, Hungary, Poland, Serbia, South Africa, South Korea, Spain, Tunisia, and the United

States.[3] Two years later, Freedom House titled its Freedom in the World 2019 report, "Democracy in Retreat." The evidence is clear: "Between 2005 and 2018, the share of Not Free countries rose to 26 percent, while the share of Free countries declined to 44 percent."[4] Most troubling in the recent past has been the challenge to American democracy, which is "testing the stability of its constitutional system and threatening to undermine political rights and civil liberties worldwide."[5]

When viewed through a world regional prism, the Middle East and North Africa (MENA) region scores the worst. The prevalence of authoritarian rule in some countries of the Persian Gulf combined with conflict and violence in such MENA countries as Iraq, Syria, Yemen, and Libya produced a negative performance. It is followed by Eurasia that has "incumbents armored against the future." Sub-Saharan Africa also has "entrenched autocrats and fragile institutions." Asia Pacific has a few rulers who are abusing their mandate and committing crimes, while stifling any opposition to their authority. Europe, a fortress of democratic solidity, is witnessing fissures in its structure, created in part by the Brexit vote and Britain's withdrawal from Europe in 2020, some populist leanings, the migrant/refugee crisis, and Russian meddling in European affairs. Finally, even the Americas region, which has enjoyed some modicum of relative peace and stability, is now experiencing aspects of populism and turmoil.

The Economist Intelligence Unit (EIU), which is "the research and analysis division of The Economist Group" and "the world leader in business intelligence,"[6] found comparable results. In its Democracy Index 2015, titled "Democracy in an Age of Anxiety," it reported a decline of democracy in North America, Eastern Europe, and the MENA but a slight rise in Asia and Australasia and in Sub-Saharan Africa. Latin America and Western Europe remained the same.[7] A year later, the status of democracy worsened when no region experienced an improvement in its average score and almost twice as many countries (seventy-two) recorded a decline in their total score as recorded an improvement (thirty-eight). Eastern Europe experienced the most severe regression. The EIU's 2016 Democracy Index report, "Revenge of the 'Deplorables'," examined the deep roots of today's crisis of democracy in the developed world, and looked at how democracy fared in every world region. Almost one-half of the world's countries can be considered undemocratic of some sort, and the number of "full democracies" declined from 20 in 2015 to 19 in 2016. The United States has been downgraded from a "full democracy" to a "flawed democracy" because of a further erosion of trust in government and elected officials there.[8]

These and other concerns about democracy or its lack thereof have been voiced in literary circles over the past two decades. In *The Future of Freedom*, Fareed Zakaria holds that democracy does not function under all conditions.

It needs robust parameters to operate properly.[9] Like James Madison in the Federalist Paper No. 51, he defends the checks and balances in the Constitution so as to avoid tyranny of the majority from ruining the whole system and producing demagogues. In *The Life and Death of Democracy*, political theorist John Keane warns about the fragile state of democracy and calls for taking curative measures before it is too late.[10] Marc F. Plattner cites three sources of doubt about democracy: "1. The growing sense that the advanced democracies are in trouble in terms of their economic and political performance; 2. The new self-confidence and seeming vitality of some authoritarian countries; and 3. The shifting geopolitical balance between the democracies and their rivals."[11] In his book, *What is Populism*, Jan-Werner Muller views populists as "a real danger to democracy" and populism as "not a corrective to liberal democracy in the sense of bringing politics 'closer to the people.'"[12] In their book, *How Democracies Die*, Steven Levitsky and Daniel Ziblatt believe that democracies can and do die. Their death does not necessarily come like a bolt, as in a revolution or military coup, but gradually as critical institutions such as the judiciary and the press, weaken.[13] In her book, *Fascism: A Warning*, Madeleine Albright, former U.S. Secretary of State, holds that fascism, which persisted even after World War II, is now threatening international security, peace, and justice around the world.[14]

Naomi Chazan artfully summarizes why democracies are regressing. This involves "three analytically distinct components that together combine to create an encompassing syndrome of democratic recession: illiberalism, neo-authoritarianism, and populism." Illiberalism includes the curbing of political freedoms of both individuals and groups, which relate to democratic rights; the restrictions imposed on nongovernmental organizations, and the reduction or halt of subsidies to cultural organizations and programs. Neo-authoritarianism weaken the institutions of good governance by "tampering with key democratic guardrails (such as constitutions and political parties), emasculating structural checks and balances (notably parliaments and the judiciary), and restraining democratic watchdogs (especially the media and civil society)."[15] As per Steven Levitsky and Daniel Ziblatt, these crush institutional checks and balances, lessen accountability, boost the centralization of power, and advance its personalization.[16] Populism, usually emanating from below, concerns the loosening of liberal norms of compromise, mutual tolerance, and pluralism, among others, especially "when manipulated either by pretenders to power or its occupants as a means to achieving or maintaining political control."[17]

As this book was nearing completion, the coronavirus pandemic erupted. Starting in the city of Wuhan in China's Hubei province in the latter part of 2019, it gave some countries the green light to use or exploit emergency powers or extreme measures in their fight against it. While coordinated, collective, and serious actions are most needed in health crises, including travel restrictions, closure of nonessential businesses, institutions, and services, as well as practicing of physical or social distancing, such actions must be temporary, must not radically encroach or obliterate civil liberties and privacy protections, and must not enable authoritarian creep. A quick tour around the world points to grave concerns. In China, "A new system uses software to dictate quarantines—and appears to send personal data to police, in a troubling precedent for automated social control."[18] In Hungary, the right-wing prime minister Viktor Orbán, who has elevated his political credentials over the years by vilifying immigrants, "told his counterparts there was a 'clear link' between migrants and the coronavirus."[19] In the United States, a similar story happened where a White House staffed by xenophobes used "the coronavirus to strengthen border controls it has long wanted to embrace."[20] In Iran, security forces ensured that streets remained empty and mass gatherings did not materialize. In Jordan, the government implemented Defense Law No. 13, which is essentially a state of emergency that applies all measures necessary to secure the health and safety of the public.[21] The coronavirus-democracy link was also clearly expressed in Israel, where Prime Minister Benjamin Netanyahu conflated "the essential struggle against the deadly pandemic with his own political and personal interests."[22] This is in addition to the government that utilized "hugely intrusive digital technology to track the movements of diagnosed Israelis—and potentially anyone in Israel—in order to inform those people who have unwittingly been in 10-minutes or more of close proximity to a virus carrier that they must immediately self-quarantine."[23] It can be argued that authoritarian regimes have become more repressive and democratic regimes have become less democratic or open. The concern is that some of the controls imposed during the pandemic may continue past the pandemic and have a long-term negative effect on basic freedoms and democratic trends.

THIS BOOK AND ITS STRUCTURE

This book, titled *Democracy in Crisis Around the World*, will weave threads of history and politics in two parts. While the first part primarily focuses on five world regions (i.e., Sub-Saharan Africa, Eastern Europe, Western Europe, Latin America, and the MENA), the second highlights four major countries (i.e., India, China, Russia, and the United States). Hence, the reader will gain more breadth from the former and more depth from the latter. These two parts will be bookended by chapter 1 offering an overview of various measures of democracy and chapter 11 assessing how different democracy indicators align with the various regions and countries that serve as the focal points of the previous chapters. Each of the eleven chapters ends with discussion, questions, and suggested readings for further analysis and study.

What is of interest about this book is that the authors happen to be all associated with Monmouth University. They represent the academic specializations of political science, history, and criminal justice; they originate from various areas of the world, specifically Jerusalem, India, Nigeria, China, and the United States; and ten of the twelve authors have had field research experiences in varying international locales, including Israel, Palestine, India, Nigeria, Russia, Argentina, England, Ireland, and China.

While the authors are fully aware of the crisis facing democracy, they hope to establish that liberty, equality, and the fundamental premises of democracy are shared values and universally sought. Although not a votary of democracy, while discussing it in his *Politics*, Aristotle emphasized that "For if liberty and equality, as is thought by some, are chiefly to be found in democracy, they will be best attained when all persons alike share in the government to the utmost."[24] Perhaps therein rests a possible solution even though not a panacea to achieving sustainable democracies. Stable institutions, civic engagement, and political participation would be key to fulfilling democratic aspirations of nations, however varied and culturally, economically, historically, and politically diverse. Moreover, in the ultimate analysis, the issue is not to give up the quest for democracy because of the challenges and shortcomings a country or world region are facing at a particular time and dismissing them as unfit for democracy. As Amartya Sen has reminded us, the question is not whether a country is fit for democracy; our aim should be to make a country fit through democracy.[25]

Chapter 1 introduces numerous measures scholars employ to quantify democracy. It begins with a general overview of the differences between qualitative and quantitative methodology as these approaches are of utmost importance for researchers to show evidence for their arguments. It delves into topics such as quantification, validity, and reliability. The chapter then proceeds to discussing specific measures including Polity IV, Freedom House, Varieties of Democracy (V-Dem) measures, the EIU Democracy Index, Democracy Barometer, and the World Values Survey. It places heavy emphasis on the Polity and Freedom House measures as they are highly common within the scholarship relating to democracy, comparative politics, and international relations. A dissection of the fundamental concepts is provided that comprise both measures. In order to have a more nuanced view of the complexity involved in measuring the multifaceted concept of democracy, a general description of additional variables scholars and students can use is given. The chapter then constitutes a good primer for the subsequent, region-specific and country-specific chapters by placing readers in a critical perspective to analyze the complexity of the historical and contemporary examples discussed.

Chapter 2 addresses democracy and its changing phases in Sub-Saharan Africa. It analyzes how Africans incorporated some elements of democracy into their political systems long before contact with the Europeans. The traces of modern democracy indicate that Africans were not oblivious of the devolution of power or rights of the people, but their conception of democracy was different from that of the Europeans. The advent of the Europeans generated a shift in the understanding and practice of democracy, which caused a reinterpretation and reorientation of African democracy. The parliamentary system, for example, introduced some elements that were nonexistent earlier. The change to the European model initially posed a challenge, but Africans adapted. One of the common elements of democracy is election, which was not fully part of African democracy, but which Africans are now familiar with and practice. The gaining of independence from colonial rule ushered African states into the global community where democracy is the acceptable form of government. This does not mean that all African states practice democracy in its true sense. The impact of the Cold War and the varying ideologies is an indication that some African countries leaned toward and experimented with some aspects of socialism, as happened in Ghana, Tanzania, and Angola in the early days of independence.

Chapter 3 examines democracy in transition, as illustrated by political trends in Eastern Europe. In 2004, for example, Hungary formally joined the European Union as an exemplar of democratization. The decades of communist repression and military control had given way to a republic that was finally in control of its own collective destiny. Its institutions promoted economic development and its constitution protected citizens' rights. By 2019, however, the political situation has unraveled. Since consolidating power, the Fidesz Party and its leader Viktor Orbán have systematically dismantled many of the features that had defined postcommunist Hungary. In doing so, Orbán has developed a new governing strategy for his country and for others in the region—the *illiberal democracy*—a state that has democratic institutions, but lacks the protections that are associated with liberal democracies.

The challenge to democracy has impacted Western Europe as well, as explained in chapter 4. Divisions, exacerbated by mistrust in the mainstream media and the rise of social media platforms, are widening. Identity politics emphasize the differences between peoples within countries and among different countries, lessening society's commitment to a common good and provoking disagreement based on unchangeable markers of identity rather than on issues or policy. Optimists hold that technology could help to facilitate democracy because of the increased access available to individual citizens and the ease with which they can form groups or political associations that might allow them to influence government or policy. Others worry about the power that the internet and surveillance technology provides governments to spy on and control their citizens. Still others stress that many people remain excluded from the public forum, even in an age of increased access to information and online forums for expression. The controversy over Britain's exit from the European Union provides a useful case study for the ways in which these general factors have played out in Western European democracies in recent years. Meanwhile, developments in Spain, Italy, France, Germany, and the European Union as a whole further illustrate many of the trends, although they also highlight how differences in culture and history can lead to different results and which issues become most prominent.

Chapter 5 considers democracy in Latin America, which predates other regions of the developing world. Yet, across the region, instability and periodic democratic collapse at the hands of the military riddled the twentieth century, and a general pattern of volatility continues to the present. This chapter reviews the literature on democratic transition and consolidation, exploring whether socioeconomic modernization theory and institutional models illuminate what ails Latin American democracy today. An alternative approach is articulated, one that links popular support as well as popular disenchantment with democracy to the concept of contemporary social contracts consummated around long-term socioeconomic development. Two country case studies—Venezuela and Argentina—test rival explanations of democratic instability and backsliding in Latin America. Venezuela's drift into civilian authoritarian rule and Argentina's chaotic yet resilient democracy present two common national trajectories that are apt to surface in the future. In the Venezuelan case, traditional political parties failed to provide voters with legitimate choices at the ballot box and voters soon ditched democratic norms and expectations in favor of mob rule. In contrast, Argentina's traditional Peronist Party continues to anchor and polarize politics, assuring that voters have choices on Election Day and an organized partisan opposition after Election Day to gravitate toward when socioeconomic conditions deteriorate.

In chapter 6, it is argued that the MENA region is far from being democratic. It consists of a few quasi-democratic countries and a large number of authoritarian or autocratic regimes where ruling elites have staying power and where moves toward good governance, accountability, and transparency are not consistent or robust. The past two decades have witnessed the ups and downs of change in Arab states, as expressed by what became known as the Arab Spring, which started in Tunisia at the end of 2010 and then spread to most other MENA countries. The results—toppling of a few authoritarian leaders as in Tunisia, Egypt, and Libya and civil wars and wars as in Syria, Libya, and Yemen—and their implications are yet to be fully expressed. The profiles of seven countries—Tunisia, Egypt, Jordan, Qatar, Iran, Israel, and Turkey—are then presented to show both similarities and differences within the region along the democratic spectrum. This is followed by measuring democracy in seventeen Arab and three non-Arab countries through consideration of multiple variables that address governance and representative government, media freedom, religious liberty, human rights, human development, and economic freedom. The chapter concludes with suggestions for advancing democratic rule in the MENA region, good governance, political accountability, the empowerment of citizens, especially women and the youth.

Chapter 7 concentrates on India's party system as being pivotal in its sojourn with democracy. Whereas the recent decades have witnessed political parties scrambling for coalition success and economic liberalization, the Bharatiya Janata Party (BJP) is moving away from the party-centric institutionalization of democratic governance to a party that has increasingly rightist identity-based nationalism. Despite the poor outcome of the demonetization policy of the Modi government and lackadaisical economic growth, Prime Minister Narendra Damodardas Modi and the BJP returned to power in 2019 with a significant mandate. The success of the BJP despite failing to keep its promise of economic development presents a puzzle. The BJP has successfully aligned and reinforced its platform with religious and nationalistic narrative, even authoritarian tactics to curb free expression of dissent. This is finding traction in a republic that was formed on principles of secularism in a nation where more than 80 percent of the people identify themselves as Hindus. With its platforms of Hindutva and nationalism, is the BJP poised to become a one-party system to rival the dominance of the Indian National Congress of the past decades, which was based on the foundation of secularism and state-sponsored growth, or will India find its argumentative culture to overcome this onslaught to the foundations of democracy?

Chapter 8 holds that free thinking and free speech are the most formidable threats to the rule of the Chinese Communist Party (CCP). In the Internet age, the CCP has remodeled its method of control in order to build a society of digital authoritarianism that consists of a real-time, nationwide surveillance network, a national system that can aggregate bank data, hospital records, real-world movements, online activity, and other records into a single "trustworthiness" score. Digital authoritarianism has three major components. First, in the name of upholding "cyber sovereignty," the CCP initiated the Golden Shield Project in 1997 and the project has evolved into a massive Internet censorship system. Second, the government controls and manages the society by creating a social credit system so everyone must conform and contribute to the state capitalism. Third, the government uses the Skynet to surveil society so that no one can step out of the boundaries defined by the

CCP. To illustrate, the chapter explains how the CCP has banned all foreign Internet services in China but has allowed the development of and release of WeChat by Tencent, a multinational conglomerate company. WeChat is a multifunction mega app used for messaging, social media, and mobile payment, which the government also employs to support its censorship activities.

More than any other event, chapter 9 maintains, the implosion of the Soviet Union in 1991 ended the Cold War and heralded the rise of liberal democracy and global capitalism in the 1990s. The transition to democracy, however, has been anything but successful. It was seriously eroded under President Boris Yeltsin in the 1990s and has all but vanished under President Vladimir Putin. Yeltsin's preoccupation with eradicating the Russian Communist Party and the legacy of communist rule in the Union of Soviet Socialist Republics led him to miss a golden opportunity in 1991–1992 to provide a constitutional foundation for democracy. A severe economic crisis and his use of military force against his political opponents in the legislature in the constitutional crisis of October 1993 caused him to make the fateful mistake of tying the future of Russian democracy to the support of Russia's wealthiest oligarchs who focused on increasing their personal fortunes rather than investing in the development of Russia's economic infrastructure and democratic institutions. Putin's election as president in 2000 was welcomed as was his policy of restoring stability and national pride by strengthening the state's power. Since then, he has methodically used his control over state and independent media, the military, and the security forces to dismantle nearly all signs of Russian democracy under Yeltsin and to disparage Western liberal democracy as an anachronistic political ideology for the twenty-first century.

Chapter 10 suggests that the partisan divisions in the United States today are much wider and deeper than in previous eras, and the political bitterness has only intensified since President Donald J. Trump's impeachment trial in 2020. Rather than simply disagreeing over policy positions, customary in campaigns, politics has become exceedingly personal and vindictive, and is now polarized into bifurcated camps of citizens who are extremely distrustful of one another. Much of the current political rancor in American democracy can be partly traced to the negative side effects of left-wing and right-wing political populism, with some dating back to the Boston Tea Party, Shays' Rebellion, and the era of Jacksonian democracy. Actually, the American government was originally designed to limit the negative effects of populist movements through federalism and the system of representative democracy. Populist movements were further checked by non-constitutional influences with the emergence of political parties, where a new class of political elites came to serve as political intermediaries between government and the people by recruiting, vetting, and funding mainly mainstream candidates, most of whom promoted shared values and pluralistic ideals.

This chapter maintains that political reforms to our presidential nomination system (i.e., primary system) and campaign finance system (i.e., Citizens United) have weakened political parties and crippled the important role political parties played in preventing the negative effects of populist movements.

The concluding section contains both chapter 11 and the Epilogue. Chapter 11 offers a deeper view of each indicator of democracy and how all of them relate to one another. It focuses on four distinct measures of democracy: Polity, Freedom House, EIU, and five of the V-Dem indices. It has a general comparison of all measures by displaying summary statistics as well as a correlation matrix to understand that while the measures have distinct features, all measures are significantly correlated. This should allow readers to recognize that different measures may be more applicable given a particular research interest. The chapter then gives summary statistics and discussion of each measure throughout Sub-Saharan Africa, South Asia, East Asia and the Pacific, Eastern Europe, Western Europe, Latin America, and the MENA, as well as the main countries of India, China, Russia, and the United States. While these geographic entities do not completely align with the chapters in the book, they make the most sense for analytical purposes. By providing summary statistics of each measure, readers gain knowledge of the performance of each indicator throughout the world. Interestingly, many of the measures vary quite widely in measuring particular countries. While it reminds readers of the difficult task of analyzing democracy and the tough choices required to measuring democracy, it expresses the hope that the serious analyses of democracy contained in this book can motivate further study and action.

The Epilogue ties the status of democracy in the different world regions and countries to how well they have fared during the novel coronavirus (COVID-19) pandemic. What is evident is how several authoritarian and populist leaders utilized the pandemic to augment their control and influence. A main point is that democracy with all its flaws stands out as the most capable in addressing the challenges of the modern world and advancing humane politics, and it is our responsibility to nurture it and keep it strong.

NOTES

1. Winston S. Churchill, quote from November 11, 1947, as cited by International Churchill Society. https://winstonchurchill.org/resources/quotes/the-worst-form-of-g overnment/.
2. Freedom House, *About Us*. https://freedomhouse.org/about-us.

3. Arch Puddington and Tyler Roylance, *Freedom in the World 2017: Populists and Autocrats—The Dual Threat to Global Democracy*. https://freedomhouse.org/report/freedom-world/freedom-world-2017.

4. Freedom House, *Freedom in the World: Democracy in Retreat*. https://freedomhouse.org/report/freedom-world/freedom-world-2019/democracy-in-retreat.

5. Ibid.

6. The Economist Intelligence Unit, "About Us." *The Economist*. https://www.eiu.com/n/?form_name=enquiry_form&enquiryType=BMP.

7. Ibid., "Democracy Index 2015: Democracy in An Age of Anxiety." *The Economist*. https://www.yabiladi.com/img/content/EIU-Democracy-Index-2015.pdf.

8. Ibid., "Democracy Index 2016: Revenge of the 'Deplorables'." *The Economist*. http://felipesahagun.es/wp-content/uploads/2017/01/Democracy-Index-2016.pdf.

9. Farid Zakaria, *The Future of Freedom: Illiberal Democracy at Home and Abroad*, Revised edition (New York, NY: W. W. Norton & Company, 2007).

10. John Keane, *The Life and Death of Democracy* (New York, NY: Simon & Schuster, 2009).

11. Marc F. Plattner, In *Democracy in Decline?*, edited by Larry Diamond and Marc F. Plattner (Johns Hopkins University Press and the National Endowment for Democracy, 2015), 7.

12. Jan-Werner Muller, *What is Populism* (Philadelphia, PA: University of Pennsylvania Press, 2016), 103.

13. Steven Levitsky and Daniel Ziblatt, *How Democracies Die* (New York, NY: Broadway Books, 2018).

14. Madeleine Albright, *Fascism: A Warning*, Reprint edition (New York, NY: Harper Perennial, 2019).

15. Naomi Chazan, "Israel's Democracy at a Turning Point." In *Continuity & Change in Political Culture: Israel & Beyond*, edited by Yael S. Aronoff, Ilan Peleg, and Saliba Sarsar (Lanham, MD: Lexington Books, 2020), chapter 5.

16. Levitsky and Ziblatt, *How Democracies Die*, 72–117.

17. Chazan, "Israel's Democracy."

18. Paul Mozur, Raymond Zhong, and Aaron Krolik, "In Coronavirus Right, China Gives Citizens a Color Code, With Red Flag." *The New York Times*, March 1, 2020. https://www.nytimes.com/2020/03/01/business/china-coronavirus-surveillance.html.

19. Borzou Daragahi, "Coronavirus could be Used by Authoritarian Leaders as Excuse to Undermine Democracy, Experts Warn." *Independent*, March 19, 2020. https://www.independent.co.uk/news/health/coronavirus-us-cases-government-pandemic-democracy-covid-19-a9407011.html.

20. Ibid.

21. Human Rights Watch, *Jordan: State of Emergency Declared*, March 20, 2020. https://www.hrw.org/news/2020/03/20/jordan-state-emergency-declared.

22. David Horovitz, "Coronavirus or Democracy? Which Crisis Should Israelis be More Worried About?" *The Times of Israel*, March 20, 2020. https://www.timesofisrael.com/coronavirus-or-democracy-which-crisis-should-israelis-be-more-worried-about/.

23. Ibid.
24. Aristotle, *Politics*, Book 4. http://classics.mit.edu/Aristotle/politics.4.four.html.
25. Amartya Sen, "Democracy as a Universal Value." *Journal of Democracy* 10, no. 3 (1999): 3–17.

Chapter 1

Variation in Measures of Democracy

Stephen J. Chapman

In order to understand the different dimensions of democracy, it is a good strategy to begin with how scholars think of the concept. This chapter offers an overview of how scholars approach the research in general as well as an overview of various measures of democracy. Readers should gain perspective in the many underpinnings of democracy scholars highlight prior to moving through the regional perspectives offered in subsequent chapters.

Throughout the international relations and comparative politics literatures, there exist multiple measures of democracy. Scholars have employed numerous indicators to analyze a host of different research questions. However, employing diverse democratic indicators can undoubtedly affect outcomes of analyses. It is the burden of the researcher to choose the most appropriate measure for their particular study. This chapter analyzes the differences between the measurement strategies of democratic indicators in order to offer a deeper view of the term.

As one will realize throughout this book, democracy works in disparate ways depending upon the region of the world, the institutional makeup of a country, the cultural and religious environment, among many other important factors. Similarly, multiple variables exist, which scholars use to measure democracy. There is not a "one-size-fits-all" method for measuring democracy. Some of these measures focus more on the credibility and stability of institutions, while others emphasize individual-level freedoms. Depending upon the goal of the researcher, one measure may be more appropriate than others. Prior to discussing these measures in detail, it is essential to take a step back and offer context to those who are not familiar with the methodological approaches of scholars interested in democracy.

METHODS

Scholars adopt various methodological approaches in order to test their theories within the social sciences. While the specific approaches are numerous, many fall into two broad categories of qualitative and quantitative methods. These are the approaches scholars use to provide evidence toward their arguments. It is important to have a general understanding of both prior to moving into a discussion of specific democracy measures. While the majority of measures within this chapter focus on the quantitative, there are measures that intertwine qualitative aspects as well.

Qualitative methods tend to rely on thick description of events or experiences in order to underline the key factors or themes that led to a particular outcome. Scholars accumulate evidence not by amassing large datasets, but rather by immersing themselves in the setting under consideration. This is done in order to provide valuable detail about what factors contributed to a societal outcome. Qualitative research tends to focus on small samples, whether it be an analysis about individuals or countries. The type of qualitative method employed by scholars is quite varied. Given that qualitative scholars are interested in the "on the ground" detail, much of their research necessitates interaction with their subjects of study. This does not necessarily have to be individuals; it can be a host of potential focal points of study that have cultural or societal importance. Even a particular historical event can be the subject of a qualitative design. Some qualitative methods include the use of focus groups, historical narratives, interviews, participant or observational research, and content or discourse analysis. Scholars who utilize these methods tend to rely on person-to-person interaction, historical documents, primary and secondary sources, to name a few. This is what allows the researcher to offer such rich detail within their analyses.

However, the benefit of qualitative research is not without its drawbacks. While qualitative research does provide vital contextual detail, it is not possible to generalize the findings in one setting to another. This creates a tradeoff between qualitative and quantitative methods. Where detail is gained in qualitative, generalizable power is lost. While generalizable power is gained in quantitative methods, it is at the cost of losing country-specific details. This is not to contend one is better than the other, rather, it is about the researcher being aware of the benefits and drawbacks of the adopted approach.

In contrast to qualitative methods, quantitative methods rely on large datasets with many observations (sometimes in the thousands or even millions!). Rather than focusing on one or a few countries, cultures, events, or individuals, quantitative scholars want as many observations as possible in order to provide evidence of their arguments. Researchers then use this data to conduct a multitude of statistical tests in order to show which factors included have a statistically significant relationship with the outcome they are attempting to explain. These are what researchers label independent and dependent variables. Scholars attempt to explain an outcome (dependent variable) with one or multiple explanatory factors (independent variables). A scholar's argument rests on the significance of the explanatory variables of interest showing a significant effect on the outcome. Some of the potential statistical tests employed by researchers include regression analysis (there are multiple types), chi-square, t-tests, analysis of variance tests. Similar to qualitative methods, the choice of test is dependent upon the scholar's approach. In addition, some methods are limited by the way variables are measured. While this is a brief overview of the methods used by scholars, it leads to an important concept for the current chapter, quantification.

Quantification, or operationalization as it is also called, is a central part of the quantitative research process. It consists of the transformation of concepts into numbers. If scholars want to use democracy as one of their variables, be it dependent or independent, they must go through the process of defining how they are numerically measuring the level of democracy within a given country. This goes for any concept a researcher is attempting to use in a quantitative analysis. Within the concept of quantification, there are two additional concepts of importance, that is, validity and reliability. Validity focuses on how well the chosen measure reflects the real-world phenomenon under consideration. Sometimes, this is straightforward. For example, if a thermometer accurately measures a person's body temperature, it is a valid measurement. However, other times, it is extremely difficult to quantify a particular variable, usually one that is multifaceted and somewhat ambiguous. For example, concepts such as culture, religiosity, or the topic of the current text, democracy.

In addition to validity, reliability relates to the consistency in the measure. If the measures of democracy highlighted within this chapter return similar results overtime by following the same processes, they are reliable measures of democracy. Returning to the thermometer, for example, if I were to gauge a person's temperature twenty times over the course of a day and it consistently returned the same reading, the thermometer has reliability. However, reliability does not automatically indicate validity. If the same thermometer was consistently five degrees off, it would have reliability for being consistent, but it would not be a valid measure as it is not actually measuring what is asked, that is, a person's body temperature.

This brief overview of qualitative and quantitative methods serves as a useful introduction into discussion of the measures of democracy. While these measures are all quantitative, many intertwine qualitative aspects into measuring democracy. This section is also important as it offers context of the various ways scholars provide evidence for their arguments. The next section delves into the quantification strategies behind multiple measures of democracy.

MEASURES OF DEMOCRACY

There is a multitude of democratic indicators of importance. While this chapter will not be able to cover them all, it will focus on two of the most widely used measures within the literature, Polity IV and Freedom House. In addition, it will also touch on other useful measures, including the varieties of democracy (V-Dem) measure, the Economist Intelligence Unit (EIU) Democracy Index, Democracy Barometer, and the World Values Survey. These measures can be more or less useful dependent upon the focus and goals of the research. One should keep in mind that one measure is not necessarily better than the other; it is the context of the scholarly inquiry that dictates the most appropriate measure. The following sections offer an overview of each measure and the societal factors used to measure the state of democracy. The last chapter of the book returns to this theme by comparing four of the measures discussed in this chapter. Moreover, it offers a breakdown of how the measures look across the many regions discussed in the intermediary chapters.

Polity IV

The Polity measure has a long history within political science. Ted Robert Gurr initiated the project in the 1970s, which has been updated many times since. Gurr's original conceptualization focused on authority patterns within a distinct social unit.[1] This measure has evolved overtime into its current version, Polity IV. The most current update led by the Center for Systemic Peace and authored by Monty G. Marshall, Keith Jaggers, and Ted Robert Gurr serving as an advisory role, focuses on two measures of authority to arrive at a unified scale of democracy.

Polity IV is a twenty-one-point scale ranging from 10 to 10, negative scores closer to autocracy, positive scores closer to democracy. The authors provide three suggested categories, including "autocracies" (scores: 10 through 6), "anocracies" (scores: 5 through 5), and "democracies" (scores: 5 through 10). The scores are created through two distinct measures of authority, Institutionalized Democracy and Institutionalized Autocracy. The Polity score is created by subtracting the autocracy measure from the democracy measure.[2] The variables are quantified using similar factors, including executive recruitment, constraints on the executive, and openness of mass participation.

The Polity measure relies on six core component variables that fall under the three main categories of executive recruitment, executive restraint, and public participation in the political process. It first focuses on the level of regulation involved within the recruitment process for executives. There are three distinct categories involving recruitment, including unregulated, designational or transitional, and regulated. Unregulated recruitment concerns the seizure of power using force. This means that the executive comes to power in absence of any formal process or election via a coup. Until the executive gains power through a formal process, the country is labeled as unregulated. The second category includes designational or transitional executive recruitment. The designational category involves countries where the executive is designated to the office by political power-holders. This includes countries that lack formal competition for recruitment, be it one-party rule or elections that are clearly illegitimate. The transitional category focuses on countries that are in a transition in one form or another. For example, this could include a movement from or to autocracy. It could also include situations where a coup has occurred, the leader steps down, but still holds an important position in the political sphere, such as head of the military. Finally, the regulated category relates to recruitment from some institutionally mandated process. This includes competitive elections, but hereditary succession as well. Also notable in this category is a measure of stability, in that the current regime does not have an impact on future selection of the executive.[3]

The second component centers on the level of competition involved in the selection of the executive. This is relatively straightforward, as countries can also fit into three categories. This first is selection, where the executive is simply chosen by hereditary succession, designated by political elite, or sometimes combination of both. For example, this includes countries where executives run unopposed, continuously win in rigged elections, have regular appointment of civilian leaders by military leaders, or repeated instances of opposition parties boycotting elections.[4] The second category consists of dual or transitional countries that are either in a transitional period or where there is a combination of power being transferred by hereditary succession and competitive elections, as in the case of a monarch or prime minister. Finally, there is the election category, where executives are chosen via competitive elections.[5]

The third component of the Polity measure focuses on the openness of executive recruitment. This involves who is included in the possible pool of executives. Closed countries have those that are determined by hereditary selection. There is also a dual executive-designation category, where there is hereditary selection combined with executive selection, stemming from executive or political elites selecting a chief minister. The dual executive-election category exists where there is hereditary selection and the chief minister is selected via an election. Finally, the open category consists of countries where executives are chosen by elites or via competitive elections.[6]

The fourth component also concentrates on the executive, or more specifically the constraints placed on the executive's decision-making once in power rather than the selection process. This consists of four main categories, with three intermediate categories between each. The first is unlimited authority, where executive authority is essentially unchecked. This can occur in various ways, including ignoring formal restrictions on the executive, the absence of a legislature or having a legislature with no real check on the executive, or the constitution of the country is revised or suspended by the executive. The second category consists of slight to moderate limitation on executive authority, where there exist some constraints but they are weak or limited in some way. These limitations include a legitimate legislature that can initiate its own legislation and constrain the executive in some manner. It also includes the existence of an independent judiciary. The next category is substantial limitations on executive authority. This category includes many of the same conditions as the last, just to a greater extent. For example, countries in this category have a legitimate legislature that regularly modifies or defeats executive proposals or funding requests. Finally, the last main category is executive parity or subordination. This encompasses countries where there exists equality in power between the facets of government. It could also include situations where another branch is more powerful than the executive. This can occur when an institutional body such as the legislature appoints the executive or in an unstable parliamentary democracy with high turnover between governments.[7]

It is clear from this brief overview of the first four components that there is heavy emphasis on the executive. However, many of the components include other institutions within their quantification process that emphasize the interaction with the executive. It also includes factors important to the public, for example, whether or not they have a say in choosing the executive. The last two components focus directly on the public's expression of preferences, mainly addressing the stability of political groups as well as the level of repression placed on such groups by the government.

The fifth component centers on the amount of regulation on participation present in a country. This involves the level of rules involved in when, if, and how political preferences are expressed.[8] This consists of five groupings ranging from unregulated to regulated. The unregulated category has countries where there are no stable political organizations and no organized restrictions on political activity. This occurs in countries where political movements stem from particular leaders, regional interests, or religious/ethnic divisions.[9] This also pertains to countries where the size and importance of these groups vary widely overtime. The second grouping is multiple identity, where there are stable political groupings competing at the national level for influence that share some level of common interests. The next grouping, sectarian, includes countries that are defined by incompatible political groupings vying for power. When one group is in power, the other(s) suffer, and vice versa. It also includes countries where an entire subset of the population is excluded from the political process. The restricted group comprises countries that hold stable political groupings that do not have a strong faction-based membership. However, there are still limitations placed on groups, issues, or types of participation. Finally, the regulated group includes stable political groupings that regularly compete in the political process with little use of coercion or intimidation and no specific groups, issues, or types of participation are excluded from the process.[10]

Finally, the sixth component operationalizes the level of competition involved in political participation. Groupings range from repressed to competitive. Repressed countries are those where there is no opposition political activity due to limitations by the ruling party. The suppressed category comprises countries where opposition groups do exist outside of government, but are severely limited in their actions. Furthermore, it includes countries where large subsets of the population are excluded from participating. The factional grouping consists of those countries that focus on an in-group/out-group mentality, that is, they fight for their own group to the detriment of the others. There is also a transitional grouping, which includes any country at some point of transition between any of the other categories. Finally, the competitive grouping is when a country holds stable, secular groupings that regularly compete for power, there exists peaceful transference of power, and there is little instance of coercion or disruption in the political process.[11]

The Polity measure clearly includes some extremely important factors underlying democracy. However, it is not without its shortcomings. First, the measure includes no information on the level of civil liberties in a country aside from the coding of limitations on participation. It also places a heavy emphasis on the executive, signaling the choices made by the scholars coding the measure. More importantly, it includes both democracies and autocracies in one measure. This, again, brings up a decision by the researcher using the Polity measure. In the original piece that initiated the Polity data, the authors note that autocracies and democracies have dissimilar forms of authority.[12] Marshall, Gurr, and Jaggers noted that those interested in studying the "varying effects of democracy and/or autocracy should employ the original Polity scheme."[13] Essentially, if one is interested in how democracies and autocracies behave differently, that researcher should use the original institutionalized democracy and institutionalized autocracy variables. This chapter now moves to discussing another major measure of democracy within the literature, the Freedom House scores.

Freedom House

The Freedom House measure is another democracy indicator and provides a useful contrast with the Polity IV measure. While Polity focuses mainly on the institutional arrangements of a country, Freedom House centers on the political guarantees accorded to the people within a given country or territory. The measure began in the 1950s, but has been developed extensively overtime into its current form. Much of the motivation behind the quantification strategy comes from the Universal Declaration of Human Rights that was adopted by the United Nations General Assembly in 1948. The measure is developed yearly by a combination of analysts, scholars, think-tank members, and the human rights community. Much of the scoring process includes the usage of both quantitative and qualitative data as ratings are given based on governmental publications as well as field research. Freedom House produces two measures, a "Freedom Rating" with a range of 1–7; scores of 1.0–2.5 are considered free, 3.0–5.0 partly free, and 5.5–7 not free. There is also the aggregate score for each country, ranging from 0 (least free) to 100 (most free). Both scores are based on two categories, political rights and civil liberties. The political rights category consists of ten indicators; the civil liberties category contains fifteen.[14] Each country is scored on a scale of 0–4 for each of the twenty-five combined indicators. The 1–7 scale represents the average score on both the political rights and civil liberties categories; the combined score is simply the aggregate score of all indicators.

The political rights category is split between three subcategories, including electoral process, political pluralism and participation, and functioning of government. Three questions can be found within the electoral process category, all of which focus on the existence and legitimacy of elections. The first two questions focus directly on the election process of executives and the legislative body of a country. These include factors such as the registration process, the secrecy of ballots, timing of election, the presence of gender or other types of discrimination, the amount of oppression involved in the electoral process, the reporting of election results, and other similar measures about the validity of executive and legislative elections. The third question in this category addresses electoral laws, specifically measures of the clarity of electoral laws for the public, the existence and independence of election commissions that maintain elections, the breadth of suffrage within a country, the fairness involved in the construction of electoral districts (presence of malapportionment or gerrymandering) and systems (proportional or majoritarian), as well as the transparency and fairness involved in the legislative process to change electoral laws.[15]

The second subcategory within the political rights is political pluralism and participation. Most questions within this category relate to the existence and freedom of political parties to organize. This includes discriminatory practices against particular political groups, legal hurdles to form new parties, the level of repression aimed at party leaders or supporters, the possibility of independent candidates to establish themselves within the existing political system, the propensity of corruption via bribes present, as well as the presence and legitimacy of an opposition voice within society. There are also questions about the public's political rights, particularly the presence or level of discrimination relevant to ethnic, religious, gender, LGBT, and other types of groups.[16]

Finally, the third subcategory concerns the functioning of government. Much of this subcategory examines the implementation of legislative duties, such as if those elected are able to form a government and conduct normal governmental business. Other questions deal with any potential undue influence from outside actors on the legislative process, including influence from nonstate actors, foreign governments, nonelected officials such as the military class and insurgent groups. There are also questions concerning the transparency within a government. That is, if there are safeguards against political corruption present in the country and if the public has access to reasonable governmental information.[17]

It is clear already from the overview of the political rights category that the design of Freedom House adopts a different measurement strategy relative to the Polity measure. The second category of Freedom House, civil liberties, is comprised of various measures not included in the Polity variable, as it does not code for any civil liberties within a country. However, one can already envision the tough decisions researchers must make when selecting the appropriate measure of democracy.

The civil liberties category within Freedom House is similarly split into subcategories. The measure consists of four subcategories: freedom of expression and belief, associational and organizational rights, rule of law, and personal autonomy and individual rights. The freedom of expression and belief subcategory has a range of questions about the freedoms granted within a country, such as the existence of a free and independent media, the level of intimidation or discrimination against members of the media, and the legal hurdles placed on the media. The subcategory also covers religious freedoms, including the practice, establishment, and expression of religious belief or nonbelief within a country; the level of academic freedom, including the limitations placed on teachers and professors in respect to their research and curriculum development; the level of political influence within the educational system; and the level of freedom enjoyed by student-led groups. Finally, this subcategory covers questions on individuals' political beliefs and the potential for government retribution or surveillance by governmental organizations. Again, this first subcategory shows the large emphasis on individual-level rights.

This theme continues in the second subcategory of associational and organizational rights. Questions include a variety of freedoms for individuals, nongovernmental organizations, and labor unions. Among the topics covered is the right to organize and peacefully protest without intimidation, retribution, or arrest. It also covers the level of freedom granted to nongovernmental organizations and labor unions to organize, fund themselves, strike, and express themselves without influence from governmental organizations.[18]

The rule of law subcategory intertwines individual-level rights with the institutional arrangement of the country. First, it includes factors such as the independence of the judiciary, the level of due process within civil and criminal matters, protections from illegitimate physical force, for instance, if the public has a path to address violations by governmental officials, and if these rights apply equally across all groups within a country.[19]

Finally, the last subcategory within the civil liberties category is personal autonomy and individual rights. The questions in this subcategory include whether individuals have freedom of movement and are free of intimidation or violence in terms of residence, employment, and education. It also contains questions focusing on the legitimacy of property rights within a country and if those rights apply equally across genders and racial/ethnic groups. Furthermore, it measures the level of freedom in terms of the family unit, for example, marriage laws, protections from domestic abuse, limitations placed on family size, fairness in divorce proceedings across genders, and the level of influence from societal groups or other family members in respect to household decisions. Finally, it also has questions concerning economic exploitation of individuals, including the level of governmental control over industry and/workers, protections against trafficking or economic discrimination, barriers that prevent social mobility, and the level of protections for workers with respect to wages, working conditions, and child or slave labor.[20]

Clearly, the Freedom House measure creates a comprehensive measure of freedoms within a country. However, there are some limitations with this measure as well. Specifically, it consists of a litany of individual-level rights. This can be viewed as strength and as weakness. It is strength to the extent that one can gain a clear understanding of the political environment within a country. From a research standpoint, however, many of the factors constituting the measure are redundant. That is, Freedom House measures the same concept multiple times. This may not cause problems with respect to outcomes of analyses, but it certainly places a heavy burden on collection. Furthermore, the Freedom House measure does not pay attention to the institutional arrangement of a country. While they contain measures of an independent judiciary and the electoral process of the executive and legislative body, they do not provide as much detail in the interchange between branches of government relative to the Polity measure. Again, this is simply a product of attempting to measure a complex term.

ADDITIONAL MEASURES OF DEMOCRACY

This section covers additional measures that scholars can employ to understand the level of democracy within a country. The discussion of Polity and Freedom House displays the tradeoffs scholars must think about when deciding on the most appropriate measure for their analysis. The following measures allow for additional options to researchers and practitioners who want to understand the factors undergirding democracy.

Varieties in Democracy (V-Dem)

V-Dem is a new type of operationalization for democracy. Developed by Michael Coppedge et al.,[21] the dataset does not equate to a singular measure of democracy. Rather, it includes over 350 unique indicators that scholars can employ in their research. The quantification process includes both qualitative and quantitative aspects, as there is some level of subjectivity involved in some of the indicators. However, the dataset also includes five "high-level" indices, including Electoral, Liberal, Participatory, Deliberative, and Egalitarian. The Electoral Democracy index includes measures that focus on legitimacy of the electoral process, the amount of suffrage within a population, freedom of nongovernmental organizations, freedom of expression and participation within the process, and freedom of the press. Coppedge et al. contend that this is the essential aspect of representative democracy and is taken into account for all other high-level indices.[22] The Liberal index focuses on the amount of individual rights within a system, protections of government interference, rule of law, and institutional arrangements such as checks and balances. The Participatory Democracy index centers on the level of public participation in both political and nonpolitical organizations. The Deliberative Democracy index centers on how decisions are made within a country. That is, if the process respects all relevant voices in the conversation in a reasonable manner and is not plagued by group-based appeals. Finally, the Egalitarian Democracy index relates to measures of the equality in protections across different groups in society, resources are offered equally across groups, and if both groups and individuals have equality in access to power. These indices measure many of the same concepts as Polity and Freedom House, but offer researchers more flexibility to include specific measures that are important to their arguments rather than selecting a single, comprehensive score. Furthermore, the V-Dem measure emphasizes the historical processes involved in democracy, which allows for a more nuanced view relative to alternative measures.

EIU Democracy Index

The EIU index is developed by *The Economist's Intelligence Unit* and covers 165 nations. The overall measure ranges from 0 to 10, with lower scores representing more authoritarian countries and higher scores indicating a more democratic nation. There are four categories of authoritarian regime, hybrid regime, flawed democracy, and full democracy.[23] These scores are constructed on five different dimensions covering sixty specific questions. The five important dimensions consist of electoral process and pluralism, civil liberties, functioning of government, political participation, and political culture. Each indicator is scored on a 0/1 basis (yes/no questions) or on a three-point scale and then converted to the standardized ten-point scale. The scores are created with a combination of expert opinion and public opinion surveys.[24] Again, many of the same factors included in other measures already discussed show up in the EIU measure. However, the measure has come under some level of criticism as the EIU does not publish the list of respondents to the survey, their expertise, or their national origin. The concluding chapter of this book will offer some insight as to whether this measure is biased relative to other potential measures of democracy.

Democracy Barometer

The democracy barometer is another newer measure of democracy. Developed principally by Wolfgang Merkel and Daniel Bochsler,[25] it is a unique measure as it does not encompass the entirety of countries throughout the world. Rather, it focuses on developed democracies, covering seventy countries as of 2019. It originally identified over 300 indicators that could be used to construct the measure, ultimately selecting 105 indicators that fit the author's criteria. However, similar to the V-Dem measure, it allows for a more nuanced view of democracy rather than a unified score. The authors of the dataset adopt a heavily theoretical framework, deducting principles, components, subcomponents, and ultimately specific indicators.[26]

The 105 indicators fit within three broad categories with three subcategories within each. There is the Freedom category (individual liberties, rule of law, and public sphere subcategories), containing a variety of indicators that covers individual rights such as freedom of movement, protection from government-sponsored abuses, freedom of religion, effective property rights, public confidence in legal system and police, freedom of the press, as well as a host of institutional arrangements to guarantee such protections. The second category is control (competition, mutual constraints, and government capability subcategories), comprising indicators on electoral laws, including the financing of political parties and campaigns, the level electoral competition, and the construction of electoral districts. In addition, this category has measures of the balance between the institutions within government, the level of judicial independence, the extent of federalism found within a country, and governmental and economic stability. The third category of equality (transparency, participation, and representation subcategories) includes variables that focus on the openness of the system such as the level of public access to information, disclosing political parties financing, the level of corruption in a country, and the level of political control over the media. It also covers variables addressing an individual's freedom to participate in the political process, including suffrage and the level of barriers of pathways offered by the government to participate in elections and other political actions such as petitions and lawful protests. Finally, the dataset includes variables that concentrate on the quality of representation, a somewhat unique aspect relative to other measures discussed. Specifically, these measure breadth of representations, that is, who is included or excluded, the constitutional allowances for direct democracy, the pathways for women and minorities to access power and participate, as well the congruence between votes and seats in the legislature.

The democracy barometer covers a wide array of factors important to democracy and is designed to be flexible to the needs of the researcher. However, it does not equate to a single measure or index that can easily be transferred for a quantitative analysis. This is a potential shortcoming, but it does have numerous factors fundamental to democracy.

World Values Survey

The last measure of democracy discussed in this chapter is the World Values Survey. This is unique relative to the others as it does not directly measure democracy per se. It is a survey-based dataset that covers a wide range of topics, some of which include public sentiment toward democracy. However, it is a useful dataset to consider as it does not rely on expert assessment. Conversely, it directly assesses public views on a host of indicators. Its main purpose is to understand social and political change within a country overtime. However, many of the important factors included in the previously discussed measures of democracy can also be found within the World Values Survey.

This measure evolved out of the European Values Study, developed by Jan Kerkhofs and Ruud de Moor and now covers nearly 100 nations.[27] It is a time-intensive process to conduct a series of surveys within differing populations, which is why the World Values Survey requires a global network of researchers. Among the topics are democratization, social capital, gender equality, economic development, religion, and subjective well-being.[28] Surveys are conducted over a five-year period, with its most current wave focusing on 2010–2014. What makes this relevant to the current chapter is that it provides opportunity for researchers to delve deeper into the factors that affect the political and social environment of an individual. It is possible to extract indicators that can serve as viable measures of democracy. Examples of survey questions address political participation and activity; membership in societal and political organizations; perceptions of media bias, government intrusion into the political process, corruption, and the legitimacy of elections; as well as confidence in the judiciary.[29] Many of these factors align with the important categories within other measures of democracy. In addition to these, the World Values Survey offers numerous questions on the political, religious, and economic culture of a country. Taken together, it is a dynamic dataset that can be used by researchers and practitioners for a variety of reasons.

This chapter has introduced readers to some of the options available to scholars of democracy. It began with a general overview of the methodological approaches of social scientists, with an emphasis on the quantification process. The chapter then thoroughly discussed two major measures of democracy, Polity and Freedom House. Alternative measures of democracy were also provided to offer a deeper perspective of how one can envision the concept of democracy. Many of these indicators will be revisited in the closing chapter where there is analysis of how democratic indicators compare with one another and how they relate to the regions covered in this book. However, many of the chapters throughout this book actively use some of the measures discussed in this chapter. Having completed this chapter provides the necessary perspective to critically analyze the many dimensions of democracy.

DISCUSSION QUESTIONS

1. What are some variables other than democracy that are hard to define? How could you use certain indicators to measure it? For example, how could you quantify the awesomeness of a student? A professor? What are the factors that underpin such a concept?
2. What factors are fundamental to being a democracy?
3. Why does the Polity measure include such a focus on the executive? What are some examples you can think of as to why that might be important? What other factors should be considered?

4. Which measure, Polity or Freedom House, reflects your proposed measure? What did your measure leave out? What did your measure include that neither indicator contains?

5. Having read through multiple measures of democracy, which do you feel captures the concept the best? As you see it, what are the strengths and weaknesses of each measure?

NOTES

1. Harry Eckstein & Ted Robert Gurr, *Patterns of Authority: A Structural Basis for Political Inquiry* (New York, NY: John Wiley & Sons, 1975).

2. Monty G. Marshall, Ted Robert Gurr & Keith Jaggers, *Polity IV Project: Dataset Users' Manual* (Center for Systemic Peace, 2018). http://www.systemicp eace.org/inscr/p4manualv2017.pdf.

3. Ibid.

4. Ibid.

5. Ibid.

6. Ibid.

7. Ibid.

8. Ibid.

9. Ibid.

10. Ibid.

11. Ibid.

12. Eckstein & Gurr, *Patterns of Authority.*

13. Marshall et al., *Polity IV Project,* 17.

14. *Methodology: Freedom in the World 2018* (Freedom House, 2018). https://fr eedomhouse.org/report/methodology-freedom-world-2018.

15. Ibid.

16. Ibid.

17. Ibid.

18. Ibid.

19. Ibid.

20. Ibid.

21. Michael Coppedge, John Gerring, Carl Henrik Knutsen, Staffan I. Lindberg, Jan Teorell, et al., *V-Dem Codebook v9* (Varieties of Democracy (V-Dem) Project, 2019).

22. Ibid., 39.

23. *Democracy Index 2018* (The Economist Intelligence Unit, 2018). https://www .eiu.com/topic/democracy-index.

24. Ibid.

25. Wolfgang Merkel, Daniel Bochsler (Project Leaders), Karima Bousbah, Marc Bühlmann, Heiko Giebler, et al., *Democracy Barometer: Methodology, Version 6* (Aarau: Zentrum fur Demokratie, 2018).

26. Ibid., 3.

27. *History of the World Values Survey* (World Values Survey, 2019). http://www
.worldvaluessurvey.org/WVSContents.jsp?CMSID=History.
28. Ronald Ingelhart, Christian Haerpfer, Alejandro Moreno, Christian Welzel,
Kseniya Kizilova, et al. (eds.), *World Values Survey: Round Six – Country-Pooled
Datafile 2010–2014* (Madrid: JD Systems Institute, 2014). http://www.worldvalu
essurvey.org/WVSDocumentationWV6.jsp.
29. Ibid.

FURTHER READING

Democracy Index 2018. The Economist Intelligence Unit, 2018. https://www.eiu
.com/topic/democracy-index.
Harry Eckstein & Ted Robert Gurr. *Patterns of Authority: A Structural Basis for
Political Inquiry*. New York, NY: John Wiley & Sons, 1975.
History of the World Values Survey. World Values Survey, 2019. http://www.worl
dvaluessurvey.org/WVSContents.jsp?CMSID=History.
Methodology: Freedom in the World 2018. Freedom House, 2018. https://freedom
house.org/report/methodology-freedom-world-2018.
Table of Country Scores: Freedom in the World 2018. Freedom House, 2018. https:/
/freedomhouse.org/report/freedom-world-2018-table-country-scores.

Part I

WORLD REGIONAL PERSPECTIVES

Chapter 2

Democracy in Africa

Changing Phases

Julius O. Adekunle

This chapter examines the transitions in African political systems and the changing phases of democracy. It acknowledges the existence of the concept and practice of democracy in Africa before contact with the Europeans, and asserts that Africans went through a period of political change and adaptation in the wake of European imperialism and colonialism. Africa, as a plural society with its multidimensional diversity, provides a dynamic paradigm of a democratic and inclusive political system. Historically, several precolonial African societies built powerful and effective political structures and governments that exhibited some aspects of democracy. The transition from the precolonial monarchical to the colonial parliamentary system and to postcolonial presidential system underscores the changing phases of democracy. A second phase of democracy began when the Europeans arrived in the late nineteenth century. The imposition of colonial rule and the introduction of a European form of democratic governance forced Africans to adapt to radical political change. In many respects, the Europeans used African rulers to run their political system.

The gaining of independence in the mid-twentieth century ushered in the third phase of democracy in Africa. While African states are now being ruled by Africans, colonial legacy of democratic political system remains. Drawing examples from Nigeria, Ghana, and Angola, this chapter traces the history of democracy and shows that the indices of democracy manifest in modern Africa: elections, human rights, formation of political parties, freedom, and gender participation in politics. However, some forces hinder the effectiveness of democracy in Africa: a high level of electoral malpractices, corruption, attempts at one-party system, and censorship of the press. The chapter concludes with challenges of effective application of democracy and suggestions for strengthening democracy in Africa.

31

HISTORY OF DEMOCRACY

The earliest world civilizations evolved a political system that left the control of the society in the hands of one person—the king. The ancient monarchical system did not allow the participation of the people in government and did not permit power sharing. The purpose of government is not only to maintain law and order, but also to provide the opportunities for people to contribute to the socioeconomic growth of the society. The concentration of power on a paramount ruler was not democratic as it denied the people some political rights and participation. Kings became absolute rulers and trampled on the natural rights of their subjects.

While the concept of absolutism was widespread, democracy (at its evolutionary stage), was not, but it was also an ancient political ideology. Today, democracy is practiced globally, but in different and various forms. The earliest recorded form of democracy came from Athens, a Greek city-state.[1] The aristocrats owned the land, controlled the religious life of the people, and dominated the politics of Athens. They constituted the Areopagus (the city council of nobles) and consolidated power in and for themselves. An assembly of citizens existed, but with little to no political empowerment.

In an attempt to avoid tyranny, the aristocrats chose Solon as sole archon—leader. Solon (630–560 BC), a poet and reform-minded aristocrat, used the position to bring about significant sociopolitical and economic changes that constituted the foundation for Athenian democracy. Solon's reforms favored the common people, especially because freeborn males over the age of eighteen were allowed to participate in government.[2] That was a limited form of democracy as slaves, women, and poor people did not have the right to vote in the Athenian assembly. As of that historical period, no other society allowed such political participation by the people. The main body of government was the *ekklesia*, the citizens' assembly.[3] The aristocrats did not embrace the seemingly "radical" sociopolitical and economic changes because they challenged and limited their power and control over the people.

After Solon, tyranny and indiscriminate use of power were setting in, but another round of changes occurred when Cleisthenes became the leader of Athens.[4] Like Solon, Cleisthenes engineered measures that allowed participation in government, thereby promoting democracy. His reforms were intended to weaken the traditional power base of the aristocrats. For example, he created a "new political organization by grouping country villages and urban neighborhoods into units called demes."[5] Through the demes, people had greater participation in government. For his political contributions, Cleisthenes has been referred to as the Father of Athenian Democracy. In the wake of the changes, Athenian democracy took away the monopoly of political control from rulers, emphasized equality before the law, and devolved power to the people. The Athenian idea was that the state was an entity that required the participation of people in governance. Pericles (495–429 BCE), an Athenian liberal political thinker, visionary leader, and statesman made reforms that expanded democracy and strengthened the vote and power of the majority. Pericles gave more political power to the people, and the "Athenians became deeply attached to their democratic system."[6] Thus, he has been described as "an ardent populist who broadened the scope of Athenian democracy."[7] He believed that Athens was a democratic city-state. He championed the course of the common people and formulated lasting policies that ensured the participation of the people in legislative and judicial matters.[8] Pericles once said,

> Our constitution is called democracy, because power is in the hands not of a minority but of the whole people. When it is a question of settling private disputes, everyone is equal before the law; when it is a question of putting one person before another in positions of public responsibility, what counts is not membership of a particular class, but the actual ability which a man possesses. No one, so long as he has it in him to be of service to the state, is kept in political obscurity because of poverty.[9]

The Athenian democracy consisted of three institutions: a sovereign body (assembly), a Council of Five Hundred (fifty representatives from each of the ten tribes), and courts where people could present their cases before jurors. Unlike the monarchical system, under democracy, all Athenian public officials were elected, not appointed or selected. This introduced the concept of elections as an integral part of democracy. The political system lasted two centuries, but it has provided a paradigm for modern democracy.

DEMOCRACY IN PRECOLONIAL AFRICA

Ancient[10] African societies developed their own political philosophy and evolved unique ways of governing themselves. According to Peter Schraeder, "a rich mosaic of political systems existed during the precolonial independence era" in Africa.[11] Two major types of political systems existed: the centralized and the stateless. The centralized were "capable of uniformly applying policies throughout a given territory, and inhabitants of this political system owe their allegiance to the state."[12] Such centralized states included the kingdoms of Kush and Axum (in northeast); the Ghana, Mali, Songhay, Oyo (in western Africa); and numerous Bantu empires (in central, eastern, and parts of southern Africa). The kingdoms adopted the monarchical and hierarchical form of government, with the king at the head of administration.

Governance and politics were complex with different political institutions performing defined functions. Like in other world political structures, religion, and politics went hand in hand, but institutions were created to protect the rights of the people and to check the arbitrary use of political power and authority. Rulers engaged in dialogue with subordinate chiefs and military officials to resolve conflicts and seek peace. As will be discussed, in outlook, the political system was not democratic, but in actual practice, some indicators of democracy were present.

One of the earliest political organizations in Africa was the kingdom of Kush. While the origins and extent of the Kush kingdom remains unclear, it is clear that it was founded by the Kushites. Historical and archaeological evidence from Napata, its capital, indicates that Kush had cultural relations with Egypt and it was governed by powerful kings with approximately seventy-two generations of both male and female rulers. In *Africa in Global History*, Robert Harms states that "Sometimes around 780 BCE, King Kasha of Kush (known as "Kashta the Kushite") left an inscription below the first cataract stating his claim to be the legitimate ruler of the Two Lands of Ancient Egypt, but it is uncertain how far north his authority extended."[13] Moreover, there was the construction of elaborate palaces and temples. Kush was known to the outside world since the Greeks referred to is as "the Land of Punt." Punt and Egypt established commercial relations, especially "during the reign of Queen Hatshepsut who flourished early in the fifteenth century B.C."[14] The construction of pyramids, which became a symbol of political power, took place during this period.

Male rulers dominated the kingdom of Axum, but Queen Sheba (c. 1020–960 BC), emerged as a powerful ruler who symbolized beauty, power, success, and wealth. Iron smelting industries were established and Adulis, an important port city, thrived in trade. There was evidence of Greco–Roman influence, the introduction of Christianity in the fourth century, and the penetration of Islam in the seventh century AD. In the kingdom of Aksum in the Ethiopian highlands, palace administrators as well as subordinate chiefs performed sociopolitical functions of state, especially in maintaining law and order in both the metropolis and suburban areas. Governance in Aksum was on a federal system with *negusa nagast* (King of Kings) at the head of the administrative hierarchy. The king was considered powerful because the government officials held their positions at his will. He could appoint and dismiss any of the officials. He, however, was expected to listen to their advice as they were the representatives of the people.

Politics and governance in the West African empires of Ghana, Mali, and Songhay were not radically different from those of the Kush and Axum kingdoms and other centralized societies in Africa. Absolute and powerful rulers such as Mansa Kankan Musa (c. 1312–1337) and Mohammad Toure

(c. 1443–1538) established effective administrative and political systems in their respective empires. Council of ministers and provincial governors were appointed to advise the king and maintained law and order, and to collect tributes (taxation). The rulers embarked on expansionist or imperialistic policies by using the military to fight neighboring communities.

The Oyo Empire existed in modern day Nigeria, which was one of the largest and strongest empires in Yorubaland. It provides a good example of an African complex political system with traces of democracy. The king (the Alaafin) was an absolute ruler. To demonstrate the extent of his power, the Yoruba believed that the Alaafin possessed the power of life and death over his subjects. Like other ancient rulers, the authority to rule emanated from the gods as he was selected after consultation with the Ifa oracle. He ruled with the assistance of two councils: the Ogboni and Oyo Mesi. As Robert Rotberg put it, "The [alaafin] owed his election to provincial councillors and . . . possessed absolutist powers, the secular and supernatural exercise of which was curtailed only in part by an aggregate of institutionalized checks."[15] The Ogboni and Oyo Mesi councils were the institutionalized agencies of check to provide a balance of political power. The king did not unilaterally make major decisions, but acted in consultation with the council of chiefs. While the Alaafin was theoretically not bound to take to the counsel of the chiefs, in practice, he could not afford to ignore them because he relied on them for his peaceful and successful reign as well as for the execution of military campaigns.

There was a symbiotic relationship between religion and politics in Africa in the precolonial times. Both were intricately intertwined. As deeply religious people, Africans did not separate the realms of religion from that of politics, thus presenting a difficulty in referring to African politics as democratic. The king, as the representative of the gods, performed both political and religious functions—in many cases, represented by a priest. The person and position of the Alaafin were considered sacred. The palace and the burial ground were sacred. The king was basically surrounded by an aura of sacrosanctity. Hence, religious and ritual observances were an integral part of the selection and ruling process. As the king must be chosen from the ruling family, the people did not have any say in the matter. The Ifa oracle was consulted before important final sociopolitical and economic decisions were made.[16]

In Uganda, the Kabaka, chosen from among the Princes of the Drum, held a sacred political position. He was "the supreme authority in the nation," and all other authority derived from him, indicating that the system was undemocratic. For efficient political administration, the kingdom was divided into counties, called *ssaza*, each under a chief, who were all expected to be loyal to the Kabaka.[17] Like the Alaafin, the Kabaka had a *lukiiko* (council),

headed by a *katikkiro* (prime minister), to advise him. As the *lukiiko* did not
have formal power to enforce its political ideas, the Kabaka could not afford
to ignore their advice. Again, like the Oyo system, the Kabaka would be
careful in antagonizing the council because they could support a rebellion to
overthrow him.[18]

Democracy also was reflected in the political culture of noncentralized
societies of Africa. In the absence of large political structures and complex
political institutions, some African societies adopted what is referred to as
stateless system, which was an egalitarian form of governance. Among the
Bedouins in northern Africa, the Nuer and Dinka of Sudan, the Maasai of
East Africa, the pastoral nomadic Somali of northern Somali, and the Igbo
and Tiv of Nigeria, there were no formal, complex, or well-defined institutions of government such as kings, no subordinate rulers, and no official
officeholders. They also did not establish any institutionalized judicial system, yet they maintained strong and orderly societies, with relative peaceful
relations. Such societies have been described as "tribes without rulers."[19]
Rather than kings, there were clan leaders or lineage heads who performed
limited political roles because they did not possess the elaborate political
powers of the king. They controlled only their clan members by maintaining
law and order and carrying out judicial duties of settling disputes among
their clans. The noncentralized political system was commonly found
among pastoralists who, more often than not, did not live in large urbanized
structures.

Anthropologist I. M. Lewis mentioned that the pastoral Somali people did
not have "any administrative hierarchy of officials and no institutionalized
positions of leadership to direct their affairs."[20] Instead, there were representatives of the different segments or villages that composed the political
community, usually, adult male members. As was the case in Athens, adult
men possessed the right to speak on political matters of the community and
to belong to councils that had specific assignments. Kinship and villages
constituted the hallmarks of their political arrangement, and all lineages
trace their descent to a common ancestor. Lineage heads were charged
with certain responsibilities such as promoting peaceful relations among
lineage members. The lineage head indirectly performed judicial, political,
and social functions in concert with other people. Government and politics
were egalitarian. Among the Igbo society in eastern Nigeria, the political
system was based on village government where village councils, elders, and
lineage heads performed political roles without formal political authority.
Title holders and age-set organizations also performed political functions.
This system allowed more people to participate in governance and politics-
related decisions. The egalitarian nature of governance provides elements
of democracy.

DEMOCRACY: CHANGE FROM
AFRICAN TO EUROPEAN MODEL

In the wake of the abolition of the Transatlantic Slave Trade and the redirection of African–European economic relations, a new phase began with the establishment of the legitimate commerce in the second half of the nineteenth century. European economic interests in Africa increased, changing from slaves to raw materials produced in Africa. With the increased presence of the Europeans in Africa and the commencement of the new European imperialism, Africa experienced radical economic and political changes. For example, economically, there was transition from food crop production to cash crop production and wage labor. There was also transition from taxation in goods and services to taxation in cash. Political changes were profound, with far-reaching effects on the African rulers and people. The erstwhile democratic system of the Africans, either in the centralized or stateless societies, radically changed to the European version. While the traditional rulers worked with and learned from the colonial officials, they were actually not at the center of administration. European democracy thus displaced African democracy.

To firmly establish their grip on African land and people, the Europeans convened the Berlin Conference, November 1884 to February 1885. The motive of the conference organizers was to set the peaceful partition and political domination of Africa by the European in motion. Through treaty signing and wars of conquest, the Europeans took over Africa, created permanent political boundaries, and changed African kingdoms into their controlled colonies. The African rulers lost political control of their people. For example, the Alaafin of the Oyo Empire and the Sultan of the Sokoto Caliphate in Nigeria were both defeated and subjected to British hegemony, and so was the Asantehene of the Gold Coast (now Ghana). Samori Toure, the warrior king of the Mandinka Empire, was subjugated by the French. In Rwanda, the Tutsi aristocratic class was displaced by the Germans. In Uganda, the Kabaka lost control, while Shaka, the powerful and military monarch of the Zulu Kingdom, fell to the British in the Anglo-Zulu War of 1879. Whether by peaceful or violent means, colonialism brought about political change throughout Africa.

The precolonial political systems, with all the features of democracy, changed to European parliamentary system, with its form of democracy. The change gave rise to political challenges to Africans, pressuring them to adjust to a new form of "democratic" political system. The Europeans legitimized, consolidated, and increased their political power by limiting the political role of African traditional rulers. As colonialism is an imposed form of government, to the Africans, it was not democratic. For example, among the Igbo people where kingship was not traditional, the British created political institutions known as the "warrant chiefs" for their administrative convenience—to make their Indirect Rule system work. The Igbo considered the warrant chiefs as traitors and collaborators with the colonial government. Their "unrestrained authority and control of the courts, were seen by the people as miniature tyrants," and many of them became targets of brutal attacks.[21] Margery Parham admits that indirect rule "in Africa at least, it had only limited success. British authority was too detached: under it the small African society certainly survived."[22]

The first phase of colonial rule in Africa was between 1900 and 1914. The Europeans practiced undemocratic political system as Africans were not involved in the governance of their own affairs. Political decisions were taken by the imperial powers with no contributions from Africans. At the early phase, elections were not held, and the fundamental rights of the people were not duly respected. In workplaces, colonial authorities discriminated against Africans, especially the women. Africans struggled to be relevant and recognized. Equity and equal rights were absent. The outbreak of World War I in 1914 did not change the colonial hegemonic political system—Africans remained subjugated and controlled. Africans were forced to fight the war on the side of their colonial masters.

FOUNDATIONS OF DEMOCRACY IN AFRICA

Democracy, as now defined, came to Africa through the Europeans. The imposed colonial rule and the adaptation to democratic system have been a long process. While Africans participated in colonial government in one form or another, the system was not completely democratic. The wave of political change began when Africans struggled for independence. The 1960s marked a political watershed in Africa as many countries gained independence only in that year. That marked the beginning of Africans practicing the form of democracy they inherited from their colonial masters. While adapting to democracy, African states also grappled with the accompanying problems. Old ethnic and religious affiliations did not, and have not completely given way to nationalism. The manifestations of these hinder the progress of democracy in Africa, as demonstrated by the series of military intervention in politics. The military in politics is not only an aberration, but also a threat to democracy. It eliminates the legitimate power of the people to choose their own leaders. Military government suspends the constitution and rule by decrees. Political parties are banned and elections are not held as the freedom of the people is reduced. By the 1970s, many African states were under military rule.

Political changes began to manifest as from the 1990s when military rule became unpopular and global condemnation became strong. The change to liberalization gained strength as prodemocracy movements emerged and gathered momentum. William Tordoff indicates, "The wave of democratization sweeping across Africa was also felt in Ethiopia and Somalia where guerrilla forces ousted the discredited military regimes of Mengistu Haile-Maryam and Siyad Barré, respectively in 1991."[23]

DEMOCRACY: FROM PARLIAMENTARY TO PRESIDENTIAL

The end of World War II in 1945 marked the beginning of the effective process of decolonization in Africa, with the hope of independence in view. Africans have the expectation that they would be able to adapt European democracy to suit their sociocultural and political needs. Certain factors were in their favor for the struggle for independence. The right to self-determination, the granting of independence to India in 1947, and the emergence of the African educated elite accelerated the process of transfer of power from the Europeans to the Africans. According to Margery Parham in *The Colonial Reckoning*, African nationalism arose because Africans were in quest of creating nations. She argued that the force of African nationalism "swept the rule of Europe out of almost the whole of tropical Africa and has bred more than twenty new nations in its place."[24] Parham asserts that, not surprisingly, Western education allowed African educated young men "to see only one way of escape from their intolerable sense of personal and racial humiliation." Their quest was "to gain independence from white man's control, to awaken the apparently docile masses who had not shared their experiences and who seemed to accept the white man's rule as part of the new immutable, perhaps not altogether undesirable, order."[25]

That burning quest for freedom and democracy led African nationalists to vigorously embark on anticolonial activities. Across Africa, nationalists such as Kwame Nkrumah of the Gold Coast, Jomo Kenyatta of Kenya, Nnamdi Azikiwe of Nigeria, and Julius Nyerere of Tanzania emerged to demand independence for their respective colonies. In the Gold Coast and Nigeria, the decolonization process was relatively peaceful, while in Namibia, Angola, and Mozambique, it was radical and violent. Parham indicates that the Gold Coast, "was no static symbol of enfranchisement: it was a power-house from which radiated currents to increase the power and heat of nationalism elsewhere."[26] The Gold Coast, which had been regarded as the British "model colony," became the first in Sub-Saharan Africa to gain independence in 1957. In the 1960s, a wave of political change occurred when approximately seventeen African countries gained independence from their respective colonial powers. Governance changed from the Europeans to the Africans and the transition from parliamentary to presidential systems also began.

At independence, African nations had great expectations of a stable and democratic political system. There was also the expectation of good governance as Africans are now in charge of their own affairs. However, a combination of sociopolitical and economic problems surfaced early, ushering in a period of chaos, conflict, and instability. One after the other across Africa, military coups occurred and democracy was swept aside. Thus, there was a transition from civilian to military rule and democracy to dictatorship. Togo, Ghana, Guinea, Nigeria, and Uganda are few examples of African countries that experienced military rule.

Some countries will be used as case studies to examine the postcolonial phase of democracy in Africa. In the contemporary period, democracy serves as a powerful political ideology of building or rebuilding a nation. How effectively has democracy achieved this reality in Africa? Understandably, the evolution of democracy is a long process, especially in Africa. However, the ingredients to facilitate the smooth running of democracy should be set in place.

DEMOCRACY IN NIGERIA

Nigeria has been chosen in this analysis because it is one of the largest, most populous, and most diverse countries of Africa. Nigeria, with its ethnic pluralism and complex sociocultural background, presents a good example for the examination of the effective practice and values of democracy in Africa. The early history of Nigerian societies has demonstrated the practice of democracy. However, the advent of the Europeans, particularly the British, brought about significant political changes that altered the understanding and practice of democracy. The road leading to the independence of Nigeria in 1960 was fraught with political maneuvers between the nationalists and the British colonial authorities. One of the developments in line with democracy was the formation of political parties and conduct of election of public officers. Unlike the African traditional system of selecting the king, the British introduced election of officers, which enabled Africans to have a say and participation in governance.

Nigeria has had problems with effective practice of democracy since the colonial period. One major factor was how Nigeria came into being as a nation. Before the British carved out Nigeria as a nation, there were numerous independent empires or kingdoms, where kings consulted with their subordinate chiefs. For example, the Oyo Empire in the southwest and the Sokoto

Caliphate in the north were powerful political structures. The British, since the late nineteenth century, created two protectorates—the Southern and the Northern—for their colonial administrative convenience. The two protectorates were initially administered separately. When Frederick Lugard, the British Governor General, defeated the Sokoto Caliphate in 1903, the process of unifying the Southern and Northern Protectorates began. That was accomplished in what is popularly known as the amalgamation of 1914.[27] According to Michael Crowder, "Lugard took a number of decisions that were to influence the whole future of Nigeria."[28] Against the proposal by Edmund D. Morel that Nigeria should be divided into four, or that of Charles Temple, Lugard's Lieutenant Governor, who suggested a division into seven provinces, "Lugard chose to maintain the distinction between North and South" to the dissatisfaction of Nigerians.[29] That unilateral decision was undemocratic. To further reflect Lugard's desperation for power, he:

reduced the already limited powers of the Legislative Council, which in 1906 had been extended to all Southern Nigeria, to a mere cipher by restricting its authority to Lagos Colony alone, and in its place set up an unwieldly Nigerian Council with a majority of officials, and only three nominated Africans from the North and three from the South.[30]

In furtherance of their pursuit for a successful and peaceful administration, the British colonial authorities shielded the Northern Protectorate, where the Indirect Rule was first introduced, from southern influences, including the spread of Christianity. The British prevented religious conflicts by preserving the predominantly Muslim north from the Christian south. That was part of the divide and rule strategy of the British. The northerners received Islamic education while the southerners received Western education. The ethnic groups and sociocultural backgrounds were different. Thus, the amalgamation was not based on the aspirations of the people to live together, but was imposed on Nigerians only for the administrative expediency of the British, not for the application and practice of democracy. The dichotomy between the two regions and the forceful unification became a potential problem for effective and successful administration and future application of democracy.

Most of the Nigerian nationalists such as Herbert Macaulay ("The Father of Nigerian Nationalism"), Ellis Okoli, Nnamidi Azikiwe, Obafemi Awolowo were from the south. Western education had been a major factor in exposing these core nationalists into the struggle for independence. Anticolonial and political activities during the decolonization period took place mainly in the south. Newspapers, such as the *Lagos Weekly Record*, attacked the British administration. In newspapers and pamphlets, nationalists published pungent anticolonial articles that called for a democracy.

Nigeria went through a constitutional process—the British creating one form of constitution or the other to move Nigeria forward to independence. A major one was the Richards Constitution in 1946, which was on the regionalization of Nigeria. Three regional councils were created in the eastern, northern, and western regions. Nigerian nationalists criticized the constitution because it was not representative of the wishes of the people and it was not democratic as it divided rather than united Nigeria. Although the constitution was intended to last nine years, it came under review within two years and was replaced by the 1951 Macpherson Constitution, which democratized the local government system and Africanized the Nigerian public office.[31]

Political activities became more vibrant after World War II when nationalists clamored for democracy by asking for independence. The formation of political parties was fundamental to democracy. It gives the people the right to choose their own government and leaders. Three major political parties played significant roles in decolonizing and democratizing Nigeria. The National Council of Nigeria and the Cameroons (NCNC), which Dr. Nnamdi Azikiwe formed in 1947; the Northern People's Congress founded in 1949 and led by Sir Ahmadu Bello (the Sardauna of Sokoto); and the Action Group founded in 1951 under the leadership of Chief Obafemi Awolowo.[32] Nigerian political parties during the decolonization period have been rightly criticized as being regionally and ethnically based. Of the three, the NCNC had the most national outlook.

Nigerian leaders did not agree on the approaches to adopt after independence. For Azikiwe and his NCNC, a unitary form of government would foster a strong democratic union. But for Awolowo and the northern leaders, a strong autonomous regional arrangement was preferable. Thus, the division did not provide a fertile soil for democracy. However, the Western and Eastern Regions attained self-government in 1957 and the Northern Region in 1959. Finally, Nigeria became independent under the Commonwealth on October 1, 1960. Alhaji Tafawa Balewa became the prime minister while Dr. Nnamdi Azikiwe served as the governor and later the first president in 1963 when Nigeria became a Republic.

The early years of independence tested the democratic system in Nigeria. Ethnic affiliation, religious conflicts, cultural and educational differences have jointly hindered the evolution of a strong background for democracy. Nigeria became a victim of political instability. A series of successful and attempted military coups derailed a smooth process of democratic rule. The first military coup occurred in 1966 (barely six years after independence). The Nigerian Civil War (1967–1970) was followed by a prolonged period of reconciliation, reconstruction, and rehabilitation under General Yakubu Gowon as the Military Head of State. Since the military does not rule by constitution but by decrees, it means that the practice of democracy was suspended. Nigeria did not return to a stable democracy until 1999.

Corruption is a roadblock to democracy. It pervades the Nigerian society in different forms and intensities. Public officials flagrantly violate democratic rules to force their way into positions of power and wealth. Nigeria has been ranked as one of the most corrupt countries in the world. Although many public officials have been arrested, tried, and jailed for corruption, the impact has been serious on Nigeria as a democratic society. Free, fair, and credible elections are an integral and important component of democracy. In Nigeria, there have been several allegations of election malpractices and political violence. Ethnopolitical division and rivalry, which characterized the colonial period, continue to manifest after independence. Several political opponents have been assassinated and a state of fear has been created in the people. In the wake of political and religious violence, Tume Ahemba quoted Adamson Gbangange as saying, "People are saturated with fear."[33] It is clear that democracy cannot succeed in an atmosphere of fear, unrest, and election manipulations.[34]

Although Nigeria has been lurching from one crisis to another, democracy remains the most viable political option. For Nigeria to be fully democratic, there should be improvement in some aspects of democracy. Freedom of the press has to be respected, human rights should be protected, security must be provided, gender equity, and political participation should be encouraged. There should be more political and religious tolerance as Nigeria claims to be a secular society. As a large and diverse society, Nigeria is in a good position to set a strong and viable example of sustainable democracy for the rest of Africa.

DEMOCRACY IN GHANA

Unlike Nigeria, Ghana is a West African country where democracy is taking firm roots. Ghana, formerly known as the Gold Coast, was a British colony. Before the British colonization, the powerful Asante Empire, under the leadership of the *Asantehene*, established its capital at Kumasi. Osei Tutu laid the foundation, Opoku Ware expanded the empire, and the sacred Golden Stool united the people. The Golden Stool served as the soul of the Asante nation. Conscious of the military prowess and success of the Asante people, the British sided with the Fante who were close to the coast. The Asante and Fante Confederacies have competed over the economic control of the region, but the Ashanti were more military superior. Hence, the British policy of divide and rule came handy when they supported the Fante in order to dislodge the Ashanti Empire. The failure of diplomacy resulted in military confrontation.

The Asantehene had nobles and administrators who were in charge of the provinces. The central administration was elaborate and effective in maintaining law and order throughout the empire. As Agnes A. Aidoo indicates,

> Without any doubt, one of the most impressive aspects of Asante history is the systematic development of a national ideology and the elaboration of complex social and political institutions for the management of the society's affairs. Outstanding early rulers like Osei Tutu (ca. 1695–1717), Opoku Ware I (1717-Osei Kwadwo (1764–1777), and Osei Bonsu (1801–1824) created an elaborate military organization and a sophisticated centralized bureaucracy to ensure order, stability, and effective administration in the huge empire. They also used diplomacy, kinship ties, religious oaths, and the ideology of the golden stool to bind together the chiefs and officials in the central government.[35]

With this elaborate political structure and institutions of governance, there is evidence that the Asantehene often had consultations with his officials, although he held wide political powers within the metropolis and in the subordinate provinces.

The Ashanti people encountered the Europeans, especially the British who, in the late nineteenth century, were aggressive and desperate to take over the Gold Coast for their economic interests. In 1900, the British Governor Frederick Hodgson humiliated the Asantehene when he demanded that the Golden Stool be brought to him to sit on. This was an abomination to the Asante people who held the Golden Stool sacred. In order to preserve their cultural belief and practice, as well as preserving the symbol of their unity, the Queen Mother, Yaa Asantewa, led a resistance against the British. The revolt was crushed, the Asantehene, Prempeh I, was sent into exile in the Seychelles Islands in 1900, and the British began to effectively control the economy and politics of the Gold Coast.[36]

The British adopted the Indirect Rule system to govern the people in Nigeria, Kenya, Uganda, and the Gold Coast. British officials held strategic positions of the government. While the power of the British increased, that of the Asantehene declined. Monarchy gave way to parliamentary system, and the British form of democracy came into being. Some elements of democracy were found such as in elections, formation of political parties, and freedom of the press, especially during the period of decolonization after World War II.

Like Nigeria, the Gold Coast went through a process of constitutional development to achieve independence. Sir Alan Burns, the governor of the Gold Coast, introduced a Constitution in 1946, which provided a major step toward self-government. Nationalists, such as Dr. J. B. Danquah and Dr. Kwame Nkrumah, criticized the constitution as weak because the governor held veto powers. Danquah, Nkrumah, and other nationalists formed the United Gold Coast Convention (UGCC) Party, with Danquah as its president and Nkrumah as its secretary. The UGCC organized a general boycott of European goods as a result of which riots broke out in February 1948 in Accra and spread to other cities. In reaction, the British colonial government arrested and imprisoned Danquah, Nkrumah, and four other members of the party. With the British approach of silencing anticolonial activists in the Gold Coast, it can be argued that there was no democracy but hegemony.

The British set up the Watson Commission to investigate the riots of 1948. In its report published in 1950, the Commission recommended political and economic changes. The recommendation led to the introduction of a new constitution in 1951. Ideological differences tore members of the UGCC. That prompted Nkrumah to form his own party, the Convention People's Party (CPP). Nkrumah, considered a radical nationalist, called for "Self-Government Now" and used the *Accra Evening Newspaper*, which he established in 1948, to disseminate his democratic ideas to the masses. The CPP won the general elections of 1951 and Nkrumah was appointed as the Leader of Government Business, but recognized as the prime minister in 1952. Being in control of internal affairs, Nkrumah used the opportunity to consolidate his political power and to bring significant changes in the Gold Coast. Due to the overwhelming victory of the CPP in the 1956 elections, the British granted independence under the Commonwealth to the Gold Coast on March 6, 1957 and Nkrumah became the first president. On the day of independence, Nkrumah changed the name of the country to Ghana. For his role in the process of decolonization and for liberating other African states, David Birmingham, a renowned professor of modern history, described Nkrumah as "the Father of African Nationalism." With Ghana's independence, Nkrumah vowed to seek the liberation of other colonized Africans. Ghana's new form of democracy began in 1957.

A few years in the postindependence period, Ghana went through a period of political struggles, which eventually led to a military coup in February 1966. Nkrumah was accused of neglecting the country by pursuing the establishment of the Organization for African Unity. He was also moving from a democratic rule to dictatorship and socialism. Thus, Ghana transitioned from democracy to military government. After a series of military coups and changes in leadership, Flight Lt. Jerry Rawlings became the head of state in December 1981. Peter Schraeder points out that

> Rawlings oversaw a deliberately slow measured liberalization of the Ghanaian political system that ultimately included the writing of a new constitution, the legalization of opposition political parties, the emergence of a private press, and the creation of independent national human rights organizations.[37]

Rawlings returned Ghana to what Peter Schraeder describes as guided democratization.[38] In 1992, Rawlings returned Ghana to a multiparty democracy. He took part in the presidential election under the auspices of the National Democratic Congress. He won and transitioned from a military head of state to a democratically elected president until 1992. Since then, Ghana has been a stable democratic state, conducting what international observers consider free, fair, and credible elections. Ghana has become an example of stable democracy in Africa.[39] Ghana has made some significant strides toward Participatory Democracy. In order to have a sustainable democracy, ethnic marginalization should be avoided, equal gender representation should be allowed, and accountability and transparency among political leaders should be fully observed.

DEMOCRACY IN ANGOLA

Located in West-Central Africa, Angola was one of the Portuguese colonized colonies. The existence of Angola and its political system, however, predated the advent of the Portuguese. Like other African countries, Angola had a long and rich political history, which included ethnic diversity and establishment of kingdoms. The Bantu-speaking people, whose cradleland was in the Cameroon, migrated through the Congo Rain Forest to central, eastern, and parts of southern Africa. They were responsible for founding kingdoms such as the Kongo, Ndongo, Lunda, and Kasanje.[40] They were advanced culturally and technologically, and possessed the ability to assimilate other people. Of all the kingdoms, the Kongo was the most powerful. Initially, there was a loose federation of small communities but, by the 1400s, they developed into a highly centralized political system under the leadership of the *manikongo* (King of Kongo), with the capital at *Mbanza Kongo* (residence of the king).[41] The kingdom prospered through trade in copper, ivory, and slaves.

To run the central administration, the *manikongo* appointed provincial governors who were mainly in charge of maintaining law and order and collecting tribute (tax). There was an advisory council of elders, which consisted of twelve high-ranking members of the aristocracy. The aristocracy came from different lineages, which means they were representatives of the people. There was a core of "civil servants" such as the tax officer, chief justice, the police, and the military, who assisted the king in advancing the good of the society. Advisers and representatives of the people working with the *manikongo* show an element of democratic process. While the king had the final say, he could not rule arbitrarily. Mark Cartwright contends that, "Kongo kings were distinguished by their symbols of office which included a headdress, royal stool, a drum, and regalia jewelry made from copper and ivory. To enforce their rule, the king controlled a standing army composed of slaves; the force in late sixteenth century CE numbered from 16,000 to 20,000 men."[42] With his strong political and military power, the *manikongo* was able to expand his territory covering "the lands of northern Angola and the north of the Congo River (present day Congo and Zaire)."[43]

The penetration of the Portuguese into the Kongo kingdom in 1482 marked the beginning of diplomatic relations and eventually of a political turning point in Angola. In their quest for a sea route to India, the Portuguese came to Kongo when Nkuwu Nzinga was the king. Their initial relations with the *manikongo* were economic and religious—goods were exchanged, Christianity was introduced, and Nzinga was baptized. The Portuguese became interested in the slave trade. Writing on the presence of the Portuguese in Angola, Robert Collins indicated that "Slaves were procured in a variety of ways: sometimes Portuguese governors demanded them as taxes, but most often they were refugees or captives from local wars that were provoked by traders."[44] Although the Portuguese experienced fierce resistance, they survived by using superior naval and military power, and became aggressive in their search for slaves. Their aggressive approach resulted in wars, insecurity, and political instability in the Kongo. As Eric Hamblin puts it, "In 1500 the Kingdom of Kongo had been a vigorous, growing, stable entity. By 1700 it had become an emasculated, shrunken, unstable conglomeration of squabbling factions; a kingdom of despair."[45] From the end of the eighteenth century to the beginning of the nineteenth century, Portugal was experiencing some political crises, and its power in Angola had begun to wane.

The abolition of the slave trade and the beginning of legitimate commerce brought about a renewed Portuguese interest in Angola and Mozambique. After the Berlin Conference (1884–1885), in which the Europeans divided up Africa, the Portuguese successfully laid claims to Angola and Mozambique as their colonies. Portuguese colonial administration in Angola and Mozambique was completely exploitative, discriminative, and undemocratic. In those two colonies, the Portuguese held "firm political control."[46] Angolans were denied participation in government and the "colonial system had created a dichotomy among the Africans population that corresponded to that of the Portuguese social structure—the elite versus the masses."[47] As Gus Liebenow explained, "the policies of the Portuguese were marked by neglect, oppression, and calculated efforts to deny Africans even a modicum of development."[48] Instead of democratic politics, what existed in Angola was racial politics. For example, in 1921, Zalazar's government "divided the civil service into European and African branches."[49] Under this bureaucratic system, Africans did not enjoy equal job mobility and equal political participation with their European counterparts. According to Janice Love, even by the 1960s, there was in Angola an "uneven and inefficient implementation of Portuguese

colonial control."[50] There is no doubt that the Portuguese "mirrored the reality of a harsh dictatorship back in Portugal, with whites (along with blacks)
having no right to organize political parties of their own."[51] This high-handed
colonial political system became a potential cause for protests and eventually
armed conflict, civil war, and bloodshed. The turbulent political experience
during the colonial period is not the subject matter of this chapter. However,
the shaky background had significant impact on the immediate and effective
implementation of democracy after independence.

Unlike the peaceful approach to independence in Ghana and Nigeria, the
struggle for independence and the search for democracy resulted in a prolonged and destructive civil war. The campaign for independence had begun
in 1961 when the National Liberation Front of Angola (FNLA) and the
People's Movement for the Liberation of Angola (MPLA) adopted guerrilla
tactics against the Portuguese. Shortly after independence in 1974, Angola
was engulfed in a civil war as a result of the competition for supremacy
between the FNLA and MPLA. The two competing sides received foreign
support. For example, the Soviet Union and Cuba backed the MPLA, while
the United States and South Africa supported FNLA. The National Union for
the Total Independence of Angola (UNITA) under the leadership of Jonas
Savimbi, an anticommunist army leader, joined forces with FNLA.

Angola, in a continuing search for peace, transitioned from one-party
system led by the Marxist MPLA into a multiparty democracy in 1975.
The UNITA was formed as a second political party. Jon Schubert contends
that the return of peace to Angola in 2002, "raised hopes that the end of the
civil war would entail a gradual opening of political space, and allow for
increasing democratic plurality and civil liberties."[52] International observers
declared the parliamentary elections held in 2008 as free and fair, which is
an indication that Angola is moving toward consolidating and stabilizing
democratization. However, Shubert points out that the Angola society is not
as democratic as portrayed because "there is no clear separation [among] the
party, the government, and the state."[53]

Political freedom has not found its ground in Angola as the government
does not tolerate criticism. Political violence is rampant, the opposition
is intimidated, and "frequently harassed or hailed." Shubert adds that "In
Luanda, people can speak their minds relatively freely, and vent their anger
at government incapacity in call-in radio shows, but in the provinces freedom
of expression is still very limited."[54] Angolans do not enjoy the dividends of
democracy and in the wake the violations of the principles of democracy, they
"describe the state as a monarchy, where the president rules by decrees and
through powerful networks of patronage for a small clique of relatives, ministers, and generals, with little or no accountability to parliament, judiciary
or the population."[55] Democracy is under siege when political participation is

reduced to the minimal. However, Angola is not an exception; many African countries are guilty of engaging in some undemocratic practices—political, economic, electoral, and social—including corruption.

Angola faces some challenges in its democratic process. First, the protracted struggle for independence, the prolonged civil war, and the magnitude of damage pose a challenge for immediate political stability. Heavy Marxist or socialist influence that accompanied the struggle makes it difficult for democracy to flourish. Creating a one-party society does not align with the principles of democracy. Angola needs time to heal, reconcile, reconstruct, unify, and build on its nascent democracy. Second, there is the challenge of political transition. Angola experienced different phases of political systems and democratic process just like other African countries, but the radical change in Angola makes it longer for democracy to take firm roots. According to a report on peace and democracy, Angola went through "a transition from colonialism to postcolonial state-building; the transformation of society from a Socialist politically oriented society into a pluralistic democracy."[56] Third, the gender ratio in politics is a challenge. The Angolan government needs to enhance women empowerment. As politics is not an exclusive role of men, women should participate more in politics by standing for elections. Democracy is not fully applied until there is equal access to power and equal gender representation.

CONCLUSION

This chapter has demonstrated that the practice of democracy existed in ancient history of Africa, but it has transitioned from one phase to the other. The precolonial form of democracy had a different interpretation and application to the one the Europeans introduced. In African political systems, the legitimacy of the ruler did not derive from the principle of popular sovereignty, but there were strategies to check the ruler's arbitrary use of power. In other cases, the opinion of the majority carried political weight. Because colonialism changed African political system, Africans were forced to adapt to the new form of democracy. Claude Ake argues, that "Africans are seeking democracy as a matter of survival; they believe that there are no alternatives to this quest, that they have nothing to lose and a great deal to gain."[57]

Africans gained independence during the Cold War, which heightened the division that already existed in the world. The spread of communism became a threat to democratic states, especially in Europe and America. African states were caught between the two Cold War superpowers as they struggled to maintain their long-fought-for democracy. The early years of independence became a period of ideological struggle for the emerging African leaders as to what political system to adopt. The spread of democratic societies made Africans believe that they had more to gain than to lose in democracy. Shehu Shagari, former President of Nigeria, pointed out that in large countries such as Nigeria, there is no alternative political system than democracy.

Ake also mentions that "some of the gains of democratization have been remarkable, particularly the peaceful transition to non-racial democracy in South Africa." The end of the apartheid regime in 1990 and the release of Nelson Mandela from prison brought about a democratic political system in South Africa. In some countries, successful elections or transfers of power have been remarkable, such as Ghana. Ake mentions some reversals, as occurred in Nigeria, Togo, Gambia, Rwanda, Zaire, Sudan, and Angola. He further mentions that "most of Africa is still far from liberal democracy and further still from the participative social democracy that our paradigm envisages. However, there has been some impetus toward this particular kind of democracy."[58]

As Africans transitioned from one political system to the other, they showed their dynamic culture of adaptation and adjustment. While not specifically referring to political adaptation, Margery Parham says, "some powers of African resilience, some capacity for adjustment, came to their aid."[59] Change is not always smooth and generally welcome because it is often accompanied by challenges, but with resilience and understanding, progress is achieved. Africans have clearly progressed in operating on the European model of democratic political system. Based on the complexity of African societies, however, some aspects of democracy need to improve. More emphasis has to be placed on free and fair elections, ethnicity has to be downplayed in favor of nationalism, and the press should be totally free.

If democracy is going to survive in Africa, politics should be sanitized. Government should be inclusive, not exclusive, and leaders should be committed to rule with transparency. Power-hungry leaders should be booted out of office through due process of election. Young leaders with fresh ideas should be given access to political power, rather than the dominance of gerontocratic leaders who have run out of progressive ideas.

Many world leaders would boast of the power of the effectiveness of democracy in their countries. In Africa, not many leaders can uphold that claim. In several African countries, power does not lie with the sovereign people, but in the hands of the leaders who manipulate the constitution to retain themselves in office. Political progress and efficacy of democracy are hindered by their drive for power. When there is a gap between the people and government, democracy is deficient. When there is governmental structural imbalance, democracy cannot be effective. This is a grim picture that is portrayed in most African countries—disparity in ethnic representation in government, economic inequality, social injustice, increased poverty, diminishing educational standards, and poor health services—all occurring in the face of rising population. There is no nexus between the principles and practice of democracy because the governments are overwhelming corrupt; fraught with violations. To be fully recognized as democratic states, African countries must devise clear and pragmatic public policies that work in tandem with the values of democracy.

DISCUSSION QUESTIONS

1. Did democracy exist in the precolonial African political systems? If yes, describe and evaluate its concept and practice. If no, explain the reasons for its absence.
2. What are the three phases of democracy in Africa and how have Africans adapted to political change?
3. How can democracy in modern Africa be more effective?
4. What are the challenges that African nations face in effectively implementing the principles of democracy?
5. Are there differences between African and European concepts of democracy? Explain.

NOTES

1. In Greek, Demokratia is derived from *demos*, "the people," and *kratos*, "power." See "Ancient Greek Democracy." *History*. https://www.history.com/topics/ancient-greece/ancient-greece-democracy.

2. Joshua Cole, Carol Symes, Judith Coffin, and Robert Stacey, *Western Civilizations: Their History and Their Cultures*, Vol. 1, 3rd edition (New York, NY: W.W. Norton & Company, 2012), 64–65.

3. Clifford R. Backman, *The Cultures of the West: A History*, Combined Volume (Oxford: Oxford University Press, 2013), 124–125.

4. In modern times, the word tyranny connotes authoritarian power, in ancient Greece, it simply represented a person who seized power for a temporary time to make political and economic changes.

5. Lynn Hunt, Thomas R. Martin, Barbara H. Rosenwein, and Bonnie G. Smith, *The Making of the West: Peoples and Cultures*, Vol. 1, 4th edition (Boston, MA: Bedford/St. Martin's Press, 2012), 68.

6. Jackson J. Spielvogel, *Western Civilization*, Vol. 1: To 1715, 10th edition (Boston, MA: Cengage Learning, 2018), 70.

7. Backman, *The Cultures of the West*, 133.

8. Hunt et al., *The Making of the West*, 71.

9. Spielvogel, *Western Civilization*, 71.

10. This section benefits from an earlier work. See, Julius O. Adekunle, "Democracy and Political Change in Pre-Colonial Africa." In *Democracy in Africa:*

Political Changes and Challenges, eds., Saliba Sarsar and Julius O. Adekunle (Durham, NC: Carolina Academic Press, 2012), 3–18.

11. Peter J. Schraeder, *African Politics and Society: A Mosaic in Transformation* (Boston, MA/New York, NY: Bedford/St. Martin's, 2000), 64.

12. Ibid., 71.

13. Robert Harms, *Africa in Global History with Sources* (New York, NY: W. W. Norton and Company, 2018), 65.

14. Vinigi L. Grottanelli, "The Peopling of the Horn of Africa." In *East Africa and the Orient: Cultural Syntheses in Pre-Colonial Times*, eds., H. Neville Chittick and Robert I. Rotberg (New York, NY: Africana Publishing Company, 1975), 68–69.

15. Robert I. Rotberg, *A Political History of Tropical Africa* (New York, NY: Harcourt, Brace and World, 1965), 12–13.

16. In the Yoruba religious belief system and cultural practices, Ifa "was the great consulting oracle." Samuel Johnson, *The History of the Yorubas: From Earliest Times to the Beginning of the British Protectorate* (Lagos, Nigeria: CSS Bookshops Limited, first published 1921, reprinted 1997), 32.

17. James L. Gibbs Jr., *Peoples of Africa* (New York, NY: Holt, Rinehart and Winston, Inc., 1965), 88–89.

18. Vincent B. Khapoya, *The African Experience* (New York, NY: Pearson, 1994), 54–55.

19. John Middleton and David Tait, eds., *Tribes without Rulers: Studies in African Segmentary Systems* (London: Routledge and Kegan Paul, 1958).

20. I. M. Lewis, *A Pastoral Democracy: A Study of Pastoralism and Politics among the Northern Somali of the Horn of Africa* (London: Oxford University Press, 1961).

21. Webster, Boahen, and Idowu, 1967, 264.

22. Margery Parham, *The Colonial Reckoning: The End of Imperial Rule in Africa in the Light of British Experience* (New York, NY: Alfred A. Knopf, 1962), 66.

23. William Tordoff, *Government and Politics in Africa*, 2nd edition (Bloomington, IN: Indiana University Press, 1993), 114.

24. Parham, *The Colonial Reckoning*, 25–26.

25. Ibid., 42.

26. Ibid., 77.

27. Michael Crowder, *The Story of Nigeria* (London: Faber and Faber, 1966), 241.

28. Ibid.

29. Ibid.

30. Ibid., 243.

31. Ibid., 274–275.

32. Richard L. Sklar, "Nigerian Politics: The Ordeal of Chief Awolowo, 1960–65." In *Politics in Africa: Seven Cases in African Government*, ed., Gwendolen M. Carter (New York, NY: Harcourt, Brace and World, 1996), 119–165.

33. Tume Ahemba, "Christians Flee Bloodshed in Northern Nigeria." *The Guardian*, May 14, 2004. https://www.theguardian.com/world/2004/may/15/2.

34. For more information on political violence in Nigeria, see Julius O. Adekunle, "Political Violence, Democracy, and the Nigerian Economy." In *Democracy in*

Africa: Political Changes and Challenges, eds., Saliba Sarsar and Julius O. Adekunle (Durham, NC: Carolina Academic Press, 2012), 89–110.

35. Agnes A. Aidoo, "Order and Conflict in the Asante Empire: A Study in Interest Group Relations." *African Studies Review*, Vol. 20, no. 1 (April 1977): 1–36.

36. A. Adu Boahen, *African Perspectives on Colonialism* (Baltimore, MA: The Johns Hopkins University Press, 1987), 46.

37. Schraeder, *African Politics and Society*, 277.

38. Schraeder, *African Politics and Society*.

39. Kofi Akosah-Sarpong, "Restructuring ECOWAS Security." *moderng-hana.com*.

40. Thomas Collelo, ed., *Angola: A Country Study* (Washington, DC: Library of Congress, 1991), 6.

41. Ibid., 6–7.

42. Mark Cartwright, *Kingdom of Kongo* (Ancient History Encyclopedia, 2019). https://www.ancient.eu/Kingdom_of_Kongo/.

43. Collelo, *Angola*, 7.

44. Robert O. Collins, *Europeans in Africa* (New York, NY: Alfred A. Knopf, 1971), 13.

45. Eric Hamblin, "Kingdom of Kongo: Kingdom of Despair." In *Europe and the Third World: Model Essays in History*, Vol. III, ed., J. B. Webster, Unpublished manuscript (Halifax, NS: Department of History, Dalhousie University, 1991), 146.

46. Janice Love, *Southern Africa in World Politics: Local Aspirations and Global Entanglements* (Boulder, CO: Westview, 2005), 40.

47. Collelo, *Angola*, 24.

48. J. Gus Liebenow, *African Politics: Crises and Challenges* (Bloomington, IN: Indiana University Press, 1986), 36.

49. Ibid., 22–23.

50. Love, *Southern Africa in World Politics*, 47.

51. Ibid., 68.

52. Jon Schubert, "'Democratisation' and the Consolidation of Political Authority in Post-War Angola." *Journal of Southern African Studies*, Vol. 36, no. 3 (September 2010): 657–672.

53. Ibid., 659.

54. Ibid., 667.

55. Ibid., 669.

56. "Building Peace and Democracy in Angola: Challenges and Opportunities." *Report of the Angola country Program (ACP): Lessons Identified Seminar (LIS)* (Launda, Angola: The African Centre for the Constructive Resolution of Disputes (ACCORD), 2009), 9–10. See https://www.files.ethz.ch/isn/131542/2008_BudlingPeaceAndDemocracyInAngola_EN.pdf.

57. Claude Ake, *Democracy and Development in Africa* (Washington, DC: The Brookings Institution, 1996), 139.

58. Ibid., 137.

59. Parham, *The Colonial Reckoning*, 37.

FURTHER READING

Bratton, Michael and Nicolas van de Walle, *Democratic Experiments in Africa*. Cambridge: Cambridge University Press, 1997.

Jacobsen, Thorkild, "Primitive Democracy in Ancient Mesopotamia." *Journal of Near Eastern Studies*, Vol. 2 (1943): 159–172.

Jeffries, Richard and Clare Thomas, "The Ghanaian Elections of 1992." *African Affairs*, Vol. 92, no. 368 (July 1, 1993): 331–366.

Joseph, Richard, ed., *State, Conflict, and Democracy in Africa*. Boulder, CO: Lynne Rienner Publishers, 1999.

Karlström, Mikael, "Imagining Democracy: Political Culture and Democratisation in Buganda." *Africa: Journal of the International African Institute*, Vol. 66, no. 4 (1996): 486–505.

Rueschemeyer, Huber E. D. and J. D. Stephens, "The Paradoxes of Cotemporary Democracy: Formal, Participatory, and Social Dimensions." *Comparative Politics*, Vol. 29, no. 3, Transitions to Democracy: A Special Issue in Memory of Dankwart A. Rustow (April 1997): 323–342.

Sarsar, Saliba and Julius O. Adekunle, eds., *Democracy in Africa: Political Changes and Challenges*. Durham, NC: Carolina Academic Press, 2012.

Wiseman, John A., ed., *Democracy and Political Change in Sub-Saharan Africa*. New York, NY: Routledge, 1995.

Chapter 3

Political Trends in Central and East Europe

A Look at Hungary

Kevin L. Dooley

Since the end of the Cold War, the states of Central and East Europe (CEE) have been overwhelmed by the dual forces of capitalism and democracy. Initially focused on two initiatives—economic shock therapy and political liberalism—these states became a laboratory that tethered the abstract with the particular. The instant erosion of central planning allowed for academics and policymakers to test their hypotheses on what constituted the best model of governance. As they began to employ democratic ideals and free market practices to their own unique cultural and political traditions, a great discrepancy emerged among them. Some have been fortunate enough to join the European Union (EU), some have not.

To understand the diversity of CEE, it is best to identify all of its states. At a macrolevel, the region has served as an amorphous term referring to the Baltic states of Estonia, Latvia, and Lithuania; the Eastern European states of Belarus, Ukraine, Moldova, Romania, and Bulgaria; the Central European states of Poland, the Czech Republic, Slovakia, and Hungary; and the Balkans consisting of the states of the former Yugoslavia: Slovenia, Croatia, Albania, Serbia, Montenegro, Macedonia, Bosnia-Herzegovina, and the partially recognized territory of Kosovo. However, most comparative analyses of the region compartmentalize the states into subregions in order to better comprehend their democratic trends. For purposes of clarity, this chapter will *not* be examining the Baltic states (Estonia, Latvia, and Lithuania) or those of the former Yugoslavia. The former is commonly examined as constituting its own unique subregion, while the latter has been complicated by genocide, regional warfare, and international agreements. The trajectories of both subregions are unique when compared with the experiences of the others in the

region. To include them would only complicate our understanding of democratization. Instead, this chapter will focus on the process of democratization
in East and Central Europe with particular attention on the state of Hungary—
an early model of democratization following the Cold War.

The selection of Hungary as the chapter's main case study is interesting
and reflective of the region for a variety of reasons. First, Hungary was one
of the region's first successfully consolidated democracies. At a time when
Ukraine was engaged in a massive transition from the direct control of the
former Soviet Union and the states of the former Yugoslavia were involved
in mass atrocities and a regional war, democratic institutions were being
stabilized and free elections were being held there. Second, Hungary (along
with the Czech Republic and Poland) has the longest regional experience in
the EU. The Czech Republic, Poland, and Hungary were some of the first of
the Eastern bloc countries to join and were considered democratic models for
subsequent Eastern expansion. It is hard to overstate the importance of EU
membership when they joined in 2004. At the turn of the twenty-first century, membership in the EU meant access to markets and political protections
unheard of in CEE a decade earlier. Membership in the EU became a symbol
of democratic consolidation and economic stability. Lastly and perhaps most
importantly, Hungary is an interesting case study because over the past few
years it has begun to see its democratic institutions and policy initiatives take
on a nondemocratic tone. Perpetuated by a variety of international crises, a
wave of populist leaders and far-right parties has begun to win elections and
reshape the political, social, and economic landscape. Blaming the forces of
globalization and the leadership of the EU as enemies of the state, these new
political firebrands have threatened to undo many of the region's democratic
successes and usher in a new understanding of democracy.

THE END OF THE SOVIET PERIOD: CENTRAL
AND EAST EUROPE IN THE 1990S

On December 25, 1991, the Soviet Union formally ended, dissolving the
splintered Communist Party apparatus that had governed most of CEE since
the end of World War II. The ideology that was supposed to ensure the
economic, political, and social well-being to millions of Central and East
Europeans as well as Russians and Central Asians, had imploded. The cracks
in the Communist Party, which had been apparent in various satellite republics for decades, finally collapsed under its own weight.

A change of this magnitude cannot be underestimated. By the mid-1980s,
the Soviet Union's land mass stretched from Europe to the Sea of Japan
(spanning eleven time zones) and its ideology governed people as diverse as

Ukrainians and Kazakhs, Belarussians and Tajiks, and Russians and Uzbeks. Its massive army defeated Nazi Germany on the Eastern Front and its post-war foreign policy shaped the structure of international relations for nearly fifty years. When the Berlin Wall fell in 1989, the satellite republics were given a glimmer of hope at self-determination, something that many of them had not been able to experience in their long histories. The removal of Janos Kadar from the leadership of Hungary (1988), the weakening of Wojciech Jaruzelski in Poland (1989), the departure of Erich Honecker from East Germany (1989), and wholesale political changes in the party structures of most of the remaining countries of Central and Eastern Europe led analysts to believe that the end of the Soviet period was at hand. When the Soviet Union finally collapsed, the region was anxious for democratic institutions and free market economics. The Communist parties' stranglehold (in most states) had ended. The region looked to capitalize on the development of newer parties that had already experienced a modicum of electoral success when given the opportunity to challenge the Communist parties of the satellite states.

Unfortunately however, the transition to democracy was uneven and messy. When one looks at democratic measurements like those published by *Freedom House*, one sees a massive difference among the states of CEE. On the positive end of the democratic spectrum were the Czech Republic, Hungary, and Poland. On the negative end were the authoritarian or quasiauthoritarian states of Belarus, Bulgaria, Moldova, Romania, Slovakia, and Ukraine. During the 1990s, the Czech Republic, Hungary, and Poland established free market systems, experienced successive free, fair, and open elections, developed independent political institutions, and allowed for high levels of individual freedoms. The states of Belarus, Bulgaria, Romania, Slovakia, and Ukraine, however, had either witnessed a reformulated Communist Party take control (Bulgaria and Romania), a dictatorial regime continue to dominate political life (Belarus and Slovakia), or an ineffective and unstable electoral system (Ukraine and Moldova).

To analyze the process of democratization in the region, I will use a recognized set of indicators that will enable a better grasp of democratic expansion and retreat. Democracy is a fluid term and best recognized on a sliding scale. As such, an increase or decrease in a given indicator will allow one to determine how economic, political, or social forces impact democratization and how states become more or less democratic. Indicators over a given period of time allow for scholars to capture trends and make better sense of how states transition to democracy.

To examine the level of democracy in a given region, one has to acknowledge that there are different approaches at play. For purposes of this chapter, I will adopt a multistream analysis. I will look at the intersection of political institutions, substantive principles, and a variety of socioeconomic factors to assess how Hungary's democracy has changed since the end of the Cold War.

According to Whitehead, the removal of an authoritarian regime, followed by two successive, fair, and free elections is a strong indicator of democratic transition.[1] The notion "fair and free" is important here because it indicates that the people have been given the freedom to express their beliefs collectively and accept the results as legitimate. If the process of voting is deemed legitimate and a government is formed, then subsequent elections strengthen its classification as a democracy. (However, as Linz and Stepan have noted, this process cannot serve as the only requisite of democratic transition, as some elections yield governments that deny the requisite freedoms afforded to democratic peoples.[2]) Constitutionally defined checks and balances are also understood as a product of democracy. States lacking institutions that have the authority to check the power of other institutions are not considered strongly democratic because they do not possess a diversity of interests and a commitment to the preservation of the rule of law.

Socioeconomic factors are another useful set of indicators. According to Lipset, there is a causal relationship between economic development and democratization.[3] In order to determine democratic stability, Lipset argued, one must examine levels of industrialization, wealth, urbanization, and education. His argument is predicated on the notion that these features—combined with the political histories of each state—provide for the support necessary for democracy to thrive. This argument is useful because it also considers the understanding that economic development, while important, is only correlative to democracy if the state's political history is not marred by violence, international antagonisms, or an undemocratic political culture.

Lastly, it is important to examine the expansion or erosion of individual freedoms. Liberal democracies are bound by their protections of speech, media, minority rights, and one's ability to make a living. States that neglect these promises or pass legislation that limit such rights receive lower scores from Freedom House. In Hungary, one will notice a radical departure from its democratic beginnings in the 1990s in all three of these areas.

THE RISE OF VIKTOR ORBÁN AND THE FIRST DECADE OF HUNGARIAN DEMOCRACY

On June 16, 1989, a student activist gave a compelling speech in Heroe's Square to solemnly commemorate the failed Hungarian Revolution of 1956. Although the speech lasted only a few minutes, it gave national attention to the man who would reshape Hungarian politics in the twenty-first century: Viktor Orbán. Surrounded by a large array of Hungarian dignitaries and politicians were six coffins, each one commemorating the sacrifices of those Hungarians who in 1956 gave their lives so that their children and grandchildren might live in a free and democratic society. Orbán, a law student along with thirty-six other like-minded students from the radically intellectual Bibo Istvan College, had most recently formed an anti-Soviet, liberal youth organization known as Fidesz—the Alliance of Young Democrats. According to Orbán's biographer, Paul Lendval, there were two prerequisites for membership in Fidesz: the age limit was fixed between 16 and 35, and membership of the Hungarian Youth Communist League was prohibited.[4]

Youthful opposition to communism in general and to the Soviet Union in particular made Fidesz an attractive option for those who were coming of age in the late 1980s. At this time, Fidesz may have had barely 1,000 members, but its message was driven by a younger set of politicians focused on liberalism and change: a combination that propelled its leadership into important roles in the early days of the post-Soviet period. In October 1989, Fidesz transformed itself into a political party so that it could participate in the first free elections that were scheduled to take place in spring 1990. Like most new democracies in CEE, as the prospect of a fair and free election grew, its political system became inundated with political parties. In Hungary's first election more than thirty-five political parties participated. Fidesz won only twenty-two out of the National Assembly's 386 seats, or just 9 percent of the vote. However, this was an impressive showing for a political party still in its infancy.

The government that was formed was led by Jozef Antall, the leader of the Hungarian Democratic Forum (MDF), who as prime minister had the unenviable role of transitioning the economy from one that was centrally planned to one that was driven by the forces of the free market. According to Lendval, "The GDP shrank by 20% between 1988 and 1993; real wages fell by 4% in 1988 and 8% in 1991; inflation was 35% in 1991, 23% in 1992, and only fell under 20% in 1993. The previously unknown phenomenon of unemployment briefly reached 12% . . . and thousands of enterprises were liquidated and a half million jobs disappeared."[5] In the early 1990s, Hungary was in an economic freefall and a political stalemate. Antall was unable to accommodate those on the left, who were arguing for a more managed transition, and those on the right from within his own party, who were losing faith in his ability to serve as prime minister.

For these reasons, Fidesz was able to remain popular. It continued to oppose the mainstream parties and carve out a niche for itself that highlighted its youthful vigor and liberal policies. In these early days, Fidesz was overtly nontraditional. Its members never wore ties, rarely shaved, and attempted to convey a pro-Western image that was designed to portray its opposition as one that was wedded to an anti-Semitic, Catholic past preventing Hungary from achieving democratic reform. This is worth mentioning because the Fidesz Party of today has become a caricature of those that it once vilified. The liberal Orbán of 1989 is unrecognizable from the populist Orbán of 2020. Nevertheless, Orbán's image was tarnished in 1993, when he and the party's treasurer were caught using party funds to "reap profits from a luxury car rental company, with money funneled through a crony's enterprises."[6] As was the case with most states in CEE, the privatization of the Hungarian economy had led to a system in which certain wealthy individuals were able to gain tremendous wealth and political influence. Orbán believed this was a necessary feature of the transition and ingratiated himself with individuals who could help him gain more power. In the short term, this decision drove away some of Fidesz's earliest and more liberal members including Zsuzsanna Szelenyi, one of Hungary's first female members of parliament. The more liberal members argued that Orbán's approach was hypocritical. On the one hand, he was courting the EU leadership and demonstrating Hungary's commitment to democratic principles and economic development so that Hungary might be one of the first Central European countries to gain entrance into an expanding Europe. But, on the other hand, Orbán was ignoring the type of political transparency within the party that had excited its active members and brought it into parliament in the first place.[7] As a result of the controversy and the split in the party, Fidesz lost two seats in the 1994 parliamentary elections; 7 percent of the vote. The Socialist-Free Democrats had come to power.

Just prior to the election, the Hungarian parliament passed a resolution to apply for formal membership in the EU. This resolution greatly reflected public opinion. In the early 1990s, support in Hungary for membership in the EU was higher than in any other potential applicant state.[8] However, public support for EU membership was not necessarily based on a realistic understanding of what membership would entail. Assumptions about EU membership were driven largely by ideological rather than practical concerns; most were made about which groups would benefit or not benefit from membership. For example, a 2006 study conducted by Folsz and Toka demonstrated that public opinion in the early 1990s varied among different social groups and was largely driven by a perception that Western values would dominate Hungarian culture. The study found that "by and large young people, residents of urban areas, more highly qualified occupational groups, politicians, and big business were rather unequivocally expected to benefit, whereas a plurality assumed small entrepreneurs, the elderly, and people working in agriculture would be unfavorably affected."[9] These opinions formed the foundations for the political spectrum of Hungary in the 1990s. Left-wing, liberal, and socialist parties embraced the cosmopolitan and technocratic attitudes concerning membership, whereas center-right parties were more skeptical and concerned about how Western values would hurt long-standing traditions. Early elections demonstrated that the public was trusting those parties that were seen as committed to membership in the EU, but were willing to reinforce Hungarian traditions and suitable economic reforms.

Following the 1994 vote, Fidesz shifted its attitude toward the EU and changed its name to the Fidesz—Hungarian Civic Party (Magyar Polggari Part or MPP) in order to demonstrate a move to the right. It is important to remember that Fidesz began as a group of young dissidents who championed cosmopolitan values and a liberal agenda. More importantly, it placed membership in the EU as its primary foreign policy goal. Following its defeat in the 1994 election, the party's leadership changed its priorities. It moved away from its liberal social agenda and began to adopt more conservative and nationalist ideas. According to Lendval, "In the speeches of Fidesz MPs . . . current political and economic questions were increasingly interwoven with professions of faith in the nation, in Magyar tradition, in the homeland, in national interests, in respectability, in middle class values, in the family, in love of mother country."[10] Fidesz was founded as an opposition group to the Soviet Union. Its power was therefore reliant on its ability to oppose. This was something that Orbán and his colleagues understood.

In the mid-1990s, Fidesz-MPP was out of power. However, due to various economic policies and a weakened Socialist-Free Democrat coalition, Fidesz-MPP was able to reemerge in a short time as a viable party. In 1995, an economic agreement known as the Bokros Plan (named after Hungary's finance minister) was introduced. Designed to curb inflation and stimulate competitiveness so as to attract foreign investment, the Bokros Plan sent shocks through the transitioning economy. Austerity measures were chosen in order to prevent financial collapse. In other words, the forint (Hungary's currency) was gradually devalued, social benefits were limited, and public wages were capped. As the forint was inflated—supported artificially by foreign governments—the cap on wages and the introduction of austerity caused a massive public outcry. In addition, it forced the resignation of several cabinet members who could not tolerate such shock measures.

Although most economists agree today that the reforms were necessary for Hungary's long-term stability, at the time, they were politically catastrophic. "A year into the program, opposition [parties] were already 19% ahead in the opinion polls."[11] And on top of all of the austerity measures came the "Tocsik scandal." As the market was privatizing, Prime Minister Horn decided to pay Marta Tocsik, a "privatization consultant," 800 million forints ($5 million) in order to work out differences between utility companies and the federal government's Privatization and State Holdings Company (APV). Not only was 800 million forints an obscene amount of money in a state where the average monthly salary at the time was 50,000 forints ($315), it was discovered that the negotiations provided favorable real estate deals for two of the coalition parties' leaders.[12] Thus, the Bokros Plan was seen as a gross conspiracy designed to attract foreign investors at the expense of average Hungarians.

This, of course, was only partly true. The Bokros Plan was designed to stimulate growth by attracting foreign investors. When measured on those grounds, the Bokros Plan was a success. In 1996 alone, amid severe austerity and scandal, Hungarian companies were able to secure massive financial deals. For example, Taurus Rt., a Hungarian rubber company, was purchased by the French tire company Michelin for more than $60 million; the Budapest Power Station was sold to a consortium of Finnish and Japanese investors for $47 million; and Budapest's Forum Hotel was sold to Intercontinental Hotels Corporation for $49.4 million.[13] The Hungarian economy had weathered the storm. However, those in positions of power could not say the same.

Almost immediately, Orbán and the leaders of the Fidesz-MPP began to attack the actions of the government. Claiming that the party leadership was turning over state authority to foreign corporations and to international organizations like the International Monetary Fund. The Bokros Plan and the subsequent Tocsik scandal led to the reemergence of Orbán and Fidesz. In 1998, Fidesz picked up 128 seats and secured a coalition of center-right parties (Independent Smallholders Party; Hungarian Democratic Forum). The coalition then installed Orbán as prime minister. Orbán had done the impossible. He was able to weather corruption charges earlier in the decade, reestablish Fidesz as a center-right party, build a coalition, and emerge as the head of government. As Bozoki stated, "The reason for Fidesz's electoral success in 1998 was that it responded to the social need for order and democratic consolidation after the turbulent years of political and economic transformation."[14] The 1990s convinced many in CEE that democracy was chaotic and that democratic consolidation required forceful stability. In much the same way that Vladimir Putin took advantage of the chaotic Yeltsin years, so too did Orbán.

Nevertheless, Hungary was still headed toward EU membership and required leadership to ensure that goal. Orbán was thirty-five years old and an international sensation. He used his youthful energy, political acumen, and most importantly a manipulation of media outlets in order to reform the way Hungarian politics was conducted. To the international community, he was a firebrand, guiding Hungary toward the EU with an eye on securing the best interests for his country and was constantly in the public eye. Orbán placed a number of his cronies into public media, therefore securing him weekly radio broadcasts and monthly television appearances.[15] More importantly, Orbán was also able to place allies in high government positions. One of the first policies that the Orbán government passed was the expiration of term limits for a variety of key government positions, namely, the state president, the supreme public prosecutor, and the governor of the National Bank.[16] As individuals vacated their positions, they were filled by those sympathetic to Orbán.

Between 1998 and 2002, Fidesz began to lay the groundwork for what we have most recently seen. For example, when Istvan Csurka the founder of the small, radical, right-wing Justice and Life Party (MIEP) claimed that the attacks of 9/11 were perpetuated by Israel and certain prominent American Jews, Orbán refused to comment.[17] This refusal coupled with the fact that another election was on the horizon, convinced Orbán that he needed to act. Therefore, Fidesz increased its public expenditures in order to pay for more comprehensive public services. It was a gamble because an increase in public spending ran contrary to Fidesz's ideology. However, it was one that Orbán believed would allow him another four years.

Unfortunately for Fidesz, the strategy did not pay off. The deficit continued to grow and the economy was suffering from stagnation. In addition, the party leadership, while attempting to stay above the fray, failed to condemn the openly racist and anti-Semitic language of its extreme right-wing members. As a result, more than 72percent of the public participated in the election; the highest turnout since 1989. To everyone's astonishment, Fidesz lost. Although they won more seats (128) than its closest rival, the Hungarian Socialist Party, it was unable to secure a large enough coalition. The Socialists were able to join with the small Alliance of Free Democrats and force Fidesz out of power.

The Socialist-Liberal coalition served from 2002 to 2010. Although scandals plagued subsequent Socialist prime ministers, Hungary was able to maintain positive Freedom House scores during their tenure. In 2003, for example, Freedom House praised the government for its protection of minorities, its largely independent private press, its separation of church and state, its protection of worker's rights to form association, strike, and petition public authorities, its fair and open elections, and its willingness to accept its tendencies toward corruption and seek legislative penalties for such behavior.[18] In 2004, Hungary formally entered the EU along with ten other formerly communist states finalizing an impressive step that began in 1989.

Not long after becoming prime minister, Peter Medgyessy (2002–2004) had failed to disclose that he had at one time served as a counterintelligence officer in the communist secret services. This along with his inability to curtail spending through a massive increase in public expenditures led to a divide among the Socialist-Liberal coalition and his removal as prime minister in 2004. When billionaire Ferenc Gyurcsany became prime minister in 2004 after an intense intraparty fight, the Socialist-Liberal coalition had someone who could match political skills with Viktor Orbán. In 2006, the two debated on live television and "54% of viewers put Gyurcsany as the winner . . . against just 23% for Orbán."[19] In 2006, the Socialist Party led by Gyurcsany picked up eight seats and was able to win reelection. This was the first time an incumbent government had been able to win reelection since 1989.

Then the bottom dropped out. Although most international observers agreed that Hungary had become more democratic since 2002—Freedom House, for example, gave Hungary a 2.0 (on a scale of 1–7) in 2006, Gyurcsany destroyed his public image and like so many of his peers was overwhelmed by the 2008 financial crisis.[20] During a private meeting of the Socialist Party on May 26, 2006, following his coalition's victory, Gyurcsany was caught on tape saying: "We don't have too many choices. The reason is because we screwed it up. Not a little bit, but very much. None of the other European countries have done such stupid things that we did. We can explain it. Eventually, we lied through the last one-and-a-half or two years. It was entirely clear that what we said was not the truth."[21] Gyurcsany's admission sent shockwaves through Hungary. Almost immediately violent protests broke out in the streets of Budapest and the conservative coalition called for his removal.

Gyurcsany's assertion that the government had been deliberately misleading the public immediately hurt his image and generated the narrative that the Socialist-led coalition could not be trusted. However, Gyurcsany turned the narrative around, claiming that his admission was something that new democracies needed and that Hungarian politics had been built on lies and a lack of public trust and he was the only one willing to admit such flaws.[22] Both narratives further polarized Hungarian politics. As Fidesz won more seats (more than 40% of the national vote), but lost its coalition partner in the April 2006 elections, it was unable to form a government. But its power never waned. Orbán was able to keep the pressure on the Socialist-led coalition and continually characterized them as traitors running an "illegitimate dictatorial" regime.[23] Unbelievably, in October 2006, Gyurcsany won a vote of confidence and was able to remain as prime minister.

By the time of the global financial crisis, however, things had changed. According to a Pew Research Center poll from 2009, Central and East Europeans had already lacked the faith that other regions had in free markets. In Hungary, though, the decline in support of free markets was astonishing. In 1991, 80 percent of Hungarians supported the move from a state-controlled economy to a free market economy. By 2009, that number fell to 46 percent, a drop of thirty-four points.[24] Hungarians were not seeing how the free market, foreign investment, and EU membership were benefiting them.

This poll, nevertheless, did have another, more nuanced finding. Although most respondents gave free markets low grades, young people and those with an education did not. Young people and those with an education in CEE, those who had lived their entire lives under capitalism and were able to achieve a college degree, were more favorable to the process of free markets, than those of older, less educated generations. This is a critical finding because it contributed to the antidemocratic, right-wing populist message of Fidesz post-2010. Fidesz understood that it was entering a new political environment. It needed to find a way to keep educated, younger Hungarians from leaving the country.

When the financial bubble burst, sending global markets into a free fall, Gyurcsany resigned, and Fidesz came to power. It was this change in leadership that led to Hungary's deteriorating democracy. When Fidesz came to power in 2010, Hungary's public debt was still more than 80 percent of GDP and its unemployment rate was almost 16 percent.[25] Its economy needed a boost and most analysts suggested that Fidesz—with its promises of cutting spending and regulations—could attract higher levels of foreign investment. This time, Fidesz came to power on an antielite, antiglobalization, and anti-EU message. The party had convinced the voters that not only were the Socialists unable to govern, but that they were conspiring with European financiers and technocrats against the Hungarian people.

THE FEDESZ MANDATE AND THE DECLINE OF DEMOCRACY

Fidesz did not simply win the election of 2010. It won a two-thirds majority without having to form a governing coalition. This was a mandate. Although it had joined with the small Christian Democratic People's Party (KDNP, *Kereszténydemokrata Néppárt*), Fidesz was the party in charge. The 2010 election was a signal to the international community that Hungary had made a decision to challenge the European and Western consensus. It openly challenged notions of public spending, immigration, the role of nongovernmental organizations, and did so through a nationalist rhetoric not seen for decades.

In addition to Fidesz, the 2010 elections also brought international attention to Jobbik, another far right party that picked up forty-seven seats. Jobbik (The Movement for a Better Hungary), which began in 2003, has relied upon a narrative of anti-Semitism and anti-EU rhetoric to gain prominence. For example, in 2007, its leader Gabor Vona "founded the Magyar Garda (Hungarian Guard) as a direct-action organization intended to 'strengthen national defense' and assist in 'maintaining public order.'"[26] This paramilitary organization—that was ultimately forced to disband by court order— wore the colors of the "Arpad Flag [a group] associated with the Second World War era Hungarian fascist organization the Arrow Cross."[27] Unlike Fidesz, Jobbik is not interested in indirect allusions to neofascist claims about Jews and minorities. They are overt in their messaging.

Yet, in 2010, Hungary still received a ranking of "Free" from Freedom House despite the growth of right-wing extremism and paramilitary activity directed at minorities. In 2012, Hungary amended its constitution, changed the method by which votes are counted, and decreased the total number of seats in its parliament from 386 to 199. These changes are significant because they gave larger, incumbent parties a higher percentage of control. For example, a study from 2014 predicted that "electoral reforms would result in nearly an 8% reduction in the possible number of seats assigned based on national lists, meaning that a smaller number of seats could be awarded to smaller and non-incumbent parties."[28] As the new law awards seats according to both a method of proportional representation (voters vote for party preference) and single-member districts (voters also vote for individual candidates), it was feared that the parties that were in control would limit the possibility of other contenders.

The 2014 parliamentary elections demonstrated that the electoral reforms did in fact benefit the incumbents. Fidesz-KDNP was able to win the most seats in the regional lists and "all but 10 of the single-member districts."[29] Furthermore, "it actually lost more than 570,000 voters compared to the 2010 elections, a drop of 8.2 percent, and finished with 44.5 percent of the vote. Still, given the disproportionality of the new elections system, this 44.5 percent of the vote leads to a 66.8 percent of the seats, a drop of only 1.3 percent."[30] The election results were, therefore, skewed to Orbán's benefit. He was granted a new term as prime minister.

The electoral changes also benefited Jobbik. In 2010, Jobbik received forty-seven seats (nearly 17% of the vote). In the 2014 election, it received only twenty-three seats. However, since the total number went from 386 to 199, Jobbik received 20 percent of the popular vote.[31] This means that a party whose platform has demonstrated overt hostility to minorities and Jews was the second largest party in parliament. Hungary's democracy was being challenged almost daily and its institutions were being governed by individuals who were changing electoral laws to benefit their parties and reviving traditional, nationalistic sentiments to openly discriminate against minorities. (In the most recent European Parliamentary elections Jobbik only received 6.64% of the Hungarian vote.)[32]

On July 26, 2014, Orbán gave a speech at the twenty-fifth Balvanyos Summer Free University and Student Camp in Bailer Tusnad, Romania that argued that the CEE countries should stop using the collapse of communism as their historical reference point and free themselves from the belief that prosperity is dependent upon Western, liberal, or democratic values. Orbán argued that if the CEE states were to become prosperous, then they must look at the most recent transformative event—the 2008 global financial crisis for how they should govern their societies. This will allow them to see that the "stars" of the future will be those that are illiberal like the states of Singapore, China, India, Russia, and Turkey.[33] In other words, states that restrict freedoms and centralize authority are the more appropriate models for the CEE countries.

Orbán's meta-narrative is one that blames Hungary's troubles on the international community and in particular those that support trade liberalization, the free movement of goods, people, and services, immigrants, minorities, elites, and nongovernmental organizations. For Orbán and his supporters, it was European technocrats within the EU institutions and American financial institutions who precipitated the 2008 financial collapse and weakened the CEE states. By the time the refugee crisis hit Europe in summer 2015, Orbán's strategy was in place. Hungary's troubles could also be blamed on those seeking asylum.

As the numbers of refugees skyrocketed across the CEE region, Orbán's government built a fence along Hungary's border with Serbia and Croatia.[34] This behavior, along with allegations that the detention facility along the Serbian border has been denying food to migrants, has raised the ire of the European Commission that has recently sued the government.[35] Orbán's rhetoric is clear. He has referred to asylum seekers as "Muslim invaders," in order to demonstrate that Hungary (and other CEE states) is under attack from those who would destroy their culture, language, and religion.[36] He has positioned himself as both the champion and defender of Hungarian culture.

This posturing has also outlined Orbán's governing philosophy. Since 2014, the government has not only taken a hardline position on immigrants and refugees, but also members of the LGBTQI community and groups within Hungary (that is, NGOs, international nonprofit groups) who seek to help the aforementioned groups. In addition, Fidesz has strengthened its grip on the media in order to mainstream its propaganda and limit the rights of those who would protest its policies.

To a large degree, it has been Orbán's control over the media that has amplified his message. According to Peter Bajomi-Lazar, the editor of *Mediakutato*, a Hungarian media journal, Fidesz returned to power to "colonize the media and that taking back control of the state-run media was a top priority in Fidesz's first term."[37] Upon coming to power, the Fidesz-led government immediately passed two laws—the Act on the Freedom of the Press and the Fundamental Rules on Media Conduct and the Media Services and Mass Media Act—that created the "Media Authority," a centralized government agency, whose leader is appointed by the prime minister and has discretion over "public and commercial broadcasting, Internet, TV, and radio, on-demand media, print and online press, and foreign media 'aimed at Hungary.'"[38] Since its creation, Hungary's Media Authority has sought to censor dissidents and ensure that Orbán's populist message is well-crafted. The information is always favorable to Fidesz and above all, allows Orbán to target groups in Hungary that have historically been either underrepresented or overtly discriminated against.

In 2015, Orbán was quoted as saying that the very topic of "LGBTQI rights 'lures one to joke,' and that 'homosexuals shouldn't behave in a provocative way like one can see in Western countries."[39] The special advisor to the prime minister, Imre Kerenyi, went a step further saying that they are devoted to 'stopping the faggot lobby.'"[40] These statements as well as the government's refusal to pass appropriate hate crime and employment protection laws, underscore the fact that members of the LGBTQI community lack the kinds of protection found in other EU countries and are continual targets of abuse. The Hungarian government's inability to educate the public on the LGBTQI community (55% of Hungarians would not welcome a homosexual as their neighbor) and to use to the media as one of its main weapons has demonstrated their unwillingness to advance democratic principles.[41]

According to *Freedom House's: Nations in Transit* summary, Hungary's National Democratic Governance rating declined from 4.25 to 4.50 in 2017 "due to the government's imitation of straightforward authoritarian practices with its attack on NGOs and academic freedoms, as well as its publicly funded negative campaigns legitimizing hatred, racism, and anti-Semitism."[42] In 2017, the Hungarian parliament passed a law that forced organizations that receive more than $26,200 from foreign actors to register with the courts. In addition, any NGO that receives more than $1,800 must list the names of all foreign donors. These measures were taken in order to further centralize authority and to ostracize minorities and foreigners.

These laws, known in Hungary as the "Stop Soros Laws," have further attempted to divide the country between those who claim to support Hungarian culture and those who seek its destruction. George Soros, a Hungarian-born billionaire and Holocaust survivor has spent decades through his Open Society Foundation to generate greater levels of education, freedom, and democracy to the world. However, recently, Orbán has used Soros as the poster child for what is wrong with liberal democracy, claiming that Soros has forced open borders to non-Christian, Europeans who will bring about the destruction of Hungarian culture. These laws have made it almost impossible for undocumented immigrants to gain any protection. They are also so broadly written that their targets are not just NGOs, but ordinary citizens who might take it upon themselves to aid and comfort undocumented immigrants.[43]

Nevertheless, it appears that Orbán and Fidesz are running out of scapegoats. As the government has limited the number of refugees and passed laws that make it almost impossible to help those that are already there, it has become more of a challenge to scapegoat minorities. As immigration is practically nonexistent and because of the government's crackdown on individual freedoms, younger, educated, and skilled workers are fleeing Hungary (and other CEE countries) by the tens of thousands for wealthier and more democratic options. Most estimates state that this exodus has resulted in about 600,000 Hungarians living abroad.[44] New immigrants to Hungary could solve many of the country's woes, but with Fidesz in power, it is impossible. It is estimated that Hungary's population has declined by more than 40,000 people a year and, if this trend continues, Hungary's population will be only around six million by 2070.[45]

Playing to its nationalist base, Fidesz has recently sought to handle its declining population through a number of financial incentives aimed at increasing Hungary's birth rate and expressions of Christianity. For example, the plan is designed to allow families that have more than three children the opportunity to pay off remaining, large-scale loans (e.g., mortgages, car payments) and to give mothers who have raised four children, the opportunity to never pay personal income taxes again. In a statement, Orbán said this plan is "Hungary's answer to challenges, instead of immigration."[46] The fear that Orbán is spreading is that if Muslims are allowed to enter Central Europe, then Christianity and therefore Hungarian culture, will die. Thus, the plan also calls for the establishment of more than "21,000 creche places" across Hungary in order to demonstrate their commitment to Christianity.[47]

In May 2019, Hungarians went to the polls to elect their representatives to the European Parliament. Fidesz was able to win 52 percent of the vote (thirteen seats) on a message of anti-immigration and division. It is now attempting to join an emerging coalition of other anti-immigrant, illiberal political parties from around the continent. Thus, Fidesz's rhetoric has shaped and has been shaped by similar right-wing populist parties in other EU states. What is occurring in Europe is not contained to the newer democratic CEE states, but to some of the oldest ones as well. Hungary's leaders have found support from U.S. President Donald J. Trump, as well as Marine Le Pen, the leader of the French right-wing populist National Front,. As recently as May 2019, Prime Minister Orbán met with President Trump at the White House. Although democracy is a difficult term to define, what we have seen in Hungary and in Western strongholds is something significant.

CONCLUSION

In the span of thirty years, Hungary and the other CEE states have seen the collapse of empire, the creation of democratic institutions, the introduction of capitalism, corruption and scandal, and finally a reemergence of nationalist leaders attempting to protect their states through racially and religiously inspired division. During the last decade of the twentieth century, Hungary was a model for the CEE region. It was used as the primary case study of this chapter because it weathered scandals, an explosion of disparate political parties, the opening up of its press, massive foreign investment, and the privatization of its economy. Its leaders made tough decisions and paid steep dividends. However, Hungary joined the EU as a full member in 2004. As we have noted, it was a messy, first fifteen years, but by most accounts, it was successful in protecting individual freedoms and expanding opportunities. Therefore, Hungary is an important case study in how states manage transitions and develop economies.

But Hungary is also significant because it demonstrates how democracies can be weakened by leaders who seek to centralize power and turn civil unrest and fear into political gains. Viktor Orbán has written a new future for the CEE region. He has made himself the defender of its values by targeting Western technocrats, members of the press, elites, and minority groups. He has used Fidesz to enhance Jobbik and other small, radical right-wing parties in order to control the political agenda and make it nearly impossible to lose future elections. But, most crucially, he has provided for the leaders of CEE states an option that looks beyond the EU in particular and the West in general.

When Francis Fukuyama argued that "history had ended" and that liberal democracy had won, he seemed to have underestimated the potency of nationalism and religion.[48] The threat of the Soviet Union had ended, China was still in the process of economic development, and the West was experiencing unprecedented levels of growth. Within this context, Fukuyama's argument seemed strong. Who in the CEE region would want a return to militarism? Who would desire a rigged system that perpetuates division? Robert Kagan even noted that Europeans were from Venus (liberal, accepting, and open) and the Americans were from Mars (sought solutions via military violence).[49] Yet in the span of a generation, those who bravely fought against tyranny are looking the other way and embracing a political model that shuts out those who seek protection. Currently, it is difficult to determine how sustainable such policies are. We know that Fidesz has popular support in Hungary as do other populist parties in Europe. However, support is usually linked to economic security, and policies of division and exclusion usually limit economic choices. Orbán and his Fidesz Party are fighting a battle against the EU, immigrants, non-Christians, and an array of groups that they have labeled enemies of the state. For the moment, these measures are rewarding them at the ballot box. However, once the scapegoats are no longer there, Fidesz will be forced to govern; a fact that they have not had to address since they assumed power.

DISCUSSION QUESTIONS

1. How has Hungarian democracy evolved since 2004, the year it joined the EU?
2. Hungary is the first country in the world to declare that it has become an "illiberal democracy." What does this term imply and could it possibly become a model for other countries around the world?
3. How has Prime Minister Viktor Orbán and his Fidesz Party begun to dismantle individual freedoms?
4. How does the presence of a unicameral legislature (a legislature with only one house) create the potential for the consolidation of power in the hands of one party?

NOTES

1. Lawrence Whitehead, *Democratization: Theory and Experience* (New York, NY: Oxford University Press, 2002).

2. Juan J. Linz and Alfred Stepan, *Problems of Democratic Transition and Consolidation: Southern Europe, South America, and Post-Communist Europe* (Baltimore, MD: Johns Hopkins University Press, 1996).

3. Seymour Martin Lipset, "Some Social Requisites of Democracy: Economic Development and Political Legitimacy." *The American Political Science Review*, Vol. 53, no. 1 (March, 1959): 69–105.

4. Paul Lendval, *Orbán: Europe's New Strongman* (New York, NY: Oxford University Press, 2017), 22.

5. Ibid., 25.

6. Zsuzsanna Szelenyi, "I Was Once Orbán's ally. I Despair at What He Has Done to Hungary." *The Guardian*, June 26, 2019. https://www.theguardian.com/co mmentisfree/2019/jun/26/viktor-Orbán-ally-hungary-courageous-democrat.

7. Ibid.

8. Agnes Batory, "Attitudes to Europe: Ideology, Strategy and the Issue of European Union Membership in Hungarian Party Politics." *Party Politics*, Vol. 8, no. 5 (September 1, 2002): 525–539.

9. Attila Folsz and Gabor Toka, "Determinants of Support for EU Membership in Hungary." In *Public Opinion, Party Competition and the European Union in Post-Communist Europe*, eds. Robert Rohrschneider and Stephen Whitefield (New York, NY: Palgrave Macmillan, 2006), 148.

10. Lendval, *Orbán*, 36.

11. Ibid., 41.

12. Ernest Beck, "Hungary's Privatization Hasn't Slowed Despite APV Scandal." *Wall Street Journal*, October 11, 1996. https://www.wsj.com/articles/SB844970865 284033000.

13. Ibid.

14. Andras Bozoki, "Consolidation of Second Revolution? The Emergence of the New Right in Hungary." *Journal of Communist Studies and Transition Politics*, Vol. 24, no. 2 (April 2008): 191.

15. Lendval, *Orbán*, 46.

16. Ibid.

17. Ibid., 48.

18. Freedom House, *Hungary: Freedom in the World 2003*.

19. Lendval, *Orbán*, 61.

20. Freedom House, *Nations in Transit 2006*, 2006. https://freedomhouse.org/report/nations-transit/2006/hungary.

21. Eugen Tomiuc, "Hungary: Gyurcsany's Controversial Comments True to Form." *Radio Free Europe/Radio Liberty*, September 20, 2006. https://www.rferl.org/a/1071493.html.

22. Kate Connelly, "Caught on Tape, Prime Minister Who Admitted Lying." *The Telegraph*, September 19, 2006. https://www.telegraph.co.uk/news/1529268/Caught-on-tape-prime-minister-who-admitted-lying.html.

23. Lendval, *Orbán*, 71.

24. Pew Research Center, *Global Attitudes and Trends, Chapter 4: Economic Values*, November 2, 2009. https://www.pewresearch.org/global/2009/11/02/chapter-4-economic-values/.

25. European Commission's Staff of the Directorate-General of Economic and Foreign Affairs, "Macroeconomic Imbalances – Hungary." *European Commission's Occasional Papers 106*, July 2012. https://ec.europa.eu/economy_finance/publications/occasional_paper/2012/pdf/ocp106_en.pdf.

26. Jeffrey Stevenson Murer, "The Rise of Jobbik, Populism, and the Symbolic Politics of Illiberalism in Contemporary Hungary." *The Polish Quarterly of International Affairs*, Vol. 2 (2015): 87.

27. Ibid.

28. Nathan Schackow, "Hungary's Changing Electoral System: Reform or Repression Inside the European Union?" Presentation, *Graduate Student Conference on the EU*, Pittsburgh, PA, March 1, 2014.

29. Cas Mudde, "The 2014 Hungarian Parliamentary Elections, or How to Craft a Constitutional Majority." *Washington Post*, April 14, 2014. https://www.washingtonpost.com/news/monkey-cage/wp/2014/04/14/the-2014-hungarian-parliamentary-elections-or-how-to-craft-a-constitutional-majority/.

30. Ibid.

31. Murer, "The Rise of Jobbik," 87.

32. Krisztina Than and Marton Dunai, "Hungary's Fidesz Wins 52% of Vote; Orbán Vows to Halt Immigration." *Reuters: World News*, May 26, 2019. https://www.reuters.com/article/us-eu-election-hungary-Orbán/hungarys-fidesz-wins-52-of-vote-Orbán-vows-to-halt-immigration-idUSKCN1SW062.

33. Viktor Orbán, *Prime Minister Viktor Orbán's Speech at the 25th Balvanyos Summer Free University and Summer Camp*, Speech, Bailer Tusnad, Romaina, July 26, 2014, Website of the Hungarian Government. https://www.kormany.hu/

en/the-prime-minister/the-prime-minister-s-speeches/prime-minister-viktor-Orbán-s-speech-at-the-25th-balvanyos-summer-free-university-and-student-camp.

34. Elizabeth Zerofsky, "Viktor Orbán's Far-Right Vision for Europe." *The New Yorker*, January 7, 2019. https://www.newyorker.com/magazine/2019/01/14/viktor-Orbáns-far-right-vision-for-europe.

35. *Al Jazeera*, "European Commission Takes Hungary to Court Over Migrant Law." July 26, 2019. https://www.aljazeera.com/news/2019/07/european-commiss ion-takes-hungary-court-migrant-law-190726063518691.html.

36. Harriet Agerholm, "Refugees are Muslim Invaders Not Running for Their Lives, Says Hungarian PM Viktor Orbán." *Independent*, January 9, 2018. https:// www.independent.co.uk/news/world/europe/refugees-muslim-invaders-hungary-vikt or-Orbán-racism-islamophobia-eu-a8149251.html.

37. Daniel Howden, "The Manufacture of Hatred: Scapegoating Refugees in Central Europe." *Huffington Post*, December 15, 2016. https://www.huffpost.com/ entry/scapegoating-refugees-central-europe_n_5852c05be4b0732b82ff1f50.

38. Center for Media and Communication Studies, *Hungarian Media Laws in Europe: An Assessment of the Consistency of Hungary's Media Laws with European Practices and Norms* (CEU School of Public Policy, 2012). https://cmds.ceu.edu/arti cle/2014-03-09/hungarian-media-laws-europe-assessment.

39. Hungarian LGBT Alliance, Transvanilla Transgender Association, Hatter Society, and Labrisz Lesbian Association, *LGBTQI Rights in Hungary* (United Nations Human Rights Committee, February, 2018), 3.

40. Ibid.

41. Ibid.

42. Freedom House, *Nations in Transit 2018: Confronting Illiberalism*, 2018. https://freedomhouse.org/report/nations-transit/2018/hungary.

43. Zack Beauchamp, "Hungary Just Passed a 'Stop Soros Law' that Makes It Illegal to Help Undocumented Immigrants." *Vox*, June 22, 2018. https://www.vox .com/policy-and-politics/2018/6/22/17493070/hungary-stop-soros-Orbán.

44. *Hungarian Spectrum*, "Leaving in Hordes: Emigration from Hungary." June 22, 2018. https://hungarianspectrum.org/2018/06/22/leaving-in-hordes-emigration -from-hungary/.

45. Gabor Sarnyai, "The Hungarian Population Decline Shows No Signs of Slowing Down." *Hungary Today*, February 27, 2019. https://hungarytoday.hu/the-hu ngarian-population-decline-shows-no-sign-of-slowing-down/.

46. *Hungary Journal*, "Orbán Announces Major Family Protection Package." February 20, 2019. https://thehungaryjournal.com/2019/02/10/Orbán-announces-maj or-family-protection-package/.

47. Ibid.

48. Francis Fukuyama, *The End of History and the Last Man* (New York, NY: Avon Books, Inc., 1992).

49. Robert Kagan, *Of Paradise and Power: America and Europe in the New World Order* (New York, NY: Random House, 2002).

FURTHER READING

Gorzelak, Grzegorz, ed. *Social and Economic Development in Central and Eastern Europe: Stability and Change After 1990.* Routledge Series on Regions and Cities. New York, NY: Routledge Press, 2019.

Lendval, Paul. *Orbán: Hungary's Strongman.* New York, NY: Oxford University Press, 2018.

Pap, Andras L. *Democratic Decline in Hungary: Law and Society in an Illiberal Society.* Routledge Series on Comparative Constitutional Change. New York, NY: Routledge Press, 2018.

Sebestyen, Viktor. *Twelve Days: The Story of the 1956 Hungarian Revolution.* New York, NY: Vintage Books, 2007.

Chapter 4

Democracy in Western Europe

Kenneth L. Campbell

In 1938, the Italian philosopher Bene detto Croce wrote, "when periods of barbarism and violence are approaching it is only for the vile and the foolish that the ideal becomes unfreedom and slavery; for others [liberty] remains that which alone can be called human, the only ideal which always works."[1] Western Europe in recent years has witnessed a marked rise in the popularity of right-wing parties, many of which have gained entrance into legislative bodies. The Northern League has even become the dominant party and formed a government in Italy. The United Kingdom Independence Party (UKIP) used its influence to help force a referendum on Britain's exit from the European Union (EU), despite limited electoral success. Nationalist parties have formed alliances they hope to influence the policies of the EU. Throughout Western Europe, people have voiced dissatisfaction with their governmental institutions and evinced a strong distrust of politicians, in general, in a variety of polls. Has democracy lost its legitimacy in Western Europe in the twenty-first century because of its own inherent or internal flaws or have its critics and opponents deliberately undermined it? Alternatively, have new technologies and social media, which make it easier than ever for people to communicate with one another, form groups and alliances, and express their views, enabled Western Europe to become even more democratic, with a greater potential for citizen input into government, than ever before? As the other chapters in this book no doubt make clear, these questions are not unique to Western Europe, but the goal of this chapter is to use the Western European example toward a greater clarification of why so many people have perceived a crisis for democracy at this time in world history.

Threats to democracy are not new in the history of Western Europe, which saw fascist regimes seize power in Italy, Germany, and Spain in the 1920s and 1930s; they all came to power in countries that had at least been moving in the direction of democracy prior to the rise of dictators in each. Threats to democracy, not only from these fascist states but also from the Stalinist tyranny in the Soviet Union and fears about the spread of communist-style dictatorships, led Western leaders to affirm the legitimacy of liberal democracy and to restore or introduce it wherever possible in the postwar period. Whereas Eastern European nations largely fell under Soviet influence and introduced communist regimes in the aftermath of World War II, the United States poured financial aid into Western Europe via the Marshall Plan for those countries that would reject communism in favor of democracy. These nations included the newly formed Federal Republic of Germany, known as West Germany, whereas the German Democratic Republic, or East Germany, fell under Soviet hegemony. The end of Franco's conservative military dictatorship in 1975, along with Portugal's transition to constitutional democracy around the same time, seemed to mark an end to the legacy of fascism that had so afflicted Western and Central Europe during the interwar years. The revolutions that swept across Eastern Europe in 1989, followed by the collapse of the Soviet Union in 1991, reinforced the conviction among many people in the West that Western liberal democracy and capitalism had triumphed over communism and, with fascism having been discredited and defeated in the 1940s, would only continue to spread around the world. A major proponent of this idea, the political thinker Francis Fukuyama proclaimed "the end of history," because Western liberal democracy had triumphed so thoroughly that he could not envision any society turning away from it.[2]

Fukuyama's thesis seems hopelessly naïve and blindly optimistic in hindsight and he has modified his own views significantly since then, particularly with regard some of the tensions that have arisen in Western democracies since the 1990s.[3] Opponents and critics of democracy, who can trace their lineage back to the French Revolution itself, have proved more resilient than he anticipated, while Fukuyama had failed to account for certain inherent weaknesses in democracy itself. In general, democracy has foundered on some inherent conflicts within its own basic principles, including a conflict over the meaning and goals of democracy itself.

While democracy has certain key characteristics on which most people would agree, that does not mean that all democracies operate in exactly the same way. These characteristics might include:

- Citizens' right to participate in fair, free, and regular elections with secret ballots.
- Accountability of elected representatives through a system of checks and balances and separation of powers.
- An independent judiciary.

- A commitment to the underlying principles of democracy, such as the idea that the government should act as much as possible in the best public interest.

However, some writers, including Fareed Zakaria and Jennifer Gandhi, make the distinction between liberal democracy and illiberal democracy, with the former adhering to certain basic principles, such as liberty and equality consistent with the general philosophy of liberalism that emerged out of the general ideological movement of the European Enlightenment of the eighteenth century. Liberal democracy generally stands for the rights of individual citizens, including, if not especially, those of minorities because of a fundamental conviction that the rights of some deserve to be the rights of all. A simple majoritarian vote might seem to be a straightforward way of making decisions, but it leaves open the possibility that a majority might vote in its own self-interest in such a way that could violate the rights of a minority. Such a system, sometimes known as "direct democracy," could therefore easily violate the principles inherent in the concept of liberal democracy. Rob Rieman has recently gone so far as to aver, "When democracy becomes mass democracy, democracy ceases to exist."[4] Even the names of parties can be confusing; the Forum for Democracy in the Netherlands is actually the name of a far-right populist party.

Moreover, modern democracies have tended to favor the wealthy, who have the potential to exploit their access to politicians or political office to ensure that laws reflect their economic interests, creating a vicious cycle in which the rich constantly get richer and widening the gap between the wealthiest and poorest citizens of a democratic nation. The creation of a wealthy elite class, based on money and power rather than birth or ancestry but an elite class nonetheless, has bred resentment and the rise of populism in any number of Western democracies, including most of those in Western Europe. In their 2018 book, *How Democracies Die*, Steven Levitsky and Daniel Ziblatt suggest, "Since the end of the Cold War, most democratic breakdowns have been caused not by generals and soldiers but by elected governments themselves."[5] Some critics, channeling Karl Marx, have gone so far as to criticize democracy as a Eurocentric political system that favors male bourgeois elites at the expense of women, minorities, and the working classes.[6]

We have to be careful then how we use the term democracy, which can have a broad, almost amorphous definition or mean many different things to different people. If democracy is in crisis, it is not because authoritarian rulers are dispensing with the outward forms of democracy, but rather because politicians and special interests are coopting outwardly democratic processes for their own ends. James Kirchuk provides a way of assessing the situation that does not depend on a strict or single definition of democracy. He proposes in his 2017 book, *The End of Europe: Dictators, Demagogues, and the Coming Dark Age*: "A key feature distinguishing real democracies from ones that exist solely on paper is respect for the culture and spirit of democracy, a quality defined, in the truest sense of the word, as 'liberalism'." He goes on, however, to list those characteristics that liberal democracies tend to share: "Checks and balances, a free press, individual rights, an independent judiciary, and respect for the process."[7]

Going back to the American and French Revolutions of the late eighteenth century, people aspiring for democracy have long regarded freedom of the press as an essential component of it, but the role of the media in contemporary society has done much to complicate the issue. For example, the press has many critics in Western society today, and not just from Donald J. Trump or right-wing critics accusing the mainstream media of having a left-wing bias. One critique, for example, involves the gender bias in the media. We are seeing more women presenting the news on television and playing roles as reporters and producers, but, as recently as 2015, the global average of news stories about women stood at 25 percent and, in one Western European country, Denmark, its 25 percent figure represented a decline from 31percent in 2010.[8] In addition, media outlets, including print, television, and online journalism have discovered profits in catering to people's political biases across the political spectrum. At the same time, news outlets have proliferated, including social media, which is notoriously unreliable yet represents a primary source of news for many people. With social media and self-selected news sources reinforcing people's opinions, politicians find they need to resort to the same tactics in order to convince those people to vote for them by appealing on an emotional, rather than a rational level, argues William Davies in his 2018 book, *Nervous States: How Feeling Took Over the World.*[9]

Another complication for contemporary democracy has arisen from the memory wars associated with identity politics in countries with conflicting visions of the past and its meaning for the present. These culture wars have emphasized the connections people have independent of their conservative or liberal political viewpoints, making such traditional political categories largely irrelevant for the increasing number of single-issue voters in Western Europe. Identity politics in Western Europe has been particularly strong where rival claims to the same land exist, such as in Northern Ireland and the Basque and Catalonian regions of Spain. In addition, identity politics can also take the form of nationalism in the face of perceived threats from immigration or as part of a Muslim–Christian divide in places such as France or Germany. Alternatively, it can result from rival historical viewpoints on the legacy of a nation's past, such as the divisions that occurred in many Western European nations occupied by the Nazis during World War II. Looking at how this played out in the Scandinavian countries, for example, Dan Stone writes that in Denmark and Norway "the recent resurgence of populist parties in the form of the People's Party (Denmark) and the Progress Party (Norway) builds on a link with the suppressed memories of those who collaborated with or were sympathetic to the Nazi cause." Stone observes that these parties are neither particularly explicit about this, nor do they reject the historical narrative lionizing those patriots who resisted the Nazis, but they would naturally appeal to those more likely to have sympathized with Hitler during the war.[10] Fukuyama points out that there is nothing inherently wrong with identity politics, regarding it as "a natural and inevitable response to injustice." He adds, however, that a problem has arisen because "current understandings of identity . . . can threaten free speech and, more broadly, the kind of rational discourse needed to sustain a democracy."[11] In the twenty-first century, both those on the left and those on the right have resorted to identity politics, often in response to one another, furthering an unbridgeable political divide because these people do not disagree about issues but about the rights or grievances of their own group.

In the twenty-first century, technological literacy has brought even more information at the fingertips of virtually every citizen in Western Europe, making the current generation potentially the most politically informed generation in history. In the nineteenth century, a similar revolution occurred when mass literacy helped to prepare the way for democratic reforms and was vital to convincing conservatives that an expanding percentage of the population should have the right to vote. In Britain, the Second Great Reform Act of 1867 preceded by only a few years the Education Act of 1870, which made primary education compulsory until the age of thirteen. Another reform act followed in 1884, before near universal adult suffrage became the law at the end of the World War I (excepting women between the ages of 18 and 30, who received the right to vote ten years later). The period since the emergence of the Internet has similarly changed the calculus, with the potential for just as important democratic changes.

However, two schools of thought have emerged regarding the internet, one stressing its positive implications for the future of democracy, the second not quite so optimistic.[12] On the one hand, the Internet makes the political conversation and agenda less exclusively the province of the governing or ruling class.[13] This has been especially important in countries such as Spain and Italy without as long or as strong a democratic tradition as, say, Britain or France. A good example of popular empowerment through digital media took place in Rome on December 5, 2009: an event promoted exclusively online that drew massive support in demanding the resignation of Italy's populist, antidemocratic Prime Minister Silvio Berlusconi.[14] Mark Warren has noted "the rapid development of citizen forums and workshops, citizen juries, citizen assemblies, stakeholder meetings, and even participatory theater" as examples of the democratic potential for enhancing democracy at the grassroots level.[15] Groups and individuals not only have the ability to promote their causes on social media, but also to circulate petitions, obtain electronic signatures and present them directly to government officials or elected representatives.

The second school of thought, on the other hand, fears the uses to which governments can use technology for propaganda or even for spying on their own citizens, not to mention the potential for espionage of surveillance by foreign powers. The 2015 revelations of protracted U.S. surveillance of German chancellor Angela Merkel provide one notorious example of the latter. In addition, the relative monopolies enjoyed by giant companies such as Microsoft and Facebook have given them undue influence, made more problematic by the extent to which crackpot individuals and rogue nations have exercised a pronounced influence on people's political views with misleading propaganda and outright lies. The ability of some global corporations to circumvent national laws and an unregulated Facebook to allow the most bizarre and unflattering representations of targeted politicians and political parties represent two of the greatest threats to democracy in the twenty-first century.

Furthermore, even those who see the positive sides of the digitalization of political activity worry about the continued exclusion of some voices from the public forum. As Laia Jorba and Bruce Bimber put it, "Although diversity is one of the positive effects of the extension and inclusion of digital media, not all voices have equal opportunity to be heard."[16] Another concern is that social media and the Internet have allowed people to voice opinions or sign petitions with very little substantive knowledge about an issue. They need to invest little time in sorting out true from false claims or misinformation from facts, much less to engage in any kind of sustained critical analysis of an issue or cause they might decide to take a position on or support.[17] In short, the availability of and easy access to information on the Internet does not guarantee that people will avail themselves of it or that their interest in politics will grow as a result; in fact, rather the opposite seems to have resulted.[18] If anything, public trust in politicians and institutions has eroded in recent decades since the advent of the internet. Significantly, Berlusconi sustained a vicious physical attack in Milan days after "No Berlusconi Day," an episode lauded by the 50,000 supporters who applauded the attack on the perpetrator's Facebook page.[19] In sum, hopes that the internet would increase people's political involvement have not fully received validation, and even when they have, that involvement has not always been consistent with the principles of liberal democracy.

With these general points in mind, let us consider a few case studies that help illuminate the problems currently facing democracy in Western Europe. One primary example of the current crisis of democracy is the division within the United Kingdom over the issue of Brexit, the name coined to refer to Britain's impending exit from the EU. The issue is fairly straightforward but has become so divisive in British society that people have begun to identify themselves politically primarily in relation to this one issue rather than based on their support for any particular political party, including the heretofore-dominant ones, the Labor and Conservative Parties. Some historical context is necessary in order to understand both the background and the significance of this vote.

In the aftermath of World War II, Europe embarked on an effort to create a EU or, in other words, a kind of United States of Europe. The EU would approximate, though not replicate, the United States in an effort to overcome regional differences. These differences had not only hindered the economic development of Europe as a whole, but had led to a series of increasingly destructive wars among rival nation states culminating in the catastrophic world wars of the first half of the twentieth century. The British, reluctant to relinquish their status as a world power in the aftermath of World War II, at first chose not to participate in this enterprise, then had their first application to join the Common Market rejected in 1963, and finally, along with the Republic of Ireland, joined the European Economic Community (EEC) in 1973. The next several decades, despite frequent complaints, criticisms, and wavering public opinion, saw British membership, first the EEC and then the EU, become an unquestioned status quo. Even a nationalist such as Margaret Thatcher, Prime Minister from 1979 to 1990, never seriously considered withdrawing British membership. Tony Blair, prime minister from the Labor Party from 1997 until 2007, wrote in his 2010 memoirs that for him, "Europe was a simple issue . . . I supported the Europe ideal, but even if I hadn't, it was utterly straightforward: in a world of new emerging powers, Britain needed Europe in order to exert influence and advance its interests."[20]

Then, on June 23, 2016, the British voted yes by a margin of approximately 52 to 48 percent, to leave the EU to the stupefaction of Conservative prime minister David Cameron. During the campaign leading up to the vote, advocates of Vote Leave, who favored Britain's exit from the EU, devoted 98 percent of their marketing resources to reach people where they now spend much of their time: online.[21] Furthermore, the heavy use of social media in the Brexit campaign bears strong similarities to the Russian interference on social media used to influence the 2016 presidential election in the United States, casting at least some doubt on the legitimacy of the vote. Cameron had called the vote under pressure from the recently formed UKIP and its bombastic leader, Nigel Farage, in the hopes of putting the matter to rest for the last time. Cameron did not support the "Leave" option and resigned from power rather than attempt to steer through a policy with which he did not agree. His successor, Teresa May, though she had also been in the "Remain" camp during the vote, had no such qualms. She took over as head of the Conservative Party and Prime Minister, promising to abide by the results of the referendum, to see through Britain's exit from the EU in a responsible manner, and to obtain the greatest advantages she could obtain for the country. Her failure to get the deal she negotiated approved by Parliament led to her resignation on June 7, 2019.

Brexiteers clung to the simple principle that the people voted in favor of Brexit and therefore the ruling party and Parliament had a constitutional duty to enact the will of the people. However, Britain has never been a direct democracy, but a representative one with the elected representatives of their constituents entrusted to make informed decisions for the public and the good of the country. The Brexit controversy is as much about this larger political issue as it is whether Britain will leave the EU. Thus, the question in the face of an impending Brexit has become what kind of political system a newly independent Britain will have. Will it continue down the path toward direct democracy initiated by the Brexit vote or will it maintain its past tradition as a representative democracy? Norway and Switzerland stand out as successful democracies outside the EU from which Britain might be able to learn something. It also remains to be seen whether Britain's two largest parties, Conservative and Labor, continue to dominate British politics or whether the newly formed Independent Party joins or replaces one or the other and if the Brexit Party that contested the 2019 EU election with great success morphs into more than just a single-issue party. The Conservative Party's reputation has certainly undergone damage with its bungling of the Brexit issue, while Labor has moved steadily leftward under its avowedly Marxist leader, Jeremy Corbyn. For a hundred years, the Conservative Party only needed to convince voters that it was preferable to Labor, but with more options available and the approval ratings of the Conservatives swooning, a revolution could occur that might prove helpful for democracy by making Parliament more representative than it as heretofore been. Under Britain's so-called first-past-the-post electoral system, a party such as the Social Democratic Party, that formed as a moderate alternative to the other two parties in 1981, could attract 11.5 percent of the vote in the 1983 election and gain only six seats in the House of Commons. This was a less than a tenth of the number it would have had (seventy-four) if representation were proportional to percentage of the vote.

As of this writing, the issue has completely deadlocked the British Parliament, led to the downfall of two Conservative prime ministers, David Cameron and Teresa May, and made a celebrity out of the Speaker of the House of Commons, John Bercow, for his role in just trying to maintain some kind of order. Bercow has managed successfully to defend the rights of Parliament in order to prevent, first Prime Minister May, and then her successor Boris Johnson, from striking a Brexit deal without parliamentary approval. May's resignation has exposed problems with British democracy in another way; only 124,000 members of the Conservative Party were eligible to cast votes for her successor, who turned out to be Boris Johnson, a controversial figure committed to leaving the EU even without a deal in place, even though he lacked the support of a majority of the British electorate. British voters do not directly vote for Prime Minister, but only for their own representative in Parliament for their electoral district. Therefore, they have never really had a direct say in who becomes Prime Minister other than to vote for the party whose head they most trust, if they are not deciding on the actual merits of the individual candidates in their district. However, Britain's constitutional crisis in 2019 derived from the deadlock in Parliament over whether Britain will leave the EU without a deal, accept the deal previously negotiated by Prime Minister May, or renegotiate a new deal with the EU, one that would need unanimous approval from every other member state. The issue became even more complicated because of a parliamentary vote in 2019 explicitly rejecting a no-deal Brexit, even as that was the favored choice of Johnson and many members of the Conservative Party.

In Spain, ironically, democracy has produced a different kind of crisis by raising the hopes of Catalonian and Basque nationalists that they might achieve their independence at the ballot box or through democratic means. An independence referendum in Catalonia overwhelmingly passed on October 1, 2017, which provoked a constitutional crisis when the national government declared the referendum unconstitutional and ordered Spanish police to prevent any movement toward breaking away from Spain. Aside from the independence questions that have long hovered over Spanish politics, Spain has become more politically divided than ever, with the emergence not only of Vox, but also of the extremist left-wing party Podemos and the right-leaning centrist party, Ciudadanos ("Citizens"). Ciudadanos was polling at around 27 percent in March 2019, the largest share of any political party in Spain but far from a majority.

The disadvantage of a such a divided party system lies in the inability of any single party to secure an effective ruling majority, making any government that assumes power likely dependent upon a coalition with one or two other parties. This produces instability and weakens the ability of the party in power to govern, resulting in frequent elections and changes in government. For example, the Conservative Party in the UK under David Cameron who called for the Brexit vote only ruled because of the support of the much smaller Liberal Democratic Party. Failing to secure a majority in the House of Commons after Cameron's resignation, Teresa May and the Conservatives then had to turn to the Democratic Unionist Party from Northern Ireland to have the necessary votes to govern. This scenario played out in Italy for decades, which replaced the authoritarian one-party rule of Mussolini with the most politically chaotic democracy in Western Europe in the postwar era.

In June 2019, a populist party, the Northern League, headed by Matteo Salvini, assumed power in Italy. Salvini's party has even attracted the attention of and accepted support from Steve Bannon, Donald J. Trump's one-time adviser and the head of the right-wing Breitbart news organization. Roger Cohen, writing in the *New York Times*, has called him "the foremost theorist and propagator of the global nationalist, anti-establishment backlash."[22] Salvini, like Bannon, has taken a strong stand against immigration, vowing to protect Italy's borders in much the same way that Trump has done in the United States. The election of Salvini in Italy has become Exhibit A demonstrating the ability of populist parties to achieve power and form governments in Western Europe.

Then there is the case of the EU itself. Some people feared after the Brexit vote that Britain's exit from the Union would trigger a mass exodus of other members, bringing the project for European unity, ongoing since the end of World War II, to an abrupt halt. The predicted exodus of other nations besides Britain, however, has not materialized, largely because those nationalist parties in other countries have aligned forces in the hopes of forming something of a nationalist bloc within the EU that would advance policies favorable to one another's interests. In a particularly ironic paradox, the delay of Brexit and the breakdown of negotiations in Parliament enabled the British to vote in a European-wide election for representatives to a government that at least half of them seem determined to leave. The hopes of the EU as a successful democratic project has always hinged on the ability of Europeans of different national traditions, cultures, and languages to set aside their differences to participate in a union that represented the larger interests of Europe as a whole. If nationalists succeed at undermining this, even though democratically elected to the European Parliament, they would put democracy in the EU at risk, in the same way that far-right parties and authoritarian leaders can destroy democracy even if they come to power in a democratic political system.

Ironically, the recent rise of populism and the Brexit controversy has the potential to galvanize interest in the EU, as demonstrated by the interest that nationalists took in the 2019 election. Voter apathy has historically plagued the EU, leading to complaints against it because of a "democracy deficit." Voter participation in EU elections declined in Western Europe between 1979 and 2004, dropping from 60 percent to 43 percent in France, 66 to 43 percent in Germany, and 58 to 39 percent in the Netherlands.[23] Whether apathy represented a cause or an effect of this lack of faith, it is real. Researchers in Spain, for example, found in a study published in 2012 that 70 percent of those surveyed indicated little or no interest in politics, while fewer than

7percent indicated they were "very interested."[24] In a 2002 survey, only 22 percent of German respondents said they trusted political parties, with that number declining to 18 percent in Britain, 16 percent in France and Italy. A 2006 Eurobarmoter poll found that only 45 percent in France said they trusted their democracy, while only 30 percent in Portugal affirmed trust in theirs.[25]

If the EU cannot guarantee the security of its elections, it may have difficulty reversing this trend and nip any revived interest in voting in the bud. In advance of the EU elections in May 2019, Daniel Jones, who previously worked for the FBI and conducted investigations for the United States. Senate, told the *New York Times* of his concerns regarding Russian interference in Europe after his nonprofit organization Advance Democracy reported a number of suspicious websites and social media accounts to the authorities. "It is to constantly divide, increase distrust and undermine our faith in institutions and democracy itself," he said. "They're working to destroy everything that was built post-World War II."[26]

Democracy has always depended on the acceptance of its legitimacy, the active participation of a large percentage of the voting public within any given nation or society. Whatever the reasons—and they are many and varied—growing numbers of people in Western Europe seem to have lost their faith in the democratic processes by which elected representatives and officials run their countries. In the case of the EU, these factors include the widespread perception of the EU as a technocracy in which bureaucrats for whom no one voted make decisions that affect the lives of millions and inhibit free enterprise, the subject of a recent novel titled *The Capital* by the German writer Robert Menasse (translated into English by Jamie Bulloch). Yet one of the strongest arguments made in the book in defense of the EU suggests that a retreat by European nations behind one's borders, à la Brexit, would only exacerbate their problems.

> The growing interlinking and interdependence of economies, the over-expanding power of multinationals and the increasing significance of international financial markets would no longer allow national democracies to fulfil their essential tasks: Intervening to shape the conditions in which people had to live their lives, and generally ensuring distributive justice.[27]

Menasse also skewers the British for their shortsightedness regarding the EU and the benefits that it confers upon its members:

> And it was Great Britain's iron policy to prevent further transfer of national sovereignty to Brussels, however minor. With E.U. money they restored Manchester, which had fallen into total disrepair, but rather than express their

gratitude they see the spruced-up facades of the city as proof that Manchester Capitalism will henceforth vanquish all competitors.[28]

Whatever the limits of the EU as a democratic body, Menasse seems to suggest, the benefits outweigh the costs, while withdrawal would not lead to democracy at home, but rather, given contemporary political and economic conditions, more likely would not lead to challenges from authoritarian nationalists.

The notion that far-right parties could seize power throughout Western Europe and bring about an end to democracy there may still seem incomprehensible, but the growth of those parties in the Netherlands, France, Britain, Germany, Italy, and Spain all have raised concerns about the future of liberal democracy in the region. Emmanuel Macron's *En Marche* Party would seem to be the exception as a more liberal, centrist party making the case for simply running the country more effectively, but it also provided something of a rebuke to France's multiparty democracy by portraying itself as a unifying force rather than just another alternative. Macron has become an eloquent spokesperson for European liberal democracy. In March 2019, he issued his public statement "For European Renewal," in which he affirmed that "Our first freedom is democratic freedom: the freedom to choose our leaders as foreign powers seek to influence our vote at each election." Macron's address appeared in twenty-eight newspapers in twenty-two languages throughout Europe. In it, he recommended the establishment of a "European Agency for the Protection of Democracies." Such an agency would send experts to oversee their election processes and to ensure their safety from cyberattacks. He also advocated banning "all incitements to hate and violence from the Internet" and funding of any European political party by foreign powers.[29]

Meanwhile, Macron had opened up a campaign for the French people to air their grievances in a campaign he called "the great national debate" because of internal opposition from a group calling themselves the *gilets jaunes* (yellow jackets). The *gilets jaunes* arose in the French provinces in opposition to the perceived advantages and condescension of the French urban elite, especially those in and around Paris, who have benefited from globalization and who seemed to have found their champion in Macron. In this sense, they bear some resemblance to the aggrieved industrial workers and farmers from the American South and Midwest who voted for Donald J. Trump out of resentment toward the coastal elites in the United States.

In the 2017 French election, the centrist Emmanuel Macron convincingly defeated Marine Le Pen, the candidate of the right-wing National Front (renamed as the National Rally Party). Furthermore, other recent European elections have not brought the victories the populists hoped they would. In 2019, the Italian Northern League did increase its representation in the

European legislature from five to twenty-eight. However, liberal and Green parties won 57 seats in the 751-seat assembly, which helped to counterbalance gains on the right. In that same EU election, the newly formed Brexit Party won the most seats from Britain and National Rally won more seats from France than did Macron's centrist party, but the number of representatives from right-wing parties fell far short of projections. The Brexit Party, the Northern League, and National Rally gained a combined 23 percent of the seats, well below the predicted percent.[30] Meanwhile, in Spain the Socialist Party, headed by Pedro Sánchez, won a significant victory, marking a defeat for the incipient right-wing Vox Party there. Vox did manage to win 10.3 percent of the vote and gain twenty-four seats in its first appearance in the Spanish legislature, but these numbers also fell far short of preelection prognostications. The Spanish people have not seemed anxious to jettison their democracy, given the freedoms and relative prosperity they have enjoyed since the end of Franco's regime in 1975.

To return to the questions raised at the beginning of this essay, it would be premature to say that democracy, which now has a long history in Europe, has completely lost its legitimacy, despite facing a combination of internal weaknesses and external threats. Internally, it is true that politicians have a serious credibility problem; in one recent poll, only 19 percent of those surveyed said that they trusted politicians, a rating only higher among those professions listed than that given to advertising executives.[31] Furthermore, democracy has not proven that it can effectively arbitrate such stark divisions as have occurred over Brexit in the United Kingdom, in which roughly half of the country feels so strong one way, while the other half regards its opponents as utterly wrong. It is conceivable that Scotland and even Northern Ireland, neither of which voted in favor of Brexit, might decide to vote to leave the United Kingdom altogether, but those on opposite sides of the issue in England are simply stuck with each other.

Externally, the appearance of Vox in Spain, the Northern League in Italy, and the *Alternative für Deutschland* (AfD) in Germany raise special concerns because of the history of fascist rule in these countries, though Franco's regime only gave way to representative democracy in the 1970s, whereas the Nazi Party and Mussolini's Fascist Party both collapsed with the end of the war in 1945. Italy also features a nascent party called CasaPound, a name of significance because it refers to the American poet and avowed fascist, Ezra Pound, who resided for years in Venice. An astonishing joint announcement in Milan on April 8, 2019 of a populist alliance between Salvini's Northern League and the AfD, led by Jörg Meuthen, was eerily reminiscent of the Rome-Berlin axis between Mussolini and Hitler in the 1930s. Even in Britain and France, mass demonstrations on both sides of the Brexit issue and the protests of the *gilets jaunes* have brought the crowd back into politics in a way that in the past has led countries to veer toward authoritarianism to bring about order and control. For example, the British Parliament responded with repressive measures in the 1790s for fear of the French Revolution repeating itself in Britain and again with the notorious Six Acts after soldiers attacked a crowd to disperse it in Manchester in 1819 in an event known as the Peterloo Massacre. Around the same time, France responded to revolutionary violence first by elevating General Napoleon Bonaparte to dictatorial status before restoring the Bourbon monarchy after Napoleon's downfall at Waterloo in 1815.

Still, we may not be seeing the end of democracy, but rather living through a remarkable period of realignment and adjustment in the face of a series of unusual events and pressures. These changes included the terrorist attacks on the World Trade Center in New York City on September 11, 2001, the financial collapse and crisis of 2008, and the longer trend toward globalization and its accompanying economic uncertainties and changes. Certainly, the developments surveyed in this essay illustrate some common patterns combined with distinctiveness in the response to them, based on a difference in cultures and traditions, but also the unique responses of specific individuals. Yes, the first decades of the twenty-first century have seen the rise of right-wing parties, but since 2008, environmentally friendly Green parties have also increased their appeal, as has a true centrist party like *En Marche* in France. The right-wing AfD Party in Germany has provoked antifascist resistance from left-wing groups there. Such opposition received further incentive with the assassination of Germany's foreign minister Walther Rathenau, by a neo-Nazi on June 2, 2019. This brought only a tepid response from AfD leaders, who downplayed its significance and in some instances seemed to condone it tacitly. Although the AfD, like other right-wing extremist parties, has gained popularity in recent years, whether a majority of Germans will this time sit idly by and see their state coopted by another Hitler remains a dubious proposition. Either way, for now, both the right and the left have gained at the expense of more traditional left-center liberal and right-center conservative parties. The virtual demise of the once powerful Republican Party in France serves as a prime example.

Any attempt to predict the future, based on broad historical trends, is doomed to falter in the face of the unknown inner resources individuals possess to meet the challenges before them, even as others attempt to exploit them and appeal to the people for their own narcissistic purposes. Just because people distrust politicians, political parties, or democracy itself, does not necessarily mean that they want to abandon the latter or that they want to live under an authoritarian regime. However, it does make them susceptible to charismatic politicians who come along and provide simple answers, such as placing more severe restrictions on immigration, to complex problems, such as the effects of globalization. Even so, to suggest that the Brexit vote could not have turned out differently or that Donald J. Trump could not have lost the 2016 election ignores the largely contingent nature of history and the numerous factors that contributed to those results. At the same time, however, to ignore the divisive nature of politics in the West in the twenty-first century and the return there to nationalist and xenophobic attitudes with their root causes in economic inequality and distrust of liberal elites would be equally unwise.

Populist demagogues have been around as long as democracy itself, going back to ancient Greece. Therefore, the survival of democracy is neither the only thing at stake nor should we ever consider it an end in itself. We should only value democracy to the extent that it offers solutions to the problems of society, demonstrates the ability to cooperate fruitfully with other nations, and works in the best interests of the people as a whole—even if this sometimes means eschewing direct democracy and ignoring the will, or the tyranny, of the majority. Europeans have the choice to realize that abandoning direct democracy does not necessarily mean abandoning liberal or representative democracy. In other words, the alternative to direct democracy is not necessarily authoritarianism. There has been no shortage of authors or pundits warning of the current dangers to democracy and the threat of rising authoritarianism, including Madeleine Albright, Timothy Snyder, and Rob Riemen, just to name a few.[32] Riemen warns that any society that denies its moral and cultural heritage becomes susceptible to demagoguery and strongmen only interested in perpetuating their own power. By 2020, such rulers had emerged in places such as Russia, Saudi Arabia, and Brazil, for example. As at the time of World War II, Western Europe may hold the key to whether democracy can survive in the twenty-first century. For, if there were one region of the world with the historical experience to know the costs of abandoning democracy and a long enough tradition of democracy to appreciate its benefits, that region would seem to be Western Europe. If democracy fails there, under those circumstances, will it be able to survive anywhere?

DISCUSSION QUESTIONS

1. What is the difference between liberal democracy and illiberal democracy? Why have many people and political parties started to reject liberal democracy in the twenty-first century?
2. Is democracy still a useful term of political analysis or have modern politics become too complicated to apply that concept as a useful tool of understanding?
3. What are some of the key differences in how Western European nations have responded to the crisis in democracy? What are some of the important factors that help account for those differences?

4. What developments in Western Europe might give hope to supporters of liberal democracy?

5. Has democracy lost its legitimacy as a form of government in Western Europe in the twenty-first century? Why or why not?

6. What are some of the main populist parties that have emerged in Western Europe in the twenty-first century? In what ways do they share an agenda and in what ways do they differ from one another?

NOTES

1. Benedetto Croce, *History as the Story of Liberty*, trans. Sylvia Sprigg (Indianapolis, IN: Liberty Fund, 2000; 1938), 256.

2. Francis Fukuyama, *The End of History and the Last Man* (New York, NY: Free Press, 1992).

3. See especially Francis Fukuyama, *Identity: The Demand for Dignity and the Politics of Resentment* (New York, NY: Farrar, Straus and Giroux, 2018).

4. Rob Riemen, *To Fight Against This Age: On Fascism and Humanism* (New York, NY: W. W. Norton and Company, 2018), 43.

5. Steven Levitsky and Daniel Ziblatt, *How Democracies Die* (New York, NY: Penguin, 2018), 5.

6. For a discussion of this critique, see Jan Løhmann Stephensen, "Dingpolitik and the Expansion of the Democratic Public Sphere? From 'Democracy as Talk' to 'Conversing-with-Things'." In *The Democratic Public Sphere*, eds. Henrik Kaare Nielsen et al. (Aarhus: Aarhus University Press, 2016).

7. James Kirchuk, *The End of Europe: Dictators, Demagogues, and the Coming Dark Age* (New Haven, CT: Yale University Press, 2017), 58.

8. Christina Fiig, "A Blind Spot? News Sources, Democracy and Gender in Mass Media." In *The Democratic Public Sphere*, eds. Henrik Kaare Nielsen et al. (Aarhus: Aarhus University Press, 2016), 271–272.

9. William Davies, *Nervous States: How Feeling Took Over the World* (London: Jonathan Cape, 2018), 16.

10. Dan Stone, *Goodbye to All That?: The Story of Europe Since 1945* (Oxford: Oxford University Press, 2014), 275.

11. Francis Fukuyama, *Identity: The Demand for Dignity and the Politics of Resentment* (New York, NY: Farrar, Straus and Giroux, 2018), 115–116.

12. See Martin Kroh and Hannes Neiss, "On the Causal Nature of the Relationship between Internet Access and Political Engagement: Evidence from German Political Data." In *Digital Media and Political Engagement Worldwide*, eds. Eva Andulza et al. (Cambridge: Cambridge University Press, 2012), 160.

13. See, for example, Marta Cantijoch, "Digital Media and Offline Political Participation in Spain." In *Digital Media and Political Engagement Worldwide*, eds. Eva Andulza et al. (Cambridge: Cambridge University Press, 2012), 119.

14. Christian Vaccari, "Online Participation in Italy: Contextual Influences and Political Opportunities." In *Digital Media and Political Engagement Worldwide*, eds. Eva Andulza et al. (Cambridge: Cambridge University Press, 2012), 138.

15. Mark E. Warren, "Can We Make Public Spheres More Democratic Through Institutional Innovation?" In *The Democratic Public Sphere*, eds. Henrik Kaare Nielsen et al. (Aarhus: Aarhus University Press, 2016), 31.

16. Laia Jorba and Bruce Bimber, "The Impact of Digital Media on Citizenship from a Global Perspective." In *Digital Media and Political Engagement Worldwide*, eds. Eva Andulza et al. (Cambridge: Cambridge University Press, 2012), 26.

17. Michael J. Jensen and Eva Anduza, "Online Political Participation in the United States and Spain." In *Digital Media and Political Engagement Worldwide*, eds. Eva Andulza et al. (Cambridge: Cambridge University Press, 2012), 82.

18. Clelia Colombo, et al., "Internet Use and Political Attitudes in Europe." In *Digital Media and Political Engagement Worldwide*, eds. Eva Andulza et al. (Cambridge: Cambridge University Press, 2012), 110.

19. Anna Maesa, "Italians Wrestle with Berlusconi Attack." *The Guardian*, December 15, 2009. https://www.theguardian.com/commentisfree/2009/dec/15/silvio-berlusconi-attack-opponents-italy.

20. Tony Blair, *A Journey: My Political Life* (New York, NY: Alfred A. Knopf, 2010), 528.

21. "Social Climbers: The Brexit Party." *Economist*, May 25, 2019, 55.

22. Roger Cohen, "Steve Bannon Is a Fan of Italy's Donald Trump." *The New York Times*, May 18, 2019, SR1.

23. Tony Judt, *Postwar: A History of Europe Since 1945* (New York, NY: Penguin Books, 2005), 730.

24. Colombo et al., "Internet Use," 123.

25. Paul Kubicek, *European Politics* (Boston, MA: Longman, 2012), 246.

26. Matt Apuzzo and Adam Satariano, "Russia Is Targeting Europe's Elections: So Are Far-Right Copycats." *The New York Times*, May 12, 2019, A1.

27. Robert Menasse, *The Capital*, trans. Jamie Bulloch (London: Maclehose Press, 2017), 76.

28. Ibid., 117.

29. Emmanuel Macron, *For European Renewal*, March 4, 2019. https://www.elysee.fr/emmanuel-macron/2019/03/04/for-european-renewal.en.

30. "All the Colours of the Rainbow." *Economist*, June 1, 2019, 41–42.

31. "The Followership Problem." *Economist*, May 4, 2019, 49.

32. Madeleine Albright, *On Fascism: A Warning* (New York, NY: Harper Collins, 2018); Timothy Snyder, *On Tyranny: Twenty Lessons from the Twentieth Century* (New York, NY: Tim Duggan Books, 2017); Riemen, *To Fight Against this Age*.

FURTHER READING

Berman, Shari. *Democracy and Dictatorship in Europe: From the Ancien Regime to the Present Day*. Oxford: Oxford University Press, 2019.

Davies, William. *Nervous States: How Feeling Took Over the World.* London: Jonathan Cape, 2018.

Deneen, Patrick. *Why Liberalism Failed.* New Haven, CT: Yale University Press, 2018.

Fukuyama, Francis. *Identity: The Demand for Dignity and the Politics of Resentment.* New York, NY: Farrar, Straus and Giroux, 2018.

Kirchuk, James. *The End of Europe: Dictators, Demagogues, and the Coming Dark Age.* New Haven, CT: Yale University Press, 2017.

Levitsky, Steven and Daniel Ziblatt. *How Democracies Die.* New York, NY: Penguin, 2018.

Menasse, Robert. *The Capital*, trans. Jamie Bulloch. London: Maclehose Press, 2017.

Riemen, Rob. *To Fight Against this Age: On Fascism and Humanism.* New York, NY: W. W. Norton and Company, 2018.

Chapter 5

Democracy in Latin America

Uneven Institutional Performance

Kenneth Mitchell and Samuel Maynard

Samuel Huntington's global "Third Wave" of democratic transitions in the late twentieth century crashed hardest on the shores of Latin America.[1] Marred by military dictatorships from independence in the 1800s to the 1980s, the region quickly transformed into the developing world's most democratic region by the 1990s. As the twenty-first century arrived, Cuba alone stood as an authoritarian outpost, a relic of the Cold War. The United States' security fears receded as the Soviet Union collapsed and, in turn, Latin America's ideological space for democratic competition and representation expanded. Leftist presidential victories in its oldest (Venezuela in 1998) and most populous (Brazil in 2002) democracies confirmed a maturing of democracy in Latin America. In short, leftists could win elections without fear of a military coup with tacit or overt U.S. support.

Optimism soon faded as electorates lost confidence in democracy's capacity to advance economic development, lower poverty, and reduce everyday street crime. Hardship from acute national economic crises combined with a generalized regional malaise associated with a drift toward greater commodity dependence and widespread deindustrialization in the face of Chinese industrial competition stoked popular skepticism. "Democracy had failed to deliver" became a common refrain. Right-of-center politicians peddled promarket, neoliberal economic policies of the International Monetary Fund (IMF) and World Bank that never deliver prosperity in the region, while left-of-center politicians pushed heterodox policies that too often ended in high inflation, balance-of-payments crises, and capital flight. All politicians proved susceptible to the corruption curse, wasting spectacular sums of money and furnishing for nightly TV news programs farcical images—such as politicians burying sacks of dollars in church gardens in Buenos Aires—as well as tragic images—such as Peruvian President Alan Garcia's suicide moments prior to his arrest on corruption charges. Meanwhile, rising crime eroded personal security in Caracas, Rio de Janeiro, Sao Paulo, Bogotá, Buenos Aires, Lima, Quito, La Paz and across much of Central America and Mexico. In 2019, widespread regional socioeconomic decline, and the twin cases of hyperinflation in leftist-run Venezuela and neoliberal-run Argentina, furnish an environment conducive to the rise of conservative (Brazil in 2018) and progressive (Mexico in 2018) populists with suspect democratic loyalty.

In sum, democracy survives yet decays or stagnates across Latin America—nowhere does it flourish. What derailed democratization and will it remain so in the future require an analysis of the conditions that encourage and stabilize democratic politics in the region. Elites and the masses choose democracy over other options—indeed history is replete with moments when Latin Americans chose to ditch democracy! A critical juncture has arrived and the fate of democracy lies in the balance, and this chapter aims to explain current circumstances and the road ahead. The analysis is organized into three parts. First, literature on democratic transitions and consolidation is reviewed to assess its relevance to current regional circumstances. Second, two country case studies are examined—democratic stagnation and *survival* (Argentina) and democratic stagnation and *collapse* (Venezuela). Democracy's fate is apt to traverse these two paths in much of Latin America. A third and final section summarizes the chapter's key points and offers a prediction.

WHAT AILS DEMOCRACY?

What drives popular disillusionment with democracy in Latin America? A place to start is the foundational literature that identifies and explains the conditions that "make democracy possible" and the conditions that "make it thrive."[2] No framework garners more attention from scholars than socioeconomic modernization as a prerequisite for democratization. Transitions from agricultural, traditional economies and societies toward ones that rely on industrialized urban sectors and feature mass literacy bring with them a more complex set of demands from the public, which warrant mass incorporation into politics. Seymour Martin Lipset's seminal work serves as a touchstone for this logic.[3] As socioeconomic modernization gives way to new political actors—in particular, labor unions tied to the urban working class and professional associations for lawyers, teachers, and small entrepreneurs linked to a bourgeoning urban middle class—new cultural attitudes develop and necessitate egalitarian institutions to channel the public's need for formal political representation.[4] Absent effective, new institutions, modernizing societies with growing popular demands on the state risk "institutional overload" and political discord.[5] Democracy, according to modernization theory, not only functions to solve heightened pluralism associated with economic modernization, but it also avoids the all too common prospect of violence when new and existing groups naturally clash over rival economic interests—for example, rural landowners and peasants desire high food prices in cities while urban industrial elites and factory workers prefer the opposite.[6] In lieu of armed conflict, opposing groups can forge compromise through legal mechanisms, the formation of political parties, and competitive voting, always with the reasonable expectation that if one side loses it can live to fight another day.[7] In this manner, democracy "tames politics" according Giovanni Sartori, and, at the elite-level, conjures the incentives for elite pacts to write democratic rules-of-the-game for contesting political power.[8] Socioeconomic modernization crucially underpins this process and cultivates an environment that is ideal for democracy's appearance as well as its maintenance. As societies become wealthier, better educated, healthier, and more interconnected through urbanization, mass education, and mass communication, democratic norms flourish and diffuse as a rational response to modernization's unavoidable diversity or pluralism.[9]

Modernization theory holds that as societies grow more pluralistic, that is, spawn multiple rival factions and interest groups, individuals that compose the larger polity develop democratic cultural attitudes.[10] Individuals soon switch their loyalty and votes among competing elites in this environment, much as Joseph Schumpeter anticipates in his classic *Capitalism, Socialism and Democracy*. Recent scholarly accounts support this notion by conversely pointing to ways in which social inequality hampers democratization.[11] Others extend this idea in order to explain current democratic malaise in Latin America. For Steven Levitsky, "extreme (regional) social inequality" corrodes fundamental democratic norms, implying, while acute inequality poses no imminent threat to democracy it feeds public perceptions that amplify animosity toward political institutions and elected officials.[12] Public opinion surveys chart such animosity. Although Latin Americans still prefer democracy to alternative regime types,[13] the 2018 Latinobarómetro survey notes that an overwhelming 71 percent of Latin Americans are unsatisfied with their democracies. Institutions and public officials, in particular, have all-but-lost the public's confidence; chilling, political parties, and courts rank below the armed forces. Citizens tend to believe that presidents, legislators, and local officials are universally corrupt, with about half responding that "all or most" in these categories engage in corrupt acts.[14]

Can inequality explain democracy dissatisfaction? If modernization theory is correct, then we should see public discontent rise alongside levels of social inequity. However, in Latin America, there is little empirical evidence to show this and plenty that challenges the idea. If we look to gross domestic product (GDP) growth—Lipset's main variable—the opposite correlation surfaces. In 2009, average GDP growth across Latin America reached its lowest point since its economic downturn in the early 1980s, retracting at a rate of 1.8 percent.[15] According to Latinobarómetro survey data published that same year, support for democracy actually grew. The report noted that "support [for democracy] increases more in the year of economic downturn, negating the hypothesis that swings in the economy have an impact on support for democracy."[16] Consider Honduras; a 2009 military coup dislodged its elected president—the first coup in Latin America since 1976—and only one-third of surveyed respondents affirmed their support of democracy. Coup support spiked among those with more education than among those without university degrees—registering at 40 and 27 percent, respectively. Ultimately, coup supporters were wealthier and better educated, or the opposite outcome anticipated by modernization theory.[17]

Beyond circumstantial indicators and focusing on inequality itself, a similar picture emerges. Argentina is illustrative. Despite a catastrophic economic collapse in 2001 pushed half of its population into poverty in just six months and caused inequality to soar,[18] popular support for democracy climbed 7 percent between 2001 and 2002. Amid rioting, looting of supermarkets, police-induced homicides, rampant poverty, and unemployment, as well as government and political party collapse, 65 percent of Argentines considered "democracy preferable to any other kind of government."[19]

Inequality may be a corrosive condition that contributes to democratic disenchantment rather than a "structural cause," as Levitsky argues.[20] Nonetheless, while it may be an inconvenient truth, high, persistent levels of inequality have plagued Latin America—in particular, its most populous and most developed democracies—both prior to and after democratic transitions yet popular attitudes toward democracy have varied considerably.[21] Public disdain tends to be directed toward democratic institutions and their performance, while support for democracy as a general form of government remains relatively high. This trend causes others to emphasize institutional explanations to identify the factors that drive negative attitudes. These accounts look to inherent conflicts that arise between democratic institutions—notably, between executive and legislative branches—that limit government responsiveness and make it more difficult to sustain democracy. Formative arguments from Juan Linz and Scott Mainwaring stress the profound influence institutional design can have on a democratic regime, and among "the choices regarding institutions, none is more important than the system of government: presidential, semi-presidential, parliamentary, or some hybrid."[22] According to these scholars, Latin America's presidential systems give way to institutional design flaws that limit government responsiveness and foster divergent incentives for officeholders, ending in suboptimal policy outcomes. Linz maintains presidents and legislators have "competing claims to legitimacy," which puts each branch of government at odds with the other.[23] If legislators choose not to back a president's policy agenda, there is little that can be done to resolve the situation. From this, gridlock ensues and democracy is stifled by impasse. Moreover, fixed term limits compound this problem in presidential systems. Whereas parliamentary democracies have safeguard measures to replace a prime minister when she loses the confidence of MPs, presidents are nearly guaranteed to serve their allotted term(s). Prolonged conflict, under certain circumstances, invites regime crisis. Multipartism combined with presidentialism concerns Mainwaring. Too often presidents enter into office with minority legislative support and must build ad hoc coalitions to pass legislation. As the number of parties in the legislature increases, the risk of immobilizing deadlock grows.

Intrinsically weak presidents struggle to deliver on the policies that voters anticipate, and this unresponsiveness spills over into public frustration. Such circumstances create two mutually reinforcing concerns vis-à-vis fledging support for institutions. First, deadlock may influence conflicted presidents to take extra-institutional measures to try and pipeline policies or outright rig the game in their favor. During the 1990s, for example, Latin American presidents frequently circumvented the legislature in order to push through neoliberal economic reforms that lacked congressional support. In Argentina, Brazil, and Peru, executives governed by decree, engaged in outright bribery and corruption, or resorted to suspending the constitution entirely in order to push through neoliberal policy agendas while simultaneously consolidating power. Guillermo O'Donnell notes that although this tactic may overcome executive-legislative impasse in the short term, it erodes institutional accountability in the future.[24] Alternatively, legislatures may decide to push actively for presidential impeachment in situations where executives face greater constraints on their power. From 1985 to 2004, fourteen Latin American presidents were prematurely forced from office either due to their inability to address conditions of societal unrest or as an institutional rebuke "after they took actions deliberately intended to suspend or undermine democracy."[25] In both scenarios, institutional conflict forges a path to political instability that, under the most extreme circumstances, can foment outright confrontation and state incapacity.

Do institutional issues explain recent public disaffection with democracy? If we compare data measuring state capacity and satisfaction with democracy in Latin America, support for this assertion looks to be circumstantial. For one, data on state-building in Latin America exhibit "striking stability" over the twentieth century while opinion data varies considerably.[26] Scholars linking institutional performance to popular discontent with democracy often point to short-term episodes such as economic crises or corruption scandals that may generate a sudden and dramatic decline in public support for a sitting government. Dramatic episodes are a regional phenomenon. Though, the effect of short-term crises on public support for democracy is unclear and seems to be mixed. For political scientists, it is natural to assume the public cares about political parties, courts, public bureaucracies, presidents, and legislatures as well as levels of corruption but maybe institutional performance, similar to inequality, is best depicted as secondary or corrosive rather than a core cause of democratic discontent.

For example, during the presidency of Carlos Andrés Pérez (1988–1993), Venezuela's democracy suffered through a pronounced economic decline, wide-spanning corruption allegations, two military coup attempts, and a collapse of government. This resulted in Andrés Pérez's impeachment from office and subsequent replacement. Despite this turmoil, support for democracy was largely un-phased.[27] On April 5, 1992, President Alberto Fujimori surprised Peruvians and the international community by suspending the congress, the judiciary, and the constitution, dubbed an *autogolpe* (self-coup), concentrating absolute power in the executive branch. Non-Peruvians panned the move yet Fujimori's popularity soared among Peruvians according to several polls. In Argentina, *satisfaction with democracy* plummeted in 2002, the year after its economic collapse.[28] However, when measured again in 2003, overall support for democracy ranked among the highest in the region (placed at 78% support for) despite an environment of institutional dysfunction. More notably, Argentines recorded relatively strong faith in the capacity of the state, believing it is equipped to solve problems.[29] Blame for "economic problems" (i.e., the 2002 crisis) fell more squarely on particular government officials and specific failed policies (i.e., neoliberalism) than on democracy or public institutions in general.

In sum, scholars diagnosing current democratic disaffection in Latin America have been unable to point to any novel conclusions. Although many of these accounts view eroding support for institutions as a relatively new threat, they point to underlying causes that have remained persistent since at least the Third Wave of democratization.[30] Inequality and the incapacity of institutions, while certainly conditions that foster public resentment, cannot on their own explain the variation in levels of support for democracy and the state throughout the region. While short-term crisis episodes prompt reactionary shocks, survey data shows that faith in democracy rebounds to precrisis levels shortly after.

POLITICAL ECONOMY, FRAGILE SOCIAL CONTRACTS, AND DEMOCRATIC DECAY

Modernization theory, short-term economic or corruption crises, and institutional design flaws do not exhaust the potential causes of democratic decay and may not furnish the analytic tools to forecast the future in Latin America. Another place to begin is to view democracy as a contingent and repeated choice that national polities in the region face with a specific set of expectations or norms in mind.[31] What might this entail? One option is a general political economy framework in which popular support for democracy is contingent on an elected government convincing a critical mass of citizens that it is building a viable socioeconomic development model capable of safeguarding public order and delivering material progress in the future. In other words, a modern social contract or state-society bargain around socioeconomic development—with the polity as a wavering partner—determines democracy's fate and causes variation in popular support. Given the lack of external security threats combined with society's recognition that socioeconomic gains are pivotal to public order, rule of law, and crime, it is logical that the above social contract might exist. Dips in popular democratic support might reflect either elected presidents advancing unconvincing socioeconomic blueprints or recycling ruinous models of the past. Latin Americans are now savvy, frustrated, skeptical, and well-versed on the socioeconomic challenges their societies face. Let us explore this approach further.

Argentina (1955, 1976), Brazil (1964), and Chile (1973) ditched elected governments for bureaucratic authoritarian regimes run by military generals promising industrialization and socioeconomic gains. Brazil's Economic Miracle (1968–1974) under authoritarian rule achieved rapid industrialization (similar to China today) and Chile's Pinochet dictatorship (1973–1990) registered economic successes as well. However, the bureaucratic authoritarian model eventually collapsed and lost its critical popular support among the elites and the middle classes. Hyperinflation, balance-of-payment crises, and rising poverty created the environment surrounding the 1980s democratic transitions, and these transitions quickly became tethered to the neoliberal Washington Consensus socioeconomic model that promised radical currency and trade liberalization, combined with social spending cuts and fiscal surpluses, would lead to Asian-style development. Elected neoliberal presidents, countless IMF and World Bank reports, and academic studies peddled this theme. Yet, the Washington Consensus produced regular economic turmoil and stagnation, nonstop deindustrialization, informalization of economic production, and a return to wholesale dependence on the export of commodities and raw materials. Today, elected right-wing or neoliberal politicians no longer utter references to Asian-style development or any other socioeconomic development model.

Jorge G. Castaneda in *Utopia Unarmed: The Latin American Left After the Cold War* famously counseled progressive or left-wing politicians and parties to substitute Cold War ideologies and policies for more pragmatic options.[32] Foreshadowing left-center triangulation or "third-way" policies of U.S. President Bill Clinton (1993–2001) and British prime minister Tony Blair (1997–2007), Castaneda warned the Latin American left faced prolonged electoral disappointment unless it devised a coherent and viable economic model that could rival the neoliberal, promarket economic model of the political right. Communism and socialism stood as ballot-box losers post-Cold War, and leftist inaction produced a political vacuum that ceded elections to conservative parties and candidates and inflamed frustrations on the political left. In short, this left no economic model, no electoral success, and no stable foundation for democratic development.

By the late 1990s, neoliberal policies had caused more poverty, more unemployment, and more crime as well as economic meltdowns in Argentina, Brazil, Venezuela, Ecuador, and Bolivia. Leftists heeded Castaneda's advice. Overall, public opinion data registered a dip in support for democracy. A Pink Tide of center-left presidents swept to power in the 2000s prioritizing poverty alleviation and third-way policies; for example, leftists often scrapped market distorting general subsidies and price controls in favor of market friendly conditional cash transfer (CCTs) programs that targeted public assistance to the poor. IMF and World Bank officials lauded CCT programs such as Brazil's Bolsa Familia and Mexico's Opportunities programs and soon multilateral lenders funded CCTs across the region. In turn, regional poverty fell dramatically, a new burgeoning lower-middle class (i.e., households lifted out of poverty) spawned a consumption boom, center-left candidates won elections, and public opinion data pointed to a rebound in support for democracy across Latin America.[33] Wall Street feared but soon fell in love with Brazilian leftist icon President Luiz Inácio "Lula" da Silva (2002–2010), indeed, the ex-Marxist union leader, and one-time supporter of Brazil's bureaucratic authoritarian model (during the boom years), morphed into the model center-left president that other Pink Tide presidents sought to emulate in Argentina (Nestor and Cristina Kirchner 2003–2015), Ecuador (Rafael Vincente Correa Delgado 2007–2017), Bolivia (Juan Evo Morales Ayma 2006-present), Chile (Veronica Michelle Bachelet Jeria 2006–2010, 2014–2018), and Uruguay (José Alberto 'Pepe' Mujica Cordano 2010–2015).

Economic boom turned to bust around 2010 due to the global financial crisis (2008), higher U.S. interest rates redirecting international capital away from Latin America, and a collapse in global commodity prices linked to slower Chinese economic growth. Poverty indicators began to deteriorate around 2012 and the economic policy reforms and efforts of elected governments from the far left, the center-left, the center-right, and the far right all proved ineffective (Chile, Mexico, Peru, Ecuador, and Colombia) or disastrous (Venezuela, Argentina, and Brazil). By late 2019, voters ushered in antisystem, some claim antidemocratic, presidents to power in Brazil and Mexico while regional public opinion data reflected a profound downturn in support for democracy as well as core democratic institutions (parties, courts, and elected leaders).

The lesson is straightforward: democracy's fate or legitimacy among Latin Americans, both recently and into the foreseeable future, is contingent on socioeconomic expectations in general. Cold War democratic idealism connected to the struggles for human rights that peeked in the 1980s as well as post-Cold War socioeconomic optimism among center-right (neoliberal model) and center-left (statist model) democratic politicians stand as relics of a bygone era that seldom informs current voters.

Yet, "it's the economy, stupid" (Bill Clinton's campaign platform in 1992) oversimplifies and misreads the Latin American situation. In North America and Europe, economic downturns cause presidents and prime ministers to lose the next election and shift power to the loyal opposition; however, in Latin America it often causes parties and party systems to collapse, threatening democratic stability. Bureaucratic or institutional development in the public sector (tax collection, customs house, public education, public healthcare, etc.), the rule of law (judges, prosecutors, the police force, etc.), and the loyal opposition (assumed to be a party-based opposition) all decay along with a country's party system. Today, no major Latin American country, besides Chile, has a stable party system, and most of the major parties from the 1990s no longer exist.[34]

Linking democratic institutions to democratic survival is nothing new. Madison's famous "Federalist #10" agrees with Aristotle's *Politics* that "mob rule" presents an imminent threat to popular rule and democracy. Madison's remedy emphasizes republican institutions (representative over direct democracy, federalism, elections, rule of law, and constitutional safeguards for individual liberty). Madison's case for indirect over direct representation (that is, a republic) rests on the assumption that free people cannot be trusted with power because they will form self-interested majority factions that lead society down a path to civil war. The social contract at the root of modern democracy is a tradeoff: the people delegate via free elections authority and political power to a political elite class that in turn must deliver order and an expectation of socioeconomic progress. Thomas Hobbes in *Leviathan* stresses the people have a right to rebel if the political class fails to uphold its end of the bargain (i.e., order and expectation of progress). Today, institutionalized political parties and party systems act as the main line of defense against Madison's mob rule in consolidated democracies.

But what if the political class fails habitually to live up to its end of the bargain? This appears to be the situation in Latin America. Observers are quick to bash "the people" for democratic decay in Latin America—the masses are impatient, sympathetic to populist outsiders, and so forth. Roberto Stefan Foa

and Yascha Mounk refer to the standard definition of democratic consolidation as the "only game in town"[35] before arguing:

> Democracy comes to be the only game in town when an overwhelming major-
> ity of a country's citizens embraces democratic values, reject authoritarian
> alternatives, and support candidates or parties that are committed to uphold-
> ing the core norms and institutions of liberal democracy. By the same token,
> it can cease to be the only game in town when, at some later point, a sizable
> minority of citizens loses its belief in democratic values, becomes attracted to
> authoritarian alternatives, and starts voting for "antisystem" parties, candidates,
> or movements that flout or oppose constitutive elements of liberal democracy.
> Democracy may then be said to be deconsolidating.[36]

This misreads or ignores the original arguments discussed above regarding
state-society bargains around democracy and its survival. These authors
allude to a drift toward mob rule but with scant attention to causality. Why
this might be occurring is the important question, not whether it is occurring. Our sense is that political elites have repeatedly broken their end of the
representative democratic social contract, and while it imperils democracy, it
also presents the path forward to a brighter democratic future. The latter is
discussed in the chapter's conclusion, but first let us consider the two case
studies that support the argument presented in this section.

WHEN DEMOCRACY COLLAPSES—THE
CASE OF VENEZUELA (2000–2018)

Venezuela is a country of 32 million people with the world's largest reserves
of oil. Democracy's appearance (1958), consolidation (1960s and 1970s),
decay (1980s, 1990s, and 2000s), collapse (2010s), and potential rebirth (to
be announced) cannot be divorced from the political economy of oil. How
a country with the region's highest per capita income and strongest prodemocracy political parties (for much of the twentieth century), and with an
educated, highly urban polity steeped in democratic norms and expectations
could permit democracy to collapse provides insights into the challenge
democracy faces in Latin America.

Commodity dependence exists across Latin America since the independence era yet what economists refer to as "Dutch Disease" (i.e., adverse economic consequences from reliance on one commodity) occurs most overtly
in Venezuela—97 percent of the population lives in urban areas, agricultural
stagnation for decades necessitates food imports, and 99 percent of export
earnings came from oil in 2018. While the collapse of a democratic regime is

not unusual in the region, why it occurred in Venezuela, one of the region's strongest and most stable democracies, is puzzling. Democracy died not at the hands of the military but instead from a slow erosion of institutions by civilians with popular support. Popular frustration for years (if not decades) with political parties unable to reverse economic decline no doubt grew acute in Venezuela, but similar circumstances exist elsewhere as the recent wave of elected populists attests. Venezuela suggests a potential twenty-first century Latin American path from democracy to dictatorship: first, establishment parties fail over a period of decades to articulate and deliver a coherent economic model that produces socioeconomic gains; second, a populist outsider advances an alternative economic model packaged in nationalistic rhetoric pinning past misfortunes on establishment parties that the polity legitimizes at the ballot box; and third, the new populist government further weakens political institutions (courts, bureaucracies, and electoral systems) before its economic model fails. Democracy with no safety net of parties, institutions, and polity expectations collapses or morphs into civil authoritarianism. Venezuela traversed this path, Honduras as well, and some fear Brazil and Mexico are at "stage two."

In 1922, oil began flowing in Venezuela and, by 1929, its daily oil production ranked only behind the U.S. political conflicts surfaced over how to distribute the bounty. By 1950, Venezuela's GDP per capita (US$7,424) ranked fourth worldwide. After decades of conflict, the main political forces—the military, the moderate political parties, and the church—signed the Punto Fijo Pact in 1958, and later the 1961 constitution, which constructed a democratic regime. In this *pacted* democratic transition,[37] a center-left party (Democratic Action or AD) and a center-right party [Christian Democrats or *Comité de Organización Política Electoral Independiente* (COPEI)] agreed to forge a two-party system that shared the oil wealth, put the oil sector under technocratic control, respected democratic rules, divided up public sector jobs, and prohibited the radical left in order to satisfy the military, the church, and the United States—Caracas, the national capital, housed the School of the Americas, the U.S. military's training facility for Latin American military officers during the Cold War.

By the late 1960s, analysts hailed Venezuela's consolidated democracy and its two-party system as a regional model to avoid the zero-sum politics that plagued commodity dependent states elsewhere. Institutions born out of the Punto Fijo Pact solidified in the 1960s before flourishing in the oil bonanza of the 1970s—Venezuela was a founding member of the Organization of Petroleum Exporting Countries. As military dictatorships ruled in Argentina, Brazil, Chile, Peru, Ecuador, and Uruguay, and the region's other petrostate, Mexico, had a civilian dictatorship, Venezuelan democracy experienced its golden years. Oil wealth distributed via elected AD and COPEI governments positioned Venezuela as a democratic outlier. At the end of the golden years in the early 1980s, less than 15 percent of Venezuelans lived below the poverty line (lowest in the region), the country boasted the region's highest GDP per capita and its lowest tax-to-GDP ratio (among major regional economies), and the radical left remained marginalized. In short, Punto Fijo arrangements delivered real socioeconomic benefits that legitimized and stabilized Venezuela's democratic regime as its neighbors remained almost uniformly authoritarian.

However, Venezuela's democratic success proved to only be as strong as its primary export. Starting in 1982, boom turned to bust as oil prices fell and the United States quickly raised its interest rates, a move that redirected global capital away from Latin America and toward the United States. Venezuela, along with Argentina, Brazil, Chile, and Mexico heeded World Bank and IMF advice in the late 1970s and early 1980s and borrowed low interest petrodollars to finance budget deficits, a reasonable bet but one that depended on commodity prices rebounding to 1970s levels. Unfortunately, commodity prices, oil in particular, collapsed in the early 1980s rendering accumulated debts unserviceable. On February 27, 1983, a date Venezuelans and analysts colloquially refer to as "Black Friday," Venezuela's currency collapsed, marking the start of regular devaluations and triple digit inflation that lasted the remainder of the decade. The Punto Fijo regime and Venezuelan democracy, designed to distribute oil wealth rather than tax citizens and cut spending, slowly succumbed to economic pressure. This set the stage for a popular radical political alternative—the precise outcome the Punto Fijo's architects feared. In sum, Venezuelan democracy amounted to an elite pact that was designed to distribute oil wealth peacefully during the Cold War rather than uphold a Lockean social contract aimed at protecting individual rights. Absent oil wealth to sustain such a configuration, the collapse of Venezuela's democratic regime was, in many ways, just a matter of time.

Government attempts to respond to the mounting economic crisis mainly proved ineffective and foreshadowed the profound political shifts occurring within Venezuelan society. In 1989, Caracas and surrounding cities erupted in bloody riots in response to President Carlos Andrés Pérez's (AD) move to increase the price of bread. No longer could Punto Fijo institutions and actors control popular frustration, and soon (1992), two (failed) military coups marked the military's return to national politics. A young officer named Hugo Chavez quickly became the face of the attempted coup when he galvanized public support in the media, a move that promptly landed him in jail. Despite its failure to overthrow the government, the short-lived insurrection served to mobilize public animosity toward traditional parties, which laid a path for AD and COPEI's decline. Rafael Caldera, COPEI's founder and Punto Fijo signatory won a four-party presidential election in 1993 by abandoning his party to head a broad centrist alliance. His administration proved to be as ruinous as that of his predecessor. More economic decline ensued, and the system Caldera helped to craft back in 1958 and 1961 took its final breath. Caldera's term (1993–1998) ended with COPEI and AD collapsing, GDP per capita dropped to US$3,874, over 60 percent of Venezuelans living below the poverty line, with no viable economic model, and a polity demanding new voices and new political ideas.

After his imprisonment, Hugo Chavez swapped his military uniform for civilian clothes and won the 1998 presidential election. His victory not only satisfied the public's demand for representation, but also gave way to a totally new party system that relegated both AD and COPEI to the political periphery. The Chavez campaign promised radical reform of the country's political and economic institutions and beat his conservative opponent easily—56 percent to 40 percent. His role in the 1992 coup earned him legitimacy with voters exhausted and livid with established parties. Chavez stayed in office from 1999 until his death in 2013. Venezuelans craved radical reform, and for better or worse, Chavez delivered it with a new constitution in 1999, which, among other changes, shifted from a bicameral to a unicameral legislative branch and ended mandatory voting. Chavez won reelection in 2000 and 2006 with over 60 percent of the vote and won again in 2012 (closer margin of victory). He walked into a dire economic situation but soon benefited when the 9/11 terrorist attacks in the United States. caused the price of oil to spike and stay elevated for a period of years. Oil bonanza wealth allowed Chavez to expand social welfare programs and reorient the oil sector away from technocratic to political control by the executive branch. Chavez bankrolled socioeconomic initiatives beyond Venezuelan borders in Cuba, Nicaragua, Bolivia, and Ecuador, including the establishment of his Bank of the South (meant to rival the World Bank and Inter-American Development Bank), and he bought a significant percentage of Argentine debt. Boom gave way to bust in the 2007–2008 global financial crisis and Chavez's oil bonanza policies slowly decayed along with his respect for democratic institutions. By his death, lacking virtually any democratic institutions, most observers questioned whether the Chavez regime remained democratic at all.

Chavez on his deathbed resigned the presidency and handed over power to Vice President Nicolás Maduro in March 2013. Maduro later in 2013 won a dubious special presidential election with 50.62 percent of the votes and has bounced from one political and economic crisis to another. Maduro had served in the Chavez government since 2006, first as Foreign Secretary (2006–2013) and later as vice president, and while he inherited a political and economic mess, his subsequent leadership has been nothing short of catastrophic. Hyperinflation started in 2016. The UN Commission for Latin

America estimates Venezuelan poverty was 48 percent in 2014 and today the figure stands at above 90 percent. Millions of Venezuelans fleeing their country have caused a major international "refugee crisis" across South America. The United Nations has declared the country to be a humanitarian crisis and, by most definitions, Venezuela fits into the "failed state" category. Today, Venezuela shares more with Haiti than other South American countries.

What lessons can be gleaned from this case study? Venezuelan democracy rooted in the Punto Fijo Pact succeeded for three decades at realizing its original aim, namely, sidelining the radical political left by distributing oil wealth in a manner that drained its popular support. The Punto Fijo model deradicalized politics, legitimized centrist rule (AD and COPEI), and permitted the country to avoid the military dictatorships common during the Cold War. Once the oil wealth fell, however, this model of democracy and its two main political parties could not devise a new political economy development model capable of reorienting, legitimizing, and anchoring democracy. Increasingly poor, riddled with Dutch Disease legacies (low taxation, unproductive agricultural sector, highly urban population, etc.), and saddled with a mismatch of public sector expectations and state revenue base, Punto Fijo collapsed. Factoring in the era of Hugo Chavez, the lesson regarding democracy seems clear: without an economic model to legitimize democratic institutions—especially political parties—the polity turns on traditional representation, and thus democracy. Democracy conceived in narrow institutional terms or on U.S.-style individual liberties cannot generate popular legitimacy in Venezuela. This was true in the context of abundant oil wealth as well as today with 90 percent of Venezuelans living below the poverty line. In sum, no economic model, democracy faces a perilous path. Looking ahead, a future transition back to democracy is apt to require a political party or leader able to article a new economic model that begins to reverse the dire economic situation that exists in Venezuela. No evidence suggests that Maduro can play this role. More troubling, no evidence exists that the forces opposed to Maduro are poised to articulate a coherent economic model as well.

WHEN DEMOCRACY SURVIVES—THE CASE OF ARGENTINA (2000–2018)

Prolonged economic decline, single-commodity dependence, and party-system collapse constitute a path to democratic decay and later authoritarianism in Venezuela. Argentina, at the other end of South America, marks a case study of democratic resiliency. Venezuela, no doubt tragic, stands as an outlier in a region where formal democracy remains comparatively resilient.

Although in recent years, democratic stagnation rather than movement toward consolidation tends to prevail.

Argentina is a democratic paradox. Since 1950, only the Democratic Republic of Congo suffered more years of recession than Argentina, and since its latest democratic transition in 1982, triple digit inflation rates (including hyperinflation in 1989 and 1991), sovereign defaults (including the largest on record in 2001), and IMF bailouts occur regularly. Furthermore, long before and after 1982, acute partisan polarization compromised political institutions and resulted in pockets of Argentines open to authoritarian rule. Yet, Argentine democracy muddles along, including today when the economy is once again headed toward a major crisis. Why? What prevents Argentine democracy from collapsing?

Like most Latin American countries, Argentina's economic development is highly dependent on primary commodity exports. Whereas Venezuela has bountiful oil reserves, Argentina still predominantly relies on agricultural goods; most notably grain, beef, and soy products in more recent years. From 1890 to 1930, export-led development proved to be remarkably successful. High foreign demand—largely driven by the outbreak of World War I—enabled Argentina to become one of the ten wealthiest nations in the world. By 1913, Argentine exports increased in value at an annual rate of 4percent and its per capita GDP "exceeded that not only of [its] neighbors, but also of Italy and France."[38] In turn, rapid growth translated into a forceful push toward modernization. As Argentina's economy expanded, immigration surged. Between 1874 and 1914, the country took in approximately 6 million immigrants, mostly from Europe.[39] The majority of these newcomers remained highly concentrated in the two largest cities of Buenos Aires and Bahia Blanca, which likewise contributed to soaring levels of urbanization. These conditions served as a backdrop for the country's earliest period of democratic consolidation. By 1912, a growing middle class began to organize and pressure the country's closed oligarchic regime for more inclusive electoral reforms. An increasingly vocal opposition movement-turned-political party, the Radical Civic Union (UCR) galvanized mass demonstrations that effectively forced the government to pass the Sáenz Peña Law. This established the secret ballot and compulsory vote. From 1916 to 1930, the UCR successfully became Argentina's dominant political force.

Despite the UCR's reformist government, it failed to expand its electoral base to incorporate those outside of the Argentine middle classes. This was important for two reasons. First, it prevented the political incorporation of a rapidly growing labor sector, which by the 1930s had grown to reflect the country's "most cohesive and best-organized" social class.[40] As a result, working-class Argentines were left to consolidate their interests outside the realm of party politics. Second, the UCR's anchorage to the middle class (and likewise neglect of labor interests) led the party to develop a de facto adherence to an export-led development model, which by 1930 had proven to be remarkably volatile. Market shocks—driven by the 1929 global depression—quickly led to sharp devaluations of agrarian exports and, in turn, sent Argentina into a deep economic recession. Unable to reconcile the country's need to further finance industrialization alongside lagging commodity prices, the UCR government quickly fell into turmoil that prompted a military coup. This sent the country back into a decade-long era of fraudulent politics, which period scholars now refer to as "the infamous decade."

The introduction of military dictatorship took its toll on an increasingly restless Argentine public. Labor interests, now at the forefront of politics, were routinely met with repression by the armed forces, which maintained a strong alliance with the country's business elites. By the end of the decade, frequent demonstrations by the General Confederation of Labor (CGT)—the country's trade union conglomerate—prompted calls for liberalization and left Argentine society ripe for new forms of representation. In 1943, a small group of military officers, including then colonel Juan Domingo Perón, successfully overthrew the regime and ascended to power. The military's unprecedented turn toward state intervention in the economy allowed Perón to leverage his political skills to build inroads with the now thoroughly mobilized labor sector. Perón quickly took advantage of his government post, soon becoming the regime's labor secretary, to spearhead a national minimum wage, paid holidays, and expand pension benefits.[41] His efforts also provided unions with more autonomy and political power by allowing trade organizations to form their own internal tribunals to handle wage disputes. These policies quickly gained Perón good faith among working-class Argentines, whom he would rely on to launch the foundational support for his *Peronist* movement. After being jailed for a brief period by the regime, which feared his growing popularity, Perón and his supporters mobilized in favor of a return to free and fair elections. In the 1946 general election, his Labor Party, which would soon change its name to the Peronist Party, easily defeated the UCR by 11 percent and initiated its era of national-political dominance.

The rise of Peronism marked the second period of democratic consolidation in Argentina. Whereas Radicalism failed to align itself with the popular sector during its period of hegemony, Peronism used its ties to organized labor in order to construct an alternative paradigm for the country's political and economic development. From 1943 to 1955, the state established real progressive norms. Via legitimate elections, working-class Argentines became more politically active as voter turnout prominently increased between 1946 and 1955. Women, in particular, experienced a marked expansion of democratic and economic rights during the first Peronist government, in large part due to the defining presence of Eva Perón as a figurehead of the movement. From 1944 to 1949, the party expanded full suffrage to women and implemented wide-spanning equal pay laws that applied to workers across the board.[42] These crucial reforms enabled the Perón government to consolidate a wide spanning and enduring electoral base for the Peronist Party that would become virtually unbeatable at the polls.[43] At the same time, labor-based support was fundamental for Perón to pursue an economic model centered on protectionism and domestic industrialization, or Import-Substitution-Industrialization. Whereas the prior military regime increased the state's role in the economy, Perón's government made it the primary actor around which the economy revolved. Exchange controls, import tariffs, and business licenses favoring Argentine industries were among many of the tools at the government's disposal and were frequently employed in order to fuel the country's rapid industrialization. On this front, the government was largely successful, as wages and salaries expanded to 50 percent of the national GDP by 1950.[44] Despite this, Perón's second term was met with severe economic difficulties, including a drop in domestic agricultural exports. Without export revenue coming in, the government quickly began to drain through its currency reserves to maintain its course for industrial growth. By the 1950s, Perón could no longer suppress growing dissent from conservative sectors of society. After a series of violent upheavals in Buenos Aires and its surrounds, Perón fled Argentina under threat of death and was replaced by a brief military regime in 1955.

By the mid-twentieth century, Argentine democracy stood in sharp contrast to Venezuela's strong and stable regime. Whereas cleavage-based conflict had been settled in the latter case through the adoption of Punto Fijo, partisan competition in Argentina was left untethered to institutional democracy. Non-Peronist actors (in particular, the middle classes and military sectors), without a well-entrenched electoral base, lacked the ability to successfully challenge Peronist candidates at the polls. In turn, these groups had few incentives to commit to free and fair elections and thus resorted to nondemocratic means of securing political power. This led to frequent democratic breakdowns between 1955 and 1983 and the recurrent band of the Peronist party. Despite being forced underground, Peronism remained potent even as a clandestine political movement. Without the ability to stand for election, the party fragmented into armed insurgent factions and waged war against regime officials. Assassinations, kidnappings, and bombings were regular occurrences during the early 1970s. By 1973, civil unrest became so intense that the military and a Radical-led coalition of political parties agreed to Perón's unconditional return from exile. Despite winning a landslide election in 1973,[45] his sudden death a year later did little to assuage the extreme level of violence. His presidential successor and wife, Isabel Martínez de Perón, quickly shifted power back into the military's hands. By 1976, the armed forces seized government once again and initiated Argentina's darkest period of authoritarian rule—often referred to as the country's "dirty war." In its attempt to rid the country of Peronist influence, the military junta engaged in a campaign of state terror, which resulted in the forced disappearance and murder of an estimated 30,000 innocent citizens that were deemed "subversive." In addition to the regime's brutalism, it unleashed a full-scale economic liberalization plan that would (1) "depart from the previous Peronist program" of the 1940s–1950s and (2) curb a persistent rise in inflation via austerity.[46] Despite its unrelenting adherence to the shock therapy, the military's plan ended in disaster. By 1980, four of Argentina's largest banks collapsed, which triggered a massive run on the currency. As a last-ditch effort to salvage its legitimacy, the military tried to galvanize support by invading the Falklands/Malvinas islands in 1982—an attempt that ended in dramatic failure and permanently relegated the military from Argentine politics. By 1983, free and fair elections returned.

While the uneven development of partisan competition served to destabilize Argentine democracy during the height of the Cold War, it may have protected it from breakdown during the country's longest and most profound democratic era (1983–Present). Throughout this period, Argentina experienced recurrent economic and political crises, the first of which resulted from a severe hyperinflationary spell. Throughout the 1980s, the UCR government of Raúl Alfonsín struggled to contain soaring levels of inflation while simultaneously juggling the country's extreme foreign debt through a serious of heterodox reform measures. By 1989, inflation soared to an annual rate of over 1000 percent, which thrusted the country into a full-blown economic crisis. Violent riots erupted across Argentina and Alfonsín promptly resigned the presidency before the end of his second term. While the government's failure largely discredited the UCR, it was an opportunity for Peronism to reemerge as an adaptable alternative. Breaking with Peronism's union orthodoxy, Alfonsín's successor, Carlos Saúl Menem (1989–1999) implemented a one-to-one peg between the Argentine Peso and the U.S. dollar. This dramatically reduced inflation to the single digits by 1993. His adherence to structural adjustment quickly drew the backing of the IMF, which authorized a series of loan packages to catalyze economic growth.

Despite an initial stage of stability, the Menem's contradictory economic program quickly began to prove unsustainable. By the late 1990s, Argentina's foreign debt was on the rise and an overvalued Peso threatened the competitiveness of domestic industries.[47] Moreover, Menem's flagrant democratic oversteps had led to considerable pressure from voters as well as those from within the ranks of his own Peronist party. In 1999, a Radical-led coalition was able to win the presidency for the second time in Argentine history. However, it would reprise the failure of the previous Radical government. By 2001, the administration's poor economic stewardship pushed the country into its second episode of social upheaval in just a decade. Both unemployment and poverty rates had reached exorbitant levels at 19 and 38 percent, respectively.[48] Radical president, Fernando de la Rúa, unable to contain the increasingly violent unrest, tendered his resignation in December 2001, and by doing so initiated the electoral collapse of the UCR. In the 2003 elections, the Radical Party suffered its worst defeat since its founding, only garnering 2 percent of the national vote. Just as occurred in 1989, Peronism remained waiting in the wings as the country's single viable party.

From 2003 to 2011, Peronism rekindled its status as Argentina's hegemonic political force. However, given the nature of the 2001 economic crisis, newly elected president Nestor Kirchner took a left turn away from the Menem's neoliberal agenda that prevailed through the 1990s. Instead, his economic program invoked the classically populist aspects of Peronism that permeated Argentine politics in the 1940s. Government subsidies, maintained by a global surge in the price of commodities, were used to maintain large-scale social programs that worked to sharply alleviate poverty in just a few short years. In an effort to circumvent term limit constraints, Kirchner opted to eschew a second term and instead lent his support to his wife, Cristina Fernández de Kirchner (CFK) who handily accepted the nomination for presidency. From 2007 to 2015, CFK largely maintained a steady stream of spending until commodity prices dropped once again in 2013. A stable uptick in inflation contributed to yet another non-Peronist victory at the polls, this time sending Buenos Aires mayor, Mauricio Macri to the *Casa Rosada* (Argentina's presidential palace).

The current state of Argentine politics seems to uphold accounts that peg the country's failure to a cycle of political-economic instability—or what Ronaldo Munck has deemed "the political economy of collapse."[49] The current government's attempts to quell Argentina's mounting economic pressures through neoliberal shortcuts have largely been unsuccessful. Tax cuts, utility increases, and currency liberalization have all proven to make Argentina's economy considerably vulnerable to external market pressures or, at worst, have been decidedly counterproductive. Yet, the routine failures of non-Peronist options, while they deliver pronounced episodes of chaos, have not led to the total erosion of democracy—as failed economic adjustment has in Venezuela.

What separates Argentina's democratic endurance from Venezuela's democratic collapse? The first lesson highlights the profound importance of political institutions. Peronism, the partisan force behind constitutional norms dating back to the 1940s, persists in power and in opposition, and it anchors and divides Argentine democracy into pro- and anti-Peronist camps along with a sizable and electorally significant "neither" camp. In Venezuelan, AD and COPEI via the Punto Fijo regime colluded to curb the radical left and limit democratic participation to two centrist parties wedded to an economic model; in contrast, in Argentina Peronists still fight partisan opponents (historically the Radicals, today Macri's PRO), and, crucially, Argentine partisan camps advocate rival economic policies. Presidential elections every four years give voters real choices, something Venezuelan voters lost by 1998 after AD (1989–1993) and COPEI (1994–1999) presidents oversaw IMF-inspired neoliberal shocks. Choices for voters breathe life into Argentine democracy despite recurrent economic crises since 1982. Second, Argentine swing voters compelled to vote by law are not ideological and instead reward and punish economic stewardship. Positive results with inflation, the peso, and employment get rewarded, poor performance is punished, and the precise economic model—neoliberal, heterodox, or statist—does not matter. Lastly, if Peronism is behind Argentine democracy's resiliency, its survival merits further comment given the frequency with which economic hardships brought down traditional parties elsewhere around the region. Peronism's economic flexibility, its ability to recreate itself to match current economic circumstances, and its capacity to "lose elections" and reconstitute itself, often by retreating to subnational/provincial strongholds, provide clues and challenge orthodox assumptions on how political parties intersect with democracy.

Robert Dahl shaped a generation of scholarship on democracy when he emphasized "voter choice" and a viable partisan opposition as crucial to democratic development.[50] Poor performance must be punished or democracy withers. Scholars, in turn, call for institutionalized parties on the pro-statist and pro-market sides of the political spectrum, implying that democratic development is a repeated tug-of-war between the same ideologically rooted partisans. Voters need clear goal posts to play the game of democracy. Argentina deviates from this script—arguably, Venezuela followed it. Since 1982, Peronist presidents oversaw the country's most successful periods of "pro-market, right-wing, economic neoliberalism" (Menem, 1990–2000) and "statist, progressive, economic Keynesianism" (Kirchners, 2003–2015). President Menem became the IMF's neoliberal poster child of the 1990s while the Kirchners topped the IMF's "bad behavior" list. Likewise, the non-Peronist presidents, all economic failures yet each was a different economic breed—heterodox (Alfonsín, 1982–1989), strong neoliberalism (de la Rúa, 2000–2002), and neoliberal-lite (Macri, 2015–2019).

CONCLUSION AND PREDICTIONS

Democracy, although it remains intact throughout much of Latin America, critically hangs in the balance between fragile resilience and outright decay. Across the region, this has generated a new wave of political disenchantment that has manifested in citizen's widespread dissatisfaction with democratic institutions that are designed to represent them, and the elected officials entrusted to maintain these institutions. Recent scholarship addressing this alarming trend has been overly diagnostic and insufficiently causal: attributing democratic malaise to either persistent structural barriers (such as high inequality and weak rule of law) that sit uneasily with fluctuating public opinion data, or surface-level analysis of the data itself, which scapegoats disenchanted voters for what appears to be a resurgent tolerance for authoritarianism (and thus, a preface to democratic *deconsolidation*) or for demanding more than what liberal democracy is equipped to offer.[51] In this chapter, we argue alternatively that democracy's resilience is not determined by the public's willingness to remain devoted to democratic norms, but instead by elites' abilities to fulfill their end of the social contract—that is, to credibly deliver on their promises to engender socioeconomic development. When elites fail, the social ramifications lead voters to lose faith in institutional democracy and consequently search for new and often unstable forms of representation. Where no real alternatives are available, outsider populists have been left to govern with few constraints from opposition parties—a condition that contributed to Venezuela's remarkable backslide into civil authoritarianism. Where partisan competition remains intact, and parties remain able to offer legitimate choices to voters, democracy remains "workable," if not sluggish—as demonstrated by the Argentine case.[52]

What does our argument foreshadow about the future of democracy in Latin America? Current stress tests unfolding throughout the region may be cause for more pessimism. At the time of writing this chapter, deadly riots in response to government austerity have paralyzed both Ecuador and Chile, while the recent return of the military as a political powerbroker in Bolivia harks back to a decidedly less democratic era in South America. Each national government's response has done little to assuage the public's concerns: the center-left government of Ecuador's Lenín Moreno proposing a new tax on businesses, while the conservative government of Chile's Sebastian Piñera doubling-down on armed repression and engaging in rhetorical attacks on demonstrators.[53] In both cases, party systems generally remain centripetally adhered to market-based economic solutions. A route toward democratic strengthening will require elites to converge around a socioeconomic paradigm that can credibly channel the public's demands. This will ultimately depend on whether or not they are willing to offer this in lieu of risking political upheaval at the hands of anti-system alternatives.

DISCUSSION QUESTIONS

1. Is economic modernization a prerequisite to democratization? What are country case studies for and against this standard argument in the social sciences?

2. Latin America is not the only developing region that has endured cyclical bouts of political and economic crises. Can we extract this argument and apply it in comparative perspective to other world regions?

3. Are well-functioning institutions endogenous or exogenous to pro-democratic opinions among citizens?

4. How do political parties make democracy "workable?" Conversely, what are the risks of weak party systems as seen in Latin America?

5. Consider the institutional differences between parliamentary and presidential systems? Would Latin America's democracies benefit from parliamentary rather than presidential systems?

NOTES

1. Samuel P. Huntington, *The Third Wave: Democratization in the Late Twentieth Century* (Norman, OK: University of Oklahoma Press, 1993).

2. Dankwart Rustow, "Transitions to Democracy: Toward a Dynamic Model." *Comparative Politics* 2, No. 3 (April 1970): 337.

3. Seymour Martin Lipset, "Some Social Requisites of Democracy: Economic Development and Political Legitimacy." *The American Political Science Review* 53, No. 1 (March 1959): 69–105.

4. Gabriel A. Almond and Sydney Verba, *The Civic Culture: Political Attitudes and Democracy in Five Nations* (Princeton, NJ: Princeton University Press, 1963), 31–32.

5. See Samuel P. Huntington, *Political Order in Changing Societies* (New Haven, CT: Yale University Press, 1968).

6. See Barrington Moore, *Social Origins of Dictatorship and Democracy* (Boston, MA: Beacon Press, 1966).

7. See Ibid.; Seymour Martin Lipset and Stein Rokkan, *Party Systems and Voter Alignments: Cross-National Perspectives* (Toronto: The Free Press, 1967); Robert A. Dahl, *Polyarchy: Participation and Opposition* (New Haven, CT: Yale University Press, 1971).

8. Giovanni Sartori, *The Theory of Democracy Revisited* (Chatham: Chatham House, 1987); John Higley and Michael G. Burton, "The Elite Variable in Democratic Transitions and Breakdowns." *American Sociological Review* 54, No. 1 (1989): 17–32.

9. This point is reinforced by the indicators Lipset chooses to analyze in measuring the effect of economic modernization on democracy. Among these are GDP growth, income per capita, numbers of doctors, cars, televisions, and radios per 1000 persons, as well as several measures of urbanization, Lipset, "Some Social Requisites," 76–77.

10. For example, see Daniel Ziblatt, "How Did Europe Democratize?" *World Politics* 58, No. 2 (2006): 311–338.

11. See Carles Boix, *Democracy and Redistribution* (Cambridge: Cambridge University Press, 2003); Carles Boix and Susan C. Stokes, "Endogenous Democratization." *World Politics* 55 (July 2003): 517–549; Daron Acemoglu and

James A. Robinson, *Economic Origins of Dictatorship and Democracy* (New York, NY: Cambridge University Press, 2006).

12. Steven Levitsky, "Democratic Survival and Weakness." *Journal of Democracy* 29, No. 4 (2018): 104.

13. "Still More than Half of Respondents in All of Latin America." *The Economist*, November 8, 2018.

14. *Latinobarómetro* Survey, 2018.

15. World Bank, 2019.

16. *Latinobarómetro, Informe*, 2009, 17–18.

17. Ibid., 6–8.

18. World Bank, 2019; Argentina's GINI coefficient clocked in at over 53 percent (0.53) for 2001–2002, according to World Bank data. This is the highest it has been in recent (democratic) history (1980–present).

19. Omar G. Encarnación, "The Strange Persistence of Latin American Democracy." *World Policy Journal* 20, No. 4 (Winter 2003/2004): 30.

20. Levitsky, "Democratic Survival," 104.

21. Peter H. Smith, *Democracy in Latin America: Political Change in Comparative Perspective* (Oxford: Oxford University Press, 2012), 231–233.

22. Juan J. Linz, "The Perils of Presidentialism." *Journal of Democracy* 1 (Winter 1990): 51–69; Scott Mainwaring, "Presidentialism, Multipartism, and Democracy: The Difficult Combination." *Comparative Political Studies* 26, No. 2 (1993): 198.

23. Scott Mainwaring and Matthew S. Shugart, "Juan Linz, Presidentialism, and Democracy: A Critical Appraisal." *Comparative Politics* 29, No. 4 (July 1997): 2.

24. Guillermo O'Donnell, "Delegative Democracy." *Journal of Democracy* 5, No. 1 (January 1994): 56; Counterintuitively, these institutional violations actually allowed sitting presidents to more forcefully respond to economic woes and thus maintain public support early in their terms. However, this support began to wane as each president (Menem in Argentina; Collor de Mello in Brazil; Fujimori in Peru) further eroded checks on executive power (Keck, 1992; Levitsky and Murrillo, 2003; Conaghan, 2006).

25. Arturo Valenzuela, "Latin American Presidencies Interrupted." *Journal of Democracy* 15, No. 4 (2004): 7.

26. Hillel David Soifer, *State Building in Latin America* (Cambridge: Cambridge University Press, 2015), 15.

27. *Latinobarómetro*, 1995, 10; This is the earliest data available.

28. Ibid., 2002, 7.

29. Ibid., 2003, 17.

30. See Roberto Stefan Foa and Yascha Mounk, "The Signs of Deconsolidation." *Journal of Democracy* 28, No. 1 (2017): 5–16; Francis Fukuyama, "Why National Identity Matters." *Journal of Democracy* 29, No. 4 (2018): 5–15; Levitsky, "Democratic Survival."

31. Rustow, "Transitions to Democracy."

32. Jorge G. Castaneda, *Utopia Unarmed: The Latin American Left After the Cold War* (New York, NY: Vintage Books, 1993).

33. See *Latinobarómetro*, 2003.

34. See Scott Mainwaring (ed.), *Party Systems in Latin America: Institutionalization, Decay, and Collapse* (New York, NY: Cambridge University Press, 2018).

35. See Juan J. Linz and Alfred Stepan, *Problems of Democratic Transition and Consolidation: Southern Europe, South America, and Post-Communist Europe* (Baltimore, MD: Johns Hopkins University Press, 1996).

36. Foa and Mounk, "The Signs of Deconsolidation," 9.

37. See Terry Lynn Karl, "Dilemmas of Democratization in Latin America." *Comparative Politics* 23, No. 1 (October 1990): 1–21.

38. Carl Solberg, "The Tariff and Politics in Argentina." *The Hispanic American Historical Review* 53, No. 2 (May 1973): 260.

39. Alberto Spektorowski, "Nationalism and Democratic Construction: The Origins of Argentina's and Uruguay's Political Cultures in Comparative Perspective." *Bulletin of Latin American Research* 19, No. 1 (2000): 84.

40. James W. McGuire, *Peronism Without Perón: Unions, Parties, and Democracy in Argentina* (Stanford, CA: Stanford University Press, 1997), 44.

41. Ibid., 52.

42. Nancy Caro Hollander, "Si Evita Viviera." *Latin American Perspectives* 1, No. 3 (Autumn 1974): 45–46; It is worth noting that these reforms were among some of the most progressive in the world at the time.

43. E. Spencer Wellhofer, "Political Parties as 'Communities of Fate': Tests with Argentine Party Elites." *American Journal of Political Science* 18, No. 2 (May 1974): 347–363; This is evidenced by Perón's sizable electoral victories in both presidential and legislative elections from 1946 to 1955.

44. Pablo Gerchunoff and Damián Antúnez, "De la Bonanza Peronista a la Crisis de Desarrollo." In *Los Años Peronistas (1943–1955)*, Juan Carlos Torre (ed.) (Buenos Aires: Sudamericana, 2002), 145.

45. Perón defeated Radical candidate Ricardo Balbín by over 4 million votes (a 40 percent margin).

46. David Pion-Berlin, "The Fall of Military Rule in Argentina: 1976–1983." *Journal of Interamerican Studies and World Affairs* 27, No. 2 (Summer 1985): 58.

47. Ronaldo Munck, "Argentina, or the Political Economy of Collapse." *International Journal of Political Economy* 31, No. 3 (Fall 2001): 75.

48. Jean Grugel and Maria Pia Riggirozzi, "The Return of the State in Argentina." *International Affairs* 83, No. 1 (January 2007): 90.

49. Munck, "Argentina."

50. Dahl, *Polyarchy*.

51. See Fukuyama, "Why National Identity."

52. John Aldrich, *Why Parties? The Origin and Transformation of Political Parties in America* (Chicago: University of Chicago Press, 1995), 3.

53. See *The Washington Post*, [October 18, 2019]; *BBC News*, [October 21, 2019].

FURTHER READING

Gonzalez, Mike. *The Ebb of the Pink Tide: The Decline of the Left in Latin America.* London: Pluto Press, 2019.

Levitsky, Steven and Daniel Ziblatt. *How Democracies Die: What History Reveals About Our Future*. New York, NY: Crown Publishing, 2018.

Linz, Juan J. and Alfred Stepan. *Problems of Democratic Transition and Consolidation: Southern Europe, South America, and Post-Communist Europe*. Baltimore, MD: Johns Hopkins University Press, 1996.

Mainwaring, Scott, ed. *Party Systems in Latin America: Institutionalization, Decay, and Collapse*. Cambridge, UK: Cambridge University Press, 2018.

O'Donnell, Guillermo. "Delegative Democracy." *Journal of Democracy* 5, No. 1 (1994): 55–69.

Przeworski, Adam. *Democracy and the Market: Political and Economic Reforms in Eastern Europe and Latin America*. Cambridge, UK: Cambridge University Press, 1991.

Smith, Peter H. and Cameron J. Sells. *Democracy in Latin America*. Oxford: Oxford University Press, 2016.

Chapter 6

Democracy in the Middle East and North Africa

Still Little to No Progress

Saliba Sarsar

The Middle East and North Africa (MENA) region lacks democracy or a clear democratic vision. While there are some quasi-democratic regimes and there is some momentum toward democratic change, ruling elites tend to have staying power and armed conflicts become impediments, postponing any moves toward good governance, accountability, and transparency.

MENA means different things to different people. Geographically, it refers to the lands extending from eastern Iran to western Morocco and from northern Turkey to the southern borders of the Arabian Peninsula. Politically, the region encompasses twenty-one states, specifically the Arab ones in Southwest Asia (i.e., Bahrain, Iraq, Jordan, Kuwait, Lebanon, Oman, Palestine, Qatar, Saudi Arabia, Syria, United Arab Emirates, and Yemen) and North Africa (i.e., Algeria, Egypt, Libya, Morocco, Sudan, and Tunisia), as well as the non-Arab states of Iran, Israel, and Turkey. While the Arab states share aspects of the common Arab culture, Arabic language, Islam, and history, they are diverse in their approaches to governance and citizen participation, socioeconomic and financial standing, and regional and international relations. The same is true of the three non-Arab states. While they share aspects with the Arab states, each is characterized by various cultural, historical, governmental, and political backgrounds and settings.

Likewise, democracy has a variety of meanings. As an ideal type, at its core, it signifies "the rule of citizens," with citizens considered sovereign and viewed as "self-conscious, critical participants in communities of common speech, common value, and common work that bridge both space and time."[1] As sovereign, citizens have political rights and civil liberties. They have freedoms that must be promoted and protected, such as political, religious, social, and economic. A free and independent media functions without hindrance. Citizens are the source of law that ensures basic, equal rights for all. An independent judiciary ensures the rule of law. Citizens also can become politically engaged through voting; joining political parties, interest groups, and civic associations; and competing for and holding public office, among other ways. Their impact is most consequential to the extent that it occurs within community, not outside of it. In addition to the political community's institutions and processes that delineate rights and responsibilities, mechanisms and rules, there are public expectations and needs, as expressed by the citizens and their political leaders in terms of the quality and coherence between values and principles, as well as between policies and decisions. Transparency and political accountability are not only expected, but are also among the fundamentals of democracy. Overall, legitimacy of rule is anchored in popular consent, and the more that people are free to govern and actualize themselves, the more democratic they become. In the MENA context, very few states approximate the democratic ideal, as will be shown below.

Conversely, as an ideal type, authoritarian regimes shy away from the democratic vision. They are based on capricious and unrestricted state power and force, if necessary, all concentrated in the hands of a single person, typically a man, or a small group. They may have constitutions, legislatures or assemblies, judicial branches or courts, and political parties, but these exist to support the regimes, not to be a check or watchful eye on them. Authoritarians or autocrats are adverse to government by consent, but may well bear civil liberties to an extent, such as speech and worship. They are content with passive obedience, not serious opposition, regime criticism, or heavy citizenship involvement in politics. In the MENA environment, authoritarian regimes reflect this type of governance. They vary from parliamentary constitutional monarchies (e.g., Jordan and Morocco), absolute monarchies (e.g., Qatar and Saudi Arabia), and theocracies (e.g., Iran) to military regimes (e.g., Sudan), military-backed republics (e.g., Egypt), quasi-democratic presidential republic (e.g., Turkey), and quasi-democratic parliamentary republics (Tunisia and Israel). Some follow an ideology like Arab Socialist Ba'athism in Syria or some religious doctrine like Wahhabism in Saudi Arabia. Others find justification in religion as Iran does. Several have more deeply divided societies than others, such as in Iraq, Lebanon, and Israel.

This chapter first will review current MENA developments that advance or detract from democracy. Second, the nondemocratic or authoritarian tendencies in MENA will be explored. Third, the profiles of seven countries—Tunisia, Egypt, Jordan, Qatar, Iran, Israel, and Turkey—will be presented to show both similarities and differences within the Arab region and between the Arab and non-Arab states. Fourth, a way to measure democracy will reveal the status of democracy in seventeen Arab and three non-Arab countries. Palestine is not included in this analysis as it is not yet a sovereign state and full data about it is lacking. Fifth and last, the chapter will conclude with suggestions for advancing democratic rule in the MENA region.

EVENTS BAD FOR DEMOCRACY DURING THE 2010S

Major developments harmful to democracy raged in the MENA region during the second decade of the twenty-first century. The Syrian Civil War that started as protests against the Bashar al-Assad's regime in 2011 evolved into an all-out war between forces of the Syrian government—supported by Iran, Hizbollah (the Shi'a Islamist political party and militant group in Lebanon), and Russia—and the antigovernment opposition—supported by Saudi Arabia, United Arab Emirates, Turkey, and the United States, among others. The cost was exceedingly high. In addition to more than half a million people killed, as of June 2019, the United Nations reports over 5.6 million Syrian refugees in neighboring countries and elsewhere[2] and 6.2 million internally displaced Syrians.[3] Moreover, while there were grave violations committed by opposition groups, the government forces engaged in arbitrary detention and enforced disappearances.[4] The Yemeni Civil War, which started in 2015 between the Yemeni government headed by Abdrabbuh Mansur Hadi and the Houthi armed movement, worsened as it became a deadly expression of the Saudi Arabia–Iran proxy armed conflict. According to Human Rights Watch, 6,872 civilians were killed and 10,768 injured as of November 2018; 3 million women and girls were at risk of violence by the beginning of 2018; and 14 million people remained at risk of starvation and death due to disease such as cholera.[5] In addition to arbitrary detentions, torture, and enforced disappearances, there were attacks on civil society.[6] Jamal Ahmad Khashoggi, the Saudi author, columnist, and dissident, was assassinated by Saudi government operatives at the Saudi Consulate in Istanbul, Turkey in October 2018. His mistake: criticism of Saudi Arabia's leadership, particularly Crown Prince Mohammed bin Salman, as related to a number of domestic, regional, and international issues, including the suppression of dissent and media in the kingdom, the Saudi war on Yemen, the blockade against Qatar, and the diplomatic row with Canada over Canada's concerns about human rights abuses in Saudi Arabia. Similar to the Khashoggi case but far less known, Iranian agents assassinated Masoud Molavi Vardanjani in Istanbul, Turkey in November 2019. Vardanjani, a cybersecurity expert who worked at Iran's Defense Ministry, became an ardent critic of the Iranian regime.[7] Authoritarian systems weaken and break down democracy. Neutralizing dissidents like Khashoggi and Vardanjani is an affront to democratic values and the rule of law.

Following weeks of huge, peaceful protests by a mass movement known as the Hirak, Algeria's President Abdelaziz Bouteflika resigned in April 2019 after twenty years in office. To protect its interests, the Algerian military worked out a political compromise and a transition toward presidential elections, which were subsequently postponed by the constitutional council. Even though interim President Abdelkader Bensalah has called for an "inclusive dialogue," the people insisted that all old regime officials be removed. In December 2019, after Abdelmadjid Tebboune was declared Algeria's new president, mass protests continued. Tebboune, an insider, previously served as minister of Housing and as prime minister. In Sudan, after nearly thirty years in power, President Omar Hassan Ahmad al-Bashir (1989–2019) was overthrown, also in April, by the military after months of civil unrest and rallies. Instead of working through differences with the prodemocracy protesters or resistance committees, the Transitional Military Council, headed by General Mohamed Hamdan "Hemeti" Dagolo, along with the police and paramilitary Rapid Support Forces, cracked down on them and restricted media freedom. In August 2019, a power-sharing arrangement was reached, whereby five generals and six civilians served on a "Sovereign Council." The council's chair, occupied by General Abdel Fattah Abdelrahman al-Burhan, is supposed to rotate for a period of three years until national elections can take place. In Libya, there was a war between the Libyan National Army (LNA) loyal to renegade General Khalifa Belqasim Haftar who challenged the United Nations-recognized Government of National Accord (GNA), headed by Fayez al-Sarraj. The outcome: more than 600 people were killed, over 3,000 wounded, some 90,000 internally displaced, and close to three million besieged in the capital Tripoli.[8] As 2020 neared, Russian mercenaries supported the LNA and Turkish troops assisted the GNA.

In October 2019, Iraq was shaken by antigovernment protests against rampant corruption, high unemployment, poor living conditions, and Iran's meddling in Iraqi affairs. More than 400 people died and over 11,000 were wounded. While a sectarian electoral system maintained the power of rival political factions, a democratic Iraqi identity and democratic governance continued to suffer. Antigovernment protests also erupted in Lebanon, which led to the resignation of Prime Minister Saad al-Hariri. Headed by mostly young people, the protesters called for an end to corruption and economic mismanagement and to reforming the political system that lacked accountability, efficiency, and effectiveness. The same happened in Iran in November when thousands of young and working-class people demonstrated in most provinces to show their dissatisfaction with the regime and the 33 percent rise in fuel prices.

Most of these events were an extension of, a reaction to, or a result of the chain of prodemocracy popular, youth uprisings that began in Tunisia in December 2010 and then swept across the MENA region. The people's demands for better economic conditions, sociopolitical freedoms, and greater civic participation led to the toppling of long-ruling authoritarians like Tunisia's Zine El Abidine Ben Ali (1987–2011) and Egypt's Muhammad Hosni Mubarak (1981–2011) and the killing of Libya's Muammar Gaddafi (1969–2011). A Yemeni uprising led to the resignation of President Ali Abdullah Saleh (President of North Yemen during 1978–1990 and President of Yemen during 1990–2012). He was killed by a Houthi sniper in 2017. Protests against the Syrian government and President Bashar al-Assad led to the Syrian Civil War and to charges of war crimes against him. A Bahraini uprising between 2011 and 2014, organized by the Shia opposition, was neutralized with the military help of the Gulf Cooperation Council (GCC) and its Peninsula Shield Force. The fear from Iranian interference in most GCC states was and remains real. In Saudi Arabia, mass unrest in 2011–2012, generated by governmental corruption, high unemployment, women's inequality, human rights abuses, and discrimination against the Shi'a community, yielded massive governmental funding in the amount of $130 billion to improve the country's education, health system, infrastructure, and economic growth, as well as some reforms such as municipal elections and the right of women to participate in them and to be nominated to the Consultative Assembly. In June 2018, Saudi females were allowed to drive for the first time. The Arab Spring also impacted Jordan and Morocco but to a lesser extent. In Jordan, the monarchy withstood the prospect of reform, while coopting it and containing its opponents.[9] In Morocco, the demonstrators demanded a constitutional monarchy, not the removal of the monarch or elimination of the monarchy. While the state's positive response with a new, liberal constitution and other reforms maintained stability, the Arab Spring opened the door to citizens for questioning political authority and arguing for change.

The non-Arab states of Iran, Israel, and Turkey also went through their protests. Actually, Iran had its own Persian Awakening or Persian Spring around a year and a half prior to the start of the Arab Spring, specifically in June 2009 to February 2010. Iranian opposition leaders protested the 2009 presidential election results, which they regarded as rigged, leading many of them and their supporters to be arrested and tortured. Israel had its social justice protests in 2011–2012. Hundreds of thousands of Israelis engaged in civil disobedience, sit-ins, rallies, and resistance to protest the high cost of housing, food, and transportation, the weakening of health and education services, and the squeezing of the middle class. The government presented a variety of solutions, including a housing plan, and the protests diminished over time. In 2013, Turkey had its own civil unrest. It was "led and dominated by young middle class professionals who were demanding access, freedom, and a new kind of urban living."[10] Initially starting as an environmental protest in Taksim Square and Gezi Park in Istanbul, it turned quickly into political demonstrations around the country against the government headed by Recep Tayyip Erdoğan.

WHY AUTHORITARIAN RULE?

In 2000, I questioned the dominance of authoritarianism in most Arab countries and asked if democracy is possible there or if the very notion of "Arab democracy" is an oxymoron.[11] In 2002, the United Nations Development Programme began releasing a series of Arab Human Development reports with the contribution of Arab intellectuals and activists. The first, titled "Creating Opportunities for Future Generations," urged Arab countries to surmount deficits in three areas: political freedom, women's empowerment, and knowledge.[12] In terms of the freedom deficit only, the report found that compared with the seven world regions (i.e., North America, Oceania, Europe, Latin America and the Caribbean, South and East Asia, Sub-Saharan Africa, and Arab countries), the Arab one had the lowest score in the late 1990s. This low level was confirmed in a different set of indicators of "voice and accountability," which measured different dimensions of the political system and process, liberties and rights, and media independence. Overall, political participation was limited, and civil associations were hampered from engaging effectively in public life.[13] A related document, the third Arab Human Development Report, titled "Towards Freedom in the Arab World," was published in 2004. It argued that reforms have been "embryonic and fragmentary," attacks have targeted "outspoken political critics and human rights advocates," the status of women remained dire, democratic institutions were "stripped of their original purpose to uphold freedom," and "Arab despots of the day ruled oppressively, restricting their countries prospects of transition to democracy."[14] In 2005, there was "a dress rehearsal" for the Arab Spring, namely "Iraqis went to the polls for the first time since the fall of Saddam, Syria withdrew from Lebanon after mass protests in downtown Beirut, Saudi Arabia staged municipal elections, and determined opposition by Egyptian activists forced Mubarak to give meaning and substance, albeit temporarily, to his promises of reforms."[15] That same year, the fourth report, titled "Towards the Rise of Women in the Arab World," was put forward. It viewed the advance of women within the common structure of human rights and human development and argued that "as human beings, women and men have an innate and equal right to achieve a life of material and moral dignity." However, it found that "Arab society does not acknowledge the true extent of women's participation in social and economic activities and in the production of the components of human well-being, and it does not reward them adequately for such participation." The report's authors concluded by hoping that "the desired transformation will be carried out by taking the path of a vibrant human renaissance based on a peaceful process of negotiation for redistributing power and building good governance."[16]

Although some great suggestions were put forward to reform conditions in Arab countries, much was *hiber ala waraq* or ink on paper, as people say in the MENA. In 2008, Marina Ottaway, at the time director of the Middle East Program at the Carnegie Endowment for International Peace, observed, "The concrete steps taken by Arab governments to reform their political systems do not come even remotely close to matching the rhetoric . . . . Intellectuals engaging in the debate over democracy in the press are careful not to cross redlines that would bring down the ire of intolerant regimes upon them."[17] Similarly, in 2008, Marwan Muasher, the Jordanian diplomat, minister of foreign affairs, and deputy prime minister in charge of reform, wrote, "no Arab country could claim a systematic process of political reform that would encourage the kind of political and civil development necessary to the infrastructure of a democratic society complete with an evolved system of checks and balances, allowing for true accountability and transparency of the political process."[18]

According to Muasher, Arab rulers found three arguments for their inaction: the Arab-Israeli conflict, the fear of Islamist parties, and the sequencing of reform. Specifically, democracy "could and should wait . . . until a resolution of the Arab-Israeli conflict brought about fuller stomachs and happier days"; "political party development . . . threatened to strengthen Islamist parties, most of which were alleged to be radical and armed"; and "economic reforms had to precede political reforms."[19] These arguments miss the point as several governmental initiatives and policies can be undertaken simultaneously, which would promote democratization while resolving conflict, follow set criteria for founding political parties, and create the proper political infrastructure in order to generate and sustain economic reform. Hence, while the Arab Spring was a shock to some, it was no surprise that it erupted when it did. It was a natural reaction to dire conditions that impacted the various MENA societies, especially the young people (fifteen to twenty-nine years) and children (below fifteen years), with each making up a third of the MENA population. It is no wonder that the Arab Human Development Report 2016 used "The Youth and the Prospects for Human Development in a Changing Reality"[20] as its title.

Other more convincing arguments account for the ruler's reluctance to institute reform and advance democracy, with some more internal in nature than external. Internal factors consist of the perceived alien character of such concepts as democracy, civil liberties, and human rights; the patriarchal structure of Arab culture; the "clannish" or "tribal" setup that gives chiefs and elders significant say in social and political matters and that discourages democratic governance from materializing; the appropriation of Islam by some rulers to perpetuate their rule; the makeup and quality of socioeconomic development that hinders the growth of civil societies essential to democracy; and the public's skepticism about the suitability of democracy to their countries.[21] External factors include the "autocratic structures [that] were inscribed into the DNA of most states"[22] in the MENA region. These were enabled by, an extension of, or a revulsion against colonial rule. Another external factor has to do with how the superpowers, for example, Great Britain and the United States, meddled (and continue to meddle) in some of the MENA countries. "Great powers have used their leverage in both the political and economic spheres to dictate policy to governments and have granted them financial assistance. Underwriting democracy was not a high priority for those powers."[23]

It is no wonder that the lack of democracy and economic opportunities in Arab countries were expressed in the Arab Spring, leading multitudes of people, especially the youth and women, to challenge authority and demand change. However, the outcome was devastating: more violence than not, human casualties, refugees and internally displaced people, dispossession, property destruction, and little to no change toward democracy. The Arab Spring was a "false dawn," as Steven A. Cook calls it.[24] A hot summer or a freezing winter might be equally illustrative!

As for the non-Arab states, their status of democracy will be explored below. Suffice to say, Iran has a clerical authoritarian regime despite some reform propensities in Iranian society. Israel, a parliamentary democracy, is steadily developing antidemocratic tendencies. Turkey, in spite of its democratic practices, is gradually relapsing into authoritarianism.

Moreover, it is striking to note that most key rulers (authoritarians, autocrats, or otherwise) throughout the MENA—Arab and non-Arab—have vast wealth and are unabashed about helping family and supporters. They have an urge to become glued to their political seats as doing so is extremely profitable. A good number of them act like chief executive or financial officers of their own countries and amass or boost their wealth during and after their tenures.

A related issue is the use of clout, intercession, or personal connections in order to influence decisions. While this practice exists in various corners of the world, the MENA region is famous for it. This becomes serious when related to public affairs as both the middle person and the recipient can benefit from it. This practice is not equivalent to corruption but can be viewed as such, at least from a *Western* perspective, as it is "an abuse of power to meet private ends."[25] It takes away from democratic life, equality, efficiency, and effectiveness in governance and beyond. "For ordinary citizens, who lack connections of elites to top officials and power holders and have limited material resources, the prevalence of *wasta* in their social and economic systems is exhausting and frustrating, at best, and often means restricted possibilities for social advancement and improved well-being."[26] An extreme form of it is nepotism, meaning favoring family or friends by giving them preferential treatment, interceding on their behalf, finding them jobs, or even hiring them. Arab kings and emirs do not always follow the rules of succession. "The succession appears to be at the whim of the ruling monarch— nepotism, or *wasta* in practice."[27] Presidents act as royals. Syria's Hafez Assad decreed that his son Bashar would be his successor. If it were not for the Arab Spring, Gamal Mubarak would have succeeded his father Hosni and Saif Gaddafi would have succeeded his father Muammar. In 2019, Egypt's President Abdel Fattah El-Sisi gave his three sons (Mahmoud, Mustafa, and Hassan) important administrative roles to strengthen his hold on power until 2030 or even beyond.

PROFILES OF DEMOCRACY OR ITS LACK THEREOF IN SEVEN MENA COUNTRIES

Given MENA's recent history, where do countries fall on the continuum between authoritarianism and democracy? Below are seven representative profiles of countries, with each developed essentially with the same variables of governance, media freedom, religious freedom, human rights, human development, and economic freedom.

Tunisia: A Quasi-democratic Parliamentary Republic

Tunisia was the first to open the door to the Arab Spring in December 2010. After decades of authoritarian control, it is transforming itself rapidly toward democracy through six consecutive free and fair elections; a new, progressive constitution; and liberal laws opposing violence against women and racial discrimination. Tunisia's path is enabled by its homogenous population, politically weak military, robust civil society, and relative balance of power between Islamists and secularists, but the future remains uncertain.[28] The president is the chief of state, and is elected directly by absolute majority vote for a five-year term. The prime minister is the head of government and chooses the cabinet that then needs approval by the unicameral 217-member Assembly of the Representatives of the People or Majlis Nuwwab ash-Sha'b. Suffrage is at eighteen years of age and "universal except for active government security forces (including the police and the military), people with mental disabilities, people who have served more than three months in prison (criminal cases only), and people given a suspended sentence of more than six months."[29] While the new constitution declares Islam as the country's religion, it upholds freedom of belief and conscience, that is, Tunisians have the right to believe or not believe and to change religion, if they wish. The highest courts in Tunisia include the Court of Cassation and the Constitutional Court, but the latter, established in 2014, remains vacant. The Internet and the press are partly free in Tunisia, and the country is ranked in *Freedom in the World 2019* survey as "free" with an aggregate freedom score of 69 out of 100, whereby 100 is most free.[30] Nevertheless, it still has to reform repressive laws and create basic institutions to protect human rights. As per Human Rights Watch, "Tunisian authorities continued to prosecute speech considered offensive to 'public morals' or 'public decency'" and "used the state of emergency to impose house arrest on hundreds of people accused of threatening state security."[31] Tunisia's Human Development Index (HDI) value for 2017 is 0.735, which places it in the high human development category and at the rank of 95 out of 189 countries and territories.[32] Tunisia's economic freedom score is 55.4, rendering its economy the 125th freest in the world.[33]

Egypt: An Authoritarian Republic

Egypt is led by President Abdel Fattah Saeed Hussein Khalil El-Sisi. He took control in July 2013 after the military ouster from power of Mohamed Morsi, the first democratically elected president and a key leader of the now-banned Muslim Brotherhood. Although Egypt has a 596-member People's Assembly or Majlis Al-Nuwaab (soon to be joined by a restored Senate), some twenty political parties, and a well-established judiciary, it is not free. There has been "a return to 'electoral authoritarianism' that was in many ways more illiberal than what [Egypt] had known before the uprising."[34] El-Sisi—private, quiet, with a neat appearance—is not shy to use whatever power at his disposal to silence his opponents and all those he considers Egypt's enemies. Even though he holds that democracy is good for the Middle East,[35] his rule thus far has been anything but democratic. Unlike the democratically receptive Tunisian military, the Egyptian military tilts more authoritarian and may be considered "a state within a state." The People's Assembly is weak and the once liberal judiciary lacks true independence. According to Freedom House, the Internet and the press are not free. Moreover, "[m]eaningful political opposition is virtually nonexistent, as both liberal and Islamist activists face criminal prosecution and imprisonment."[36] Human Rights Watch reports that El-Sisi "secured a second term in a largely unfree and unfair presidential election" and "his security forces have escalated a campaign of intimidation, violence, and arrests against political opponents, civil society activists, and many others who have simply voiced mild criticism of the government."[37] Amnesty

International adds that "[m]ass unfair trials continued before civilian and military courts, with dozens sentenced to death. Women continued to be subjected to sexual and gender-based violence and were discriminated against in law and practice."[38] Although the El-Sisi regime is making some progress in religious freedom, Egypt is challenged in areas that relate to "attacks on Christians, recognition of Baha'is and Jehovah's Witnesses, the rights of Shia Muslims to perform religious rituals publicly, and the discrimination and religious freedom abuses resulting from official designations on national identity and other official documents."[39] It is these and other concerns that have led the United States Commission on International Religious Freedom (USCIRF) to place Egypt on its Tier 2 under the International Religious Freedom Act.[40] In terms of human development, which considers "a long and healthy life, access to knowledge, and a decent standard of living," Egypt's HDI value for 2017 is 0.696. This positions the country in the medium human development category, but "when the value is discounted for inequality, the HDI falls to 0.493."[41] As for economic freedom, Egypt's economy is the 144th freest out of 169, making it below the regional and world averages.[42]

Jordan: A Parliamentary Constitutional Monarchy

Jordan, or the Hashemite Kingdom of Jordan, gained its independence in 1946. With a large Palestinian community, sizable Iraqi and Syrian refugees, and fewer natural resources than several of its neighbors, it promotes a culture of pluralism and, since 1989 especially, political reforms and a National Charter that emphasizes civic participation and shared responsibility. The monarchy is hereditary, and the monarch, King Abdallah II since February 1999, is the chief of state, with the power to appoint the head of government or prime minister and to be consulted on cabinet appointments. He has a supreme role in governance, always ensuring Jordan's public order, stability, and survival. Its parliament is bicameral, consisting of a 65-member Senate appointed by the king and a 130-member House of Representatives elected by the people. Suffrage is universal and set at eighteen years of age. The judicial branch has the Supreme Court and the Constitutional Court as highest courts as well as subordinate courts, but due process is not constantly assured. While Jordan has some forty-five political parties, it is not free from challenges. "Citizen's needs exceed the capacities of governing bodies, citizen participation is limited, and local organizations exercise weak political and social influence."[43] Parliamentary and partisan pluralism has not reduced the curtailment of reform and democratization.[44] The Internet is partly free but the press is not free. In addition, Jordan is ranked in *Freedom in the World 2019* survey as "partly free" with an aggregate freedom score of 37 out of 100, whereby 100 is most free. However, Jordan or the Hashemite King is known for respecting religious freedom and advancing interfaith dialogue. As for human rights, "Jordanian authorities continued to curtail freedom of expression, detaining and bringing charges against activists, dissidents, and journalists, sometimes under broad and vague provisions of the country's counterterrorism law or electronic crimes law."[45] Jordan's HDI value for 2017 is 0.735, which places it in the high human development category and at the rank of 95 out of 189 countries and territories.[46] Jordan's economic freedom score is 66.5, making its economy the 53rd freest in the world.[47]

Qatar: An Absolute Monarchy

Since gaining independence from the United Kingdom in September 1971, Qatar's oil and natural gas revenues have enabled it to become among the richest countries in the world. A hereditary monarchy, it is ruled by the Al Thani family, and the current chief of state or ruler is Emir Tamim bin Hamad Al Thani. He appoints the head of government or prime minister, the deputy prime minister, and the Council of Ministers. The emir controls all the executive powers, and although there is an Advisory Council or Majlis al-Shura and highest courts (e.g., Supreme Court or Court of Cassation and Supreme Constitutional Court), the ultimate legislative and judicial authority rests with him. Political parties are banned, and so are public affairs associations, trade unions, and protests. As per constitution, Islam is the state religion and legislation has sharia as "a main source." All religious groups must register with the government in order to function and, in addition to Sunni and Shia Muslims, eight Christian denominations have registered.[48] Qatar is not free, scoring 25 out of 100, whereby 100 is most free.[49] According to Freedom House, "While the country's flagship satellite television channel, Al-Jazeera, is permitted to air critical reports on foreign countries and leaders, journalists are subject to prosecution for criticizing the Qatari government, the ruling family, or Islam."[50] Qatar's HDI value for 2017 is 0.856, which places it in the high human development category and at the rank of 37 out of 189 countries and territories.[51] Qatar's economic freedom score is 72.6, making its economy the 28th freest in the world, and its score is above the regional and world averages.[52]

Iran: A Theocratic Islamic Republic

Iran was proclaimed as the Islamic Republic in April 1979. "It is a theocracy founded on the political privileges of a clerical oligarchy."[53] The chief of state is the Supreme Leader who is appointed for life by the Assembly of Experts and who has absolute authority over both religious and secular affairs. Ali Hoseini-Khamenei has occupied this position since June 1989. The president is the head of government, and is directly elected by absolute majority vote for a four-year term that is open for a second term and another nonconsecutive term. The cabinet or Council of Ministers is chosen by the president with legislative approval, in addition to the Supreme Leader who has decisive power over appointments and affairs in the defense, intelligence, security, and judicial areas. Iran's legislature consists of a unicameral 290-member Islamic Consultative Assembly or Majles, with all candidates first approved by the rigid Guardian Council. The judiciary has the Supreme Court and subordinate courts such as the Islamic Revolutionary Courts, Courts of Peace, and Special Clerical Court. Suffrage is at eighteen years of age, and more than twenty political parties are active, with over half of them having a Muslim orientation. The Internet and the press in Iran are not free, and its aggregate freedom score is 18 out of 100, whereby 100 is most free, according to Freedom House.[54] Human Rights Watch details how the security forces and judiciary have resorted to "arbitrary mass arrests and serious due process violations" in response to protests.[55] These concerns and other severe religious freedom violations have led the USCIRF to designate Iran as "a country of particular concern" under the International Religious Freedom Act.[56] Iran's HDI for 2017 is 0.798, which places it in the high human development category and 60 out of 189 countries and territories.[57] In terms of economic freedom, Iran scores 51.1, making its economy the 155th freest out of 169, which is below many of the other MENA countries.[58]

Israel: A Quasi-democratic Jewish State

Israel, created in May 1948, was "a just social democracy" in its early days[59] but has evolved to become a quasidemocracy with illiberal tendencies today. Modeled after some of the European political systems, it has a president as chief of state, a prime minister as head of government, a cabinet, a unicameral 120-member Knesset or legislature, and an independent judicial branch, consisting of the Supreme Court and subordinate courts. Israel still does not have a formal constitution, but relies instead on its Declaration of Establishment, Basic Laws, and the Law of Return, as modified. Israelis are engaged in public affairs through numerous political parties and in other aspects of life through a variety of civil society organizations with foci ranging from democracy, human rights, and women empowerment to religious freedom and social justice. While resilient, civil society is encountering a serious struggle between "the rising conservative nationalist social forces and the dwindling liberal and humanist camp represented by human rights organizations."[60] Israel's press is partly free, and it is ranked in *Freedom in the World 2019* survey as "free" with an aggregate freedom score of 78 out of 100, whereby 100 is most free.[61] Though free, the Palestinian Arab citizens of Israel (20.9%

of the population) and other minorities suffer from some discrimination in rights and opportunities. It is not a surprise to hear that "41% of the Jewish public, and only 14% of the Arab public, define the state of democracy in Israel as 'good' or 'very good.' Moreover, 41% of Jews (most of whom identify with the Left or Center) and 70% of Arabs feel that Israeli democracy is in grave danger."[62] For Naomi Chazan, this reality is a result "an accelerated pattern of democratic recession marked by a yawning societal polarization and the unraveling of overarching norms of social solidarity."[63] Comparably, Ilan Peleg views it as part of the move toward "ethno-nationalist, majoritarian, and hegemonic democracy" that has caused an assault on democratic institutions, particularly after 2009, including the press, the police, the courts, and even the rule of law.[64] Conditions are worse for the Palestinians in the Gaza Strip and the West Bank. "The Israeli government continued to enforce severe and discriminatory restrictions on Palestinian's human rights; restrict the movement of people and goods into and out of the Gaza Strip; and facilitate the unlawful transfer of Israeli citizens to settlement in the occupied West Bank."[65] Israel's Declaration of Independence commits to freedom of religion but Orthodox and ultra-Orthodox Judaism exercise great influence on the lives of most Israeli citizens. Israel fits within very high human development. Its rank is 22 out of 189, with its HDI at 0.903, which is higher than any country in MENA and higher than the world's 0.728.[66] Israel's economic freedom score is 72.6, with a rank of 27 out of 189, and is in between the UAE (ranked #9) and Qatar (ranked #28).[67]

Turkey: A Quasi-democratic Presidential Republic

Turkey was a parliamentary system until June 2018. It was changed to a presidential system of governance as a result of a national referendum in April 2017. Over the past few years, power has become increasingly concentrated in the hands of President Recep Tayyip Erdoğan who is both chief of state and head of government, in addition to leading the hegemonic Justice and Development Party (AKP), which has been the ruling party since 2002. The president is directly elected by an absolute majority popular vote for a five-year term, and is eligible for a second term. In July 2016, Turkey faced a national emergency when elements of the Turkish military initiated a coup that soon failed, leading to the killing of 246 people and the injury of at least of 2,000. "The government accused followers of the Fethullah Gülen transnational religious and social movement ('Hizmet') for allegedly instigating the failed coup and designates the movement's followers as terrorists."[68] Aside from imposing a state of emergency for two years, the Turkish government responded with an iron fist by imprisoning more than 70,000 people, including 150 journalists and media workers; closing down 170 media outlets and

1500 associations and foundations; prosecuting for peace appeal 360 academics; and summarily dismissing in access of 130,000 public sector workers, particularly those in the judiciary, prosecutor's offices, police, and civil service. The Internet and the press in Turkey are not free, and the country is ranked in *Freedom in the World 2019* survey as "not free" with an aggregate freedom score of 31 out of 100, whereby 100 is most free.[69] Around the start of the Arab Spring, Turkey was thought of as a model of democracy for Arab countries exiting authoritarian regimes, such as Tunisia, Egypt, and Libya, but that is no longer the case. While Turkey has a strong civil society and other democratic strengths, it has weaknesses as well, including constant banning of political parties and individual candidates and a bleak record of human and minority rights, especially regarding the Kurds who mostly live in southeastern Turkey.[70] The restrictions on religious freedom, the threats against minority religious communities, the smear campaign by government entities and progovernment media—all contributed to "a growing climate of fear among religious minority communities," and led the USCIRF to place Turkey on its Tier 2 under the International Religious Freedom Act.[71] Turkey's HDI value for 2017 is 0.791, which places it in the high human development category and at the rank of 64 out of 189 countries and territories.[72] Turkey's economic freedom score is 64.6, rendering its economy the 68th freest in the world.[73]

MEASURING DEMOCRACY

Given the above profiles, how do we measure democracy and how do we compare or contrast countries to each other? What factors must we examine to gauge the level of democracy in each country? For the past two decades, I have used a composite measure, the Status of Democracy Index (SDI), which quantifies democratization through consideration of multiple variables: four variables address governance and representative government. These mark how heads of state and members of the legislature are selected, as well as political party development, suffrage, and the maturity of political rights and civil liberties. The latter is covered in the annual Freedom House survey, as is the fifth variable measuring media freedom. Measurements of religious liberty, the sixth variable, can be derived from the International Religious Freedom Report of the United States. Department of State and the reports of the U.S. Commission on International Religious Freedom, as relevant. A seventh addresses the observance of human rights with the information from Amnesty International, Human Rights Watch, and the U.S. Department of State. The United Nations Development Program's HDI provides a measurement of human development, the eighth variable. The Heritage Foundation's

Country	A Free Election Head of State	B Free Election Legislature/ National Council	C Civil Liberty/ Political Rights	D Suffrage	E Media Freedom	F Religious Freedom	G Human Rights	H Human Development	I Economic Freedom	Total SDI	% SDI	Arab SDI Ranking	MENA SDI Ranking
Algeria	1	1.5	0	2	0	1	0.5	1.5	0	7.5	41.6	6	8
Bahrain	0	1	0	0.5	0	1	0.5	2	1	6	33.3	11	13
Egypt	1	1	0	1.5	0	1	0	1	0.5	6	33.3	11	13
Iran	1	1	0	1	0	0.5	0	1.5	0.5	5.5	30.5		16
Iraq	1	1.5	0	1.5	0	1	0.5	1	0.5*	7	39	7	9
Israel	1.5	2	2	2	1	1	0.5	2	2	14	77.7		1
Jordan	0	1	1	2	0	1.5	1	1.5	1	8.5	47.2	4	6
Kuwait	0	1.5	1	1	1	1	0.5	2	1	8.5	47.2	4	6
Lebanon	1	1	1	1.5	0	0.5	1	1.5	0.5	9.5	52.7	2	3
Libya	0	1.5	0	2	0	1	0.5	1	0.5	7	39	7	9
Morocco	0	1.5	1	2	0	1	1	1	1	9.5	52.7	2	3
Oman	0	1	0	1	0	1	0.5	2	1	6.5	36.1	9	11
Qatar	0	0.5	0	0.5	0	1	0.5	2	2	6.5	36.1	9	11
Saudi Arabia	0	0.5	0	0	0	0	0	2	1	3.5	19.4	16	19
Sudan	0	1	0	1.5	0	0	0	0.5	0	3	16.6	17	20
Syria	1	1	0	1	1	1	0	0.5	0.5*	5	27.7	14	17
Tunisia	2	2	1	2	1	1	1	1.5	0.5	11.5	63.8	1	2
Turkey	2	1.5	0	0	0	1	0.5	1.5	1	9.5	52.7		3
United Arab Emirates	0	0.5	0	0	0	1	0.5	2	2	6	33.3	11	13
Yemen	1	1	0	1.5	0	0	0	0.5	0*	4	22	15	18

Legend

A: 0 = no; 1 = indirect or partially free; 2 = yes

B: 0 = no; 1 = indirect or limited; 2 = yes

C: 0 = nonexistent or prohibited; 1= controlled by government approval; 2 = reasonably free

D: 0 = no; 1 = some; 2 = yes

E: 0 = not free; 1 = partly free; 2 = free

F: 0 = no; 1 = some; 2 = yes

G: 0 = not observed; 1 = partly observed; 2 = fully observed

H: 0 = low; 1 = medium; 2= very high

I: 0 = strong government interference; 1 = medium government interference; 2 = low government interference

*Estimated by author

Figure 6.1 Democracy Ranking of Twenty MENA Countries, 2019.

Index of Economic Freedom quantifies economic freedom, the ninth variable. A basic assumption is that human rights, human development, and economic freedom are all interconnected with democracy. As is explained in different United Nations documents, democracy enables

> greater participation, equality, security, and human development. [It] provides an environment that respects human rights and fundamental freedoms, and in which the freely expressed will of people is exercised. People have a say in decisions and can hold decision-makers to account. Women and men have equal rights and all people are free from discrimination.[74]

SDI assigns each of these nine variables 2 points for a total of 18 points. Each score ranges from 0 to 2, with 0 being nonexistent and 2 being the highest measurement. For example, if the head of state or legislature is not elected, then that country receives a score of zero. Prohibition of political parties would also equate to a 0 while tight controls would merit a 1, and reasonably free functioning would lead to a 2. Media freedom, religious liberty, and respect for human rights are each easy to quantify: 0 for not free, 1 for partly free, and 2 for free. Human development is scored by level: 0 for low, 1 for medium, and 2 for high. Economic freedom, the last variable, is scored on the level of governmental interference in the economy, with 0 for strong, 1 for moderate, and 2 for low interference. It is then possible to convert the totals to a percentage for easy digestion.

In measuring democracy in the Arab countries of the MENA region in 2019, Tunisia tops the list, followed by Morocco, Lebanon, Jordan, and Kuwait. Syria, Yemen, Saudi Arabia, and Sudan finish last, as presented in figure 6.1. Between 1999 and 2019, eight of the seventeen Arab countries never surpassed the 40th percentile. The results for the non-Arab states in 2019 reveal Israel as first, followed by Turkey and Iran. When the Arab and non-Arab states are compared to each other in 2019, Israel comes out first at the 77th percentile, Tunisia second at the 63rd percentile, and Lebanon, Morocco, and Turkey third at the 52nd percentile. A longitudinal look at the SDI data in Arab countries, as shown in figure 6.2, indicates some backsliding since 2005 in Algeria, Bahrain, Egypt, Jordan, Lebanon, Saudi Arabia, Sudan, Syria, and Yemen. While significant democratic advance appears in Tunisia, there is some progress elsewhere such as in Morocco and Qatar. The percentages for Iraq, Kuwait, and United Arab Emirates remain the same.

PROMOTING DEMOCRACY

Democratization takes more than political promises. Its promotion comes not from a quick fix. It emanates from empowerment, engagement, and a

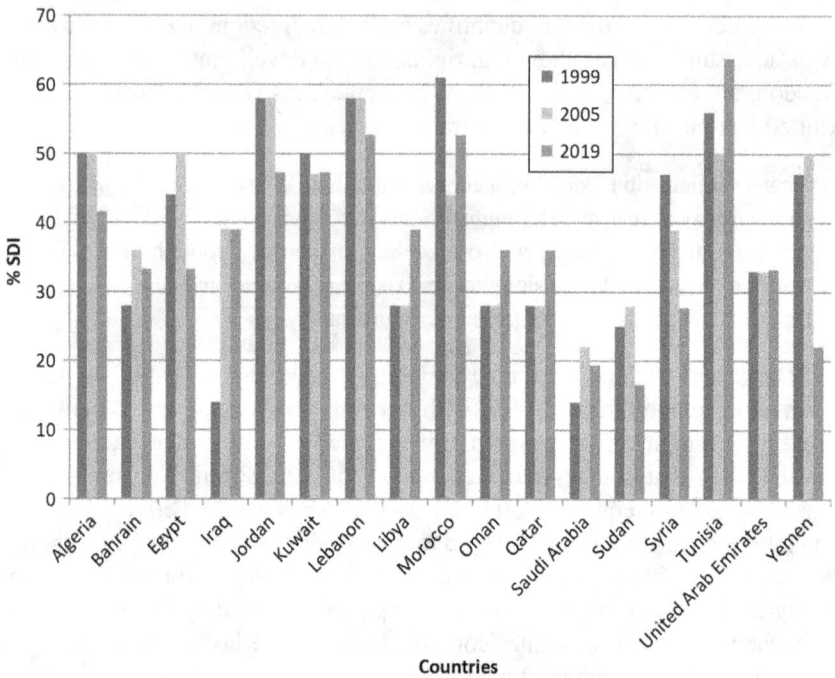

Figure 6.2   Backsliding of Democracy in Several Arab Countries.

generational commitment. As Roland Rich argues, "Democracy is a never-ending journey. Democracy is an aspiration toward which we must work."[75]

The failure of MENA countries to democratize rests with key political leaders who cling to power, preferring political stability, regime survival, and wealth to freedom and public participation. It is long overdue that political and civic leaders think beyond themselves in order to construct a present and a future that are respective of the past but equally receptive to the needs of all in society, particularly the youth and women. With a shared vision of social change and mastery of social media, the young people especially, with over half of them female, are linked across borders and intent on turning "the page on decades of sclerotic and rigged politics in favor of a more democratic alternative."[76]

What is obvious is that citizens can challenge authority and stand up to authoritarian rulers, as they have done in the recent past. What is equally important is that states can view their SDI scores and work on improving their democratic standing by enhancing their individual performance in those areas where they are deficient. Governments should foster good governance and be made accountable for the lives of all their citizens. Bureaucrats should be held responsible for their actions, and promotions should be made on merit, not on patronage. There should be investment in democracy by building and consolidating a stable middle class, which should result in greater democratic openness and political accountability. Governments, nongovernmental organizations, and academic institutions should involve students of all ages in civic education and critical thinking, not blind obedience and rote memorization. Similarly, these are advised to prioritize the empowerment of women in all facets of their lives. Empowering women is empowering a whole society. Engaged minds, empowered citizens are vital for meaningful change and democratic transformations.

DISCUSSION QUESTIONS

1. Why is MENA a long way from democracy? Explain main reasons and use examples to illustrate.
2. How do Arab and non-Arab states in MENA compare with each other on the issue of democracy?
3. What are some possible explanations for the persistence of authoritarian rule in many MENA countries?
4. Why Tunisia is considered a quasi-democratic republic? Has it always enjoyed such a characteristic or status? Explain.
5. Israel is viewed as a quasi-democratic Jewish state. How can Israel be both democratic and Jewish at the same time?
6. This chapter uses a composite measure, the SDI, which quantifies democratization through consideration of multiple variables. What are they? Evaluate them and suggest others that can be added in order to arrive at a comprehensive list.
7. How would you promote democracy in the MENA region?

NOTES

1. Benjamin Barber, *An Aristocracy of Everyone: The Politics of Education and the Future of America* (New York, NY: Oxford University Press), 265.
2. Cited in UNHCR, the UN Refugee Agency, *Syria Regional Refugee Response*. https://data2.unhcr.org/en/situations/syria.
3. Ibid., *Internally Displaced People*. https://www.unhcr.org/internally-displace -people.
4. *Syria: Events of 2018, World Report 2019*, Human Rights Watch. https://www .hrw.org/world-report/2019/country-chapters/syria.
5. *Yemen: Events of 2018, World Report 2019*, Human Rights Watch. https://ww w.hrw.org/world-report/2019/country-chapters/yemen.

6. Ibid.

7. Seth J. Frantzman, "Another Khashoggi? Iran Murdered Dissident in Istanbul, Why the Cover-Up?" *The Jerusalem Post*, March 29, 2020. https://www.jpost.com /middle-east/another-khashoggi-iran-murdered-dissident-in-istanbul-why-the-cover -up-622737.

8. Cited in Guma El-Gamaty, "Is a Military Solution the Only Option Left in Libya?" *AlJazeera.com*, June 7, 2019. https://www.aljazeera.com/indepth/opinion/ military-solution-option-left-libya-190606195532883.html.

9. Curtis R. Ryan, *Jordan and the Arab Uprising: Regime Survival and Politics Beyond the State* (New York, NY: Columbia University Press, 2018).

10. Farzana Shain and Bulent Gokay, "The Protests in Turkey: Urban Warfare in 'Rebel Cities'." *openDemocracy*. https://www.opendemocracy.net/en/protests-in- turkey-urban-warfare-in-rebel-cities/.

11. Saliba Sarsar, "Arab Politics: Can Democracy Prevail?" *Middle East Quarterly*, Vol. 7, No. 1 (March 2000): 39–48.

12. United Nations Development Programme, *Arab Human Development Report 2002: "Creating Opportunities for Future Generations."* http://www.arab-hdr.org/r eports/2002/english/ahdr2002e.pdf?download.

13. Ibid., 108–110.

14. United Nations Development Programme, *Arab Human Development Report 2004: "Towards Freedom in the Arab World."* http://www.arab-hdr.org/reports/2004 /english/execsummary-e%202004.pdf?download, 5–22.

15. Mehran Kamrava, "Introduction." In *Beyond the Arab Spring: The Evolving Ruling Bargain in the Middle East*, ed. Mehran Kamrava (Oxford and New York, NY: Oxford University Press, 2014), 2.

16. United Nations Development Programme, *Arab Human Development Report 2005: "Towards the Rise of Women in the Arab World."* http://www.arab-hdr.org/r eports/2005/english/execsummary-e2005.pdf?download, 1–24.

17. Marina Ottaway, "Evaluating Middle East Reform: Significant or Cosmetic." In *Beyond the Façade: Political Reform in the Arab World*, eds. Marina Ottaway and Julia Choucair-Vizoso (Washington, DC: Carnegie Endowment for International Peace, 2008), 4.

18. Marwan Muasher, *The Arab Center: The Promise of Moderation* (New Haven, CT and London: Yale University Press, 2008), 231.

19. Ibid., 231–232.

20. United Nations Development Programme, *Arab Human Development Report 2016: "The Youth and the Prospects for Human Development in a Changing Reality."* http://www.arab-hdr.org/reports/2016/english/AHDR2016En.pdf.

21. Rahman, "Democracy in the Middle East."

22. James L. Gelvin, *The New Middle East: What Everyone Needs to Know* (New York, NY: Oxford University Press, 2018), 14.

23. Ibid., 16.

24. Steven A. Cook, *False Dawn: Protest, Democracy, and Violence in the New Middle East* (New York, NY: Oxford University Press, 2017).

25. Mohamed A. Ramady, ed., *The Political Economy of Wasta: Use and Abuse of Social Capital Networking* (Switzerland: Springer International Publishing, 2016), vii.

26. Melani Cammett and Ishac Diwan, "The Political Economy of Development in the Middle East." In *The Middle East*, 14th edition, ed. Ellen Lust (Thousand Oaks, CA: SAGE/CQ Press, 2017), 121.

27. Neville Teller, "Nepotism or Inherited Genes – A Middle East Conundrum." *The Jerusalem Post*, July 22, 2017. https://www.jpost.com/Blogs/A-Mid-East-Journa l/Nepotism-or-inherited-genes-a-Middle-East-conundrum-501032.

28. Sharan Grewal, "Democracy & Disorder: Tunisian Democracy at a Crossroads." *Policy Brief*. The Brookings Institution, February 2019. https://www.brookings.edu/ research/tunisian-democracy-at-a-crossroads/.

29. *The World Factbook: Tunisia*, Central Intelligence Agency. https://www.cia .gov/library/publications/the-world-factbook/geos/ts.html.

30. Freedom House, *Democracy in Retreat – Freedom in the World 2019: Tunisia*. https://freedomhouse.org/report/freedom-world/2019/tunisia.

31. Human Rights Watch, *World Report 2019: Tunisia – Events of 2018*. https:// hrw.org/world-report/2019/country-chapters/tunisia.

32. United Nations Human Development Programme, *Human Development Indicators: 2018 Statistical Update – Tunisia*. http://hdr.undp.org/sites/all/themes/ hdr_theme/country-notes/TUN.pdf.

33. The Heritage Foundation, *2019 Index of Economic Freedom: Tunisia*. https:// www.heritage.org/index/country/tunisia.

34. Eva Bellin, "The Puzzle of Democratic Divergence in the Arab World: Theory Confronts Experience in Egypt and Tunisia." *Political Science Quarterly*, Vol. 133, No. 3 (Fall 2018): 451.

35. Brigadier General Abdelfattah Said ElSisi, "Democracy in the Middle East." *US Army War College Strategy Research Project*, Carlisle Barracks, PA, March 15, 2006. https://assets.documentcloud.org/documents/1173610/sisi.pdf.

36. Freedom House, *Democracy in Retreat – Freedom in the World 2019: Egypt*. https://freedomhouse.org/report/freedom-world/2019/egypt.

37. Human Rights Watch, *World Report 2019: Egypt – Events of 2018*. https://ww w.hrw.org/world-report/2019/country-chapters/egypt.

38. Amnesty International, *Egypt 2017/2018*. https://www.amnesty.org/en/cou ntries/middle-east-and-north-africa/egypt/report-egypt/.

39. U.S. Department of State, *2018 Report on International Religious Freedom: Egypt*. https://eg.usembassy.gov/2018-report-on-international-religious-freedom-egypt/.

40. United States Commission on International Religious Freedom, *Egypt*. https:// www.uscirf.gov/sites/default/files/Tier2_EGYPT_2019.pdf.

41. United Nations Human Development Programme, *Human Development Indicators: 2018 Statistical Update – Egypt*. http://hdr.undp.org/en/countries/profile s/EGY.

42. The Heritage Foundation, *2019 Index of Economic Freedom: Egypt*. https:// www.heritage.org/index/country/egypt.

43. USAID, *Democracy, Rights & Governance: Jordan*. https://www.usaid.gov/jordan/democracy-human-rights-and-governance.

44. Mohammed Bani Salameh and Ayman Hayajneh, "The End of the Syrian Civil War: How Jordan Can Cope." *Middle East Quarterly*, Vol. 26, No. 3 (Summer 2019): 2–3.

45. Human Rights Watch, *Jordan*. https://www.hrw.org/middle-east/n-africa/jordan.

46. United Nations Human Development Programme, *Human Development Indicators: 2018 Statistical Update – Jordan*. http://hdr.undp.org/sites/all/themes/hdr_theme/country-notes/JOR.pdf.

47. The Heritage Foundation, *2019 Index of Economic Freedom: Jordan*. https://www.heritage.org/index/country/jordan.

48. U.S. Department of State, *2018 Report on International Religious Freedom: Qatar*. https://eg.usembassy.gov/2018-report-on-international-religious-freedom-qatar/.

49. Freedom House, *Democracy in Retreat – Freedom in the World 2019: Qatar*. https://freedomhouse.org/report/freedom-world/2019/qatar.

50. Ibid., *Freedom of the Press 2017*. https://freedomhouse.org/report/freedom-press/2017/qatar.

51. United Nations Human Development Programme, *Human Development Indicators: 2018 Statistical Update – Qatar*. http://hdr.undp.org/sites/all/themes/hdr_theme/country-notes/QAT.pdf.

52. The Heritage Foundation, *2019 Index of Economic Freedom: Qatar*. https://www.heritage.org/index/country/qatar.

53. Ladan Boroumand and Roya Borumand. "Is Iran Democratizing? Reform at an Impasse." In *Islam and Democracy in the Middle East*, eds. Larry Diamong, Marc F. Plattnet, and Daniel Brumberg (Baltimore, MD: Johns Hopkins University Press, 2003), 132.

54. Freedom House, *Democracy in Retreat – Freedom in the World 2019: Iran*. https://freedomhouse.org/report/freedom-world/2019/iran.

55. Human Rights Watch, *World Report 2019: Iran – Events of 2018*. https://hrw.org/world-report/2019/country-chapters/iran.

56. United States Commission on International Religious Freedom, *Iran*. https://www.uscirf.gov/sites/default/files/Tier1_IRAN_2019.pdf.

57. United Nations Human Development Programme, *Human Development Indicators: 2018 Statistical Update – Iran*. http://hdr.undp.org/sites/all/themes/hdr_theme/country-notes/IRN.pdf.

58. The Heritage Foundation, *2019 Index of Economic Freedom: Iran*. https://www.heritage.org/index/country/iran.

59. Ari Shavit, *My Promised Land: The Triumph and Tragedy of Israel* (New York, NY: Spiegel & Grau, 2013), 151.

60. Amal Jamal, "The Rise of 'Bad Civil Society' in Israel." *SWP (Stiftung Wissenschaft und Politik) Comment*, January 2018. https://www.swp-berlin.org/en/publication/israel-the-rise-of-bad-civil-society/.

61. Freedom House, *Democracy in Retreat – Freedom in the World 2019: Israel*. https://freedomhouse.org/report/freedom-world/2019/israel.

62. Tamar Herman et al., *The Israeli Democracy Index*. The Israel Democracy Institute. https://en.idi.org.il/publications/25031, 10.

63. Naomi Chazan, "Israel's Democracy at a Turning Point." In *Continuity & Change in Political Culture: Israel & Beyond*, eds. Yael S. Aronoff, Ilan Peleg, and Saliba Sarsar (Lanham, MD: Lexington Books, 2020), Chap. 5.

64. Ilan Peleg, "Majority-Minority Relations in Deeply Divided Democratic Societies: The Israeli Case in a Globalized Context." In *Continuity and Change in Political Culture: Israel and Beyond*, eds. Yael S. Aronoff, Ilan Peleg, and Saliba Sarsar (Lanham, MD: Lexington Books, 2020), Chapter 6.

65. Human Rights Watch, *World Report 2019: Israel and Palestine – Events of 2018*. https://hrw.org/world-report/2019/country-chapters/israel/palestine.

66. United Nations Human Development Programme, *Human Development Indicators: 2018 Statistical Update – Israel*. http://hdr.undp.org/en/countries/profiles/ISR.

67. The Heritage Foundation, *2019 Index of Economic Freedom: Israel*. https://www.heritage.org/index/country/israel.

68. *The World Factbook: Turkey*, Central Intelligence Agency. https://www.cia.gov/library/publications/the-world-factbook/geos/tu.html.

69. Freedom House, *Democracy in Retreat – Freedom in the World 2019: Turkey*. https://freedomhouse.org/report/freedom-world/2019/turkey.

70. Agnes Czajka and Bora Isyar, "Turkish Democracy: A Flawed Model." *open-Democracy*, October 5, 2011. https://www.opendemocracy.net/en/turkish-democracy-flawed-model/.

71. United State Commission on International Religious Freedom, *Turkey*. https://www.uscirf.gov/sites/default/files/Tier2_TURKEY_2019.pdf.

72. United Nations Human Development Programme, *Human Development Indicators: 2018 Statistical Update – Turkey*. http://hdr.undp.org/sites/all/themes/hdr_theme/country-notes/TUR.pdf.

73. The Heritage Foundation, *2019 Index of Economic Freedom: Turkey*. https://www.heritage.org/index/country/turkey.

74. United Nations, *Democracy*. https://www.un.org/en/sections/issues-depth/democracy/index.html.

75. Roland Rich, *Democracy in Crisis: Why, Where, How to Respond* (Boulder, CO and London: Lynne Rienner Publishers, 2017), 193.

76. Al-Monitor, "A New Generation Lays its Predecessors' Ghosts to Rest." *Al Monitor*, April 9, 2020. https://www.al-monitor.com/pulse/originals/2020/03/young-protesters-algeria-lebanon-iraq.html.

FURTHER READING

Bellin, Eva. "The Puzzle of Democratic Divergence in the Arab World: Theory Confronts Experience in Egypt and Tunisia." *Political Science Quarterly*, Vol. 133, No. 3 (Fall 2018): 435–474.

Çinar, Kürşat. *The Decline of Democracy in Turkey: A Comparative Study of Hegemonic Party Rule.* Abingdon, UK: Routledge, 2019.

Cook, Steven A. *False Dawn: Protest, Democracy, and Violence in the New Middle East.* New York, NY: Oxford University Press, 2017.

Herman, Tamar et al. *The Israeli Democracy Index.* The Israel Democracy Institute. https://en.idi.org.il/publications/25031.

Kamrava, Mehran ed. *Beyond the Arab Spring: The Evolving Ruling Bargain in the Middle East.* Oxford and New York, NY: Oxford University Press, 2014.

Milton-Edwards, Beverley. "Chapter 6: The Ephemerals of Democracy in the Middle East." In *Contemporary Politics in the Middle East*, 4th edition. Cambridge, UK: Polity Press, 2018.

Rahman, Natalya. "Democracy in the Middle East and North Africa: Five Years after the Arab Uprisings." *Arab Barometer – Wave IV*, 2018. https://www.arabbaro meter.org/wp-content/uploads/Democracy_Public-Opinion_Middle-east_North -Africa_2018.pdf.

Part II

COUNTRY CASE STUDIES

Chapter 7

A 'Modi'-fied India

Parties, Promises, and Portends of Democracy amid an Uncertain Glory

Rekha Datta and Sam Maynard

Immediately after its break from British colonial rule in 1947, the country began to establish democratic institutions that remain relatively stable after seven decades of a politically independent identity as the Republic of India. Indian democracy benefits from many of the standard characteristics of well-consolidated Western democracies, such as free and frequent elections, a free press, respect for the constitution, and politically detached armed forces.[1]

PARTIES AND PORTENDS OF DEMOCRACY
IN INDIA: AN OVERVIEW

In the context of economic growth and development, the strength of India's democracy is challenged by its struggle to maintain political accountability. Early on, since independence, the country has had a parallel and often conflicting vision of development. Between 1950 and 2010, India's gross domestic product per capita has risen from 1.8 percent to 6 percent, and reached even higher rates until the global economic slowdown of 2008. Life expectancy during this period has doubled from thirty to sixty-six years. Sen and Dreze (2013) have identified two areas in which the challenges for India's growth and democratic portends lie. The first is the "continued *disparity*" between economic classes, and the second is the "persistent *ineptitude and unaccountability* in the way the Indian economy and society are organized."[2]

This chapter examines the role of India's party system as pivotal in its sojourn with democracy and how the party system has adapted itself as well as shaped the country's need to align economic development, while

145

upholding democratic processes, efficient governance, and accountability. Loyalties based on caste and social group identities and political personalities have often challenged parties, leading to realignment and coalitions. Political parties have had to toggle between holding on to institutional identities and a variety of points of loyalty to their base, and rising to national prominence in a federal system of government. Since the broad programmatic platform of the Indian National Congress (INC) under Jawaharlal Nehru, the party system has transformed from a bureaucratic organizational structure to a coalitional body of regional interests.[3] This has led to a reliance on a brand of decentralized populism, which enjoys a significant level of autonomy from the party organizations. Since 2014, the now ruling *Bharatiya Janata Party* (BJP), or India's People Party has steadily been gaining wider electoral support at the national and increasingly at regional levels. Previously, the party's strength was based on various regional offshoots unified under the center-right National Democratic Alliance (NDA). The rise of Narendra Modi, coupled with the lack of a viable opposition party or a coalition, are ushering in an interesting phase in India's party system and democratic governance. Currently, the BJP's and, more specifically, Prime Minister Modi's appeal is attributable to his charisma and promise of economic growth (albeit not always fulfilled), as well as to their rallying cries of Hindu nationalism.

Since the 1990s, the Congress Party's electoral support has been in steady decline. This had led to a system of vertical plebiscitarian appeal that has thrived on the absence of institutional support. While many have argued that this type of political autonomy allows the party to maintain efficiency, competing analyses point to the decrease of populist style leadership under Rajiv Gandhi in the 1980s, and how this was stifled by the fluid nature of Indian democracy.[4] This narrative indicates an electoral system that is dominated by populist regional alliances, rather than policy-oriented linkages. While India preserves stable democratic norms in terms of electoral competition, it still faces problems like corruption and patronage, which result in damaging democratic legitimacy. This confirms Huntington's assertion that ailing institutions erodes the functionality of democracy as a system of representation. Populist networks in India maintain these patronage networks, rather than empower crucial blocs of support.[5]

This chapter views party "deinstitutionalization" as a key concept in explaining the general lack of institutional accountability within other sectors of the Indian state. We define this term as the utilization of *behavioral routinization* to reinforce party adaptability in terms of governing agenda and electoral support.[6] While local political bosses associate themselves with some variation of the mainstream party system, they are able to tailor a platform that does not necessarily draw on the traditions of their respective association. This phenomenon has, in a sense, weakened democratic institutions in India by consolidating power in political offices rather than maintaining a system of electoral accountability. The interaction between candidate and voter is closely marked by a variation of populism based on the regional support base in which a local party is operating. Parties, in turn, benefit from this weak structure by forgoing bureaucratic obstacles that could limit their responsiveness to small portions of the national electorate.[7] This flexibility carries itself over into political office once a candidate has been elected, using provincial offices to maintain party activity through the politician.

In India, the liquidation of party bureaucracy has led to a centralized executive authority at the national level. As this chapter will analyze, the roles of Nehru, Indira Gandhi, and subsequent heads of state throughout the 1980s and 1990s have generally acted without significant institutional barriers or checks on power. At the time of independence, democratic institutions were reliant on Nehru's charisma and personal appeal to the electorate. This allowed him to broadly define the trajectory of India's socialist development. Under Indira Gandhi, this programmatic idea was deconstructed to allow for her populist appeal and political autonomy away from the old guard establishment. This deinstitutionalization created difficulties for successors in that they could not do away with the machine politics that became prevalent during the 1970s. Currently, the most effective way to win office is to appeal directly to varied constituencies in order to create incentives for coalitional support.

Although this system has obvious flaws, it does allow for parties to fulfill social needs that are not being met by an insufficient state. However, recent decades have demonstrated the resilience of India's party system, through its coalition politics, to rise up to the challenge.

This raises a question for the current political agenda India is facing: *in the context of weak institutions and decentralized plebiscitarian parties, is it likely that Modi will be able to keep his promises of economic growth and combat corruption effectively?* Given the history of India's party system and the embedded nature of populist linkages, it will remain a challenge to deviate from this path.

1947–1970S: THE DOMINANT PARTY ERA, THE DEINSTITUTIONALIZATION OF THE INDIAN NATIONAL CONGRESS, AND THE RISE OF PLEBISCITARY POLITICS

At the initial stages of post-independence, India's democratic infancy can be characterized by what many political scientists refer to as the "dominant party era" headed by Nehru and the INC. The introduction of the INC and Indian democracy could not have been fully envisioned without the personality of Nehru and his vision for a unified secular country. Instead of relying on splintered identities to make up the political makeup of the country, Nehru offered broad ideas to appeal to the electorate. The social democratic identity that he injected into the political discourse constructed the political institution that would modernize the country. In short, Nehru, the social leader of India, facilitated the growth and progress of the nation by virtue of his personalized and mass-based system of appeal.

Although maintaining a dominant presence within India's initial stages of democracy, the INC only garnered power with 43–48 percent of the popular vote; however, the INC's institutional malleability allowed for mass appeal and an overall consolidation of the Indian electorate. Because the INC contained itself within a multiplicity of political views, which maintained its identity as a center party while gaining support from the right and left, it took advantage of the early competitive stage of electoral politics. Nehru himself referred to the INC as the "mirror of the nation" and can be viewed as a reflection of the ever-changing political appetites and desires of the people instead of a unified programmatic entity.[8] Moreover, ideological ambiguity in the realm of policy implementation facilitated a strong corporatist structure, which Nehru utilized to mold the party as it consolidated organizational dominance.[9]

The broad appeal of the INC, along with Nehru's objective to shape India into a socialistic state, led to the inevitable fracture and the commencement of regionalism with respect to leftist parties.[10] In introducing socialism into the blueprint of India's political and constitutional construction, Nehru weakened the efficacy of Marxist and socialist opposition parties.[11] This subsequently consolidated the INC's power, which allowed Nehru to provide post-independent India with its constitutional spirit and guide the country toward a consensus via the single-party system. However, as one might view this period as a necessary measure to ensure unity and inclusion within the democratic system, some notions of democratic development view the Nehruvian period as unusual.[12]

As the INC became deinstitutionalized in the localities and developed regional coalitions, all enjoying a heightened level of autonomy from the organizational structure, Nehru consolidated power at the expense of the national party system. It is important to note that the introduction of regionalism, along with Nehruvian socialism, instigated a unique structure of corporatism that contained the molecular-style offshoots within various localities. As the INC maintained Nehru's personality at the head of its organization, regional parties provided the ability to tap patronage and consolidate power through the instrument of the political office.

Further, Nehru's single-party system allowed India to modernize without the conflicts that could have stymied development in light of the country's high level of diversity and established, from the Western perspective, stable democratic institutions. Nehru, by virtue of the INC's structure and his own personality, managed to consolidate the country, quell impediments to democratization, and embed a goal of modernization within the Indian political identity.[13] However, without Nehru's personalistic style of rule that the INC provided, stable democratic institutions would not have been able to take root as fast as they did.[14] At the risk of destabilizing established institutional norms (e.g., voting, constitutionality, and rule of law), Nehru's consolidation of power preserved the modernizing characteristics of Indian democracy without being enveloped in authoritarianism.

After Nehru's death, the INC underwent a period of drastic reformation. The election of 1967 reduced the INC's legislative majority to 54 percent and factional alliances rising in various regions throughout the country decreased the party's power in parliament. Moreover, the INC was presiding over a period of economic stagnation and an embittered split within its own ranks. The old guard of the party was in a desperate fight with young socialists to remove the new prime minister, Indira Gandhi, Nehru's daughter, and control the future of governmental affairs. Ultimately, Mrs. Gandhi received the support of the socialist sect and forced a split into what would be the "New Congress."[15]

Mrs. Gandhi's new INC ushered in the era of plebiscitary politics. Unlike her father, where his broad plan for Indian democracy facilitated a consolidation of the Indian electorate and there was a level of separation between the man and the party, Mrs. Gandhi and the INC became one. In the election of 1971, Mrs. Gandhi ran on broad antipoverty initiatives, which allowed voters to appeal directly to her sense of leadership rather than INC-backed policy plans that mobilized a wide array of interest groups.[16] Whereas in other cases, clientelism was seen as incompatible with strengthening party loyalty; the case of Mrs. Gandhi and the INC, in a way, strengthened Indian's loyalty to the party (i.e., the personality of Mrs. Gandhi) through her association with eradicating poverty.[17] Thus, the traditional INC machine cycle was broken and Mrs. Gandhi could appeal directly to the masses herself, without the restriction of the old guard INC members. The purpose of the party shifted; whereas before each faction had distinct ideological differences, now the INC was a broad money-making instrument for Mrs. Gandhi's personality, which proceeded to fill the hole left by a fading political identity.

In 1975, deinstitutionalization ultimately led to Mrs. Gandhi's unprecedented "State of Emergency" wherein she suspended democratic elections and solidified her authoritarian-style rule.[18] The breakdown of the organizational structure allowed Mrs. Gandhi to solidify her populism and make public appointments that would consolidate her power. Ultimately, personalistic power created a viable political center at the expense of parliament, regional autonomy, and other political institutions.[19] The consolidation of power in the office of prime minister and the personality of Mrs. Gandhi herself, leading one to suspect the ultimate decay of democratic, can also be seen as a producer of political efficacy. As Atul Kohli states:

> The balance sheet of political development . . . was not only toward the weakening of Indian democracy . . . elections were held regularly throughout the period, and political power remained a function of securing popular majority support. Even Indira Gandhi's personal power was a function of her widespread electoral appeal to India's poor masses . . . . The fact that she was voted out of power following the Emergency only confirmed the efficacy of Indian democracy: those who tamper with the basic system will lose popular support.[20]

The Indian electorate as a whole had become aware of the importance of elections and the change that could be brought by a cast of the ballot; voter turnout between 1967 and 1984 had averaged 60percent.[21]

Although Mrs. Gandhi's institutional power had instilled an engrained respect for electoral politics, the effects led to a proliferation of national, religious, and political identities. These identities would eventually generate a conflict between India's overall liberal principles of democracy and a desire to challenge the overarching design of the dominant Congress Party system. The 1970s and the era of Indira Gandhi can be seen as the precursor to the institutional decay of the INC in later decades; although the institution of voting and electoral party politics was solidified, further deinstitutionalization via personalism rendered the office positions malleable to the personas of politicians themselves. Elections became about securing power and political corruption became engrained in the public sphere. Moreover, the proliferation of nationalist and religion-based parties, in light of economic stagnation forced the INC and oppositional BJP to rely on competing notions of Indian identity that became possible due to India's entrenched liberal democratic values.[22]

The contributions of Nehru and Mrs. Gandhi fostered India's democratic spirit and required government to adopt an effective method of action in light of the country's overwhelming presence of diversity. Nehru's plan for modernization under the broad umbrella of the INC shaped India into a liberal democratic society while Mrs. Gandhi's personalistic rule embedded the importance of Nehru's original values into the Indian electorate and allowed the Indian people to form a direct stake in politics. Although these actions may have been necessary in the formation of India's unique political identity, as we will see in later years, the outcomes of Mrs. Gandhi's clientelism, in

light of India's liberalized commerce and democracy, will have an undermining effect on INC and its dependence on the constrained choices of the lower
strata.[23]

1980–1990S: POST-JANATA PERIOD AND ECONOMIC LIBERALIZATION

The Indian party system in the 1980s was characterized by the increased
decentralization of the electorate and further liquidation of political institutions. After a brief loss of power in 1977, Indira Gandhi was reelected as
prime minister in 1984, furthering her plebiscitarian mandate. At this time,
the traditionally central electorate of the INC began to shift its base to southern regions of the country (aligned with leftist platforms), forcing the party
to share portions of its electorate with opposition or closely aligned groups.[24]
The systematic deinstitutionalization of the INC had larger consequences for
the Indian party system as a whole. As electoral alliances have traditionally
played a crucial role in the path to the prime ministership, it became more
efficient for opposition parties to use direct appeals as well, rather than relying on programmatic strategies. This allowed regional parties and the main
Janata opposition to effectively "eat away" at the INC's representation in the
parliament.

While the rule of Indira Gandhi had implications for the quality of Indian
democracy, it also made the state more accountable to popular demands.
Voting blocs based on caste and religion began to emerge as important
electoral forces that needed to be absorbed into the national majority if one
party was to gain a parliamentary majority.[25] Opposition parties began to benefit from this peripheral mobilization, which caused a drop in the Congress
Party's share of representation.

Though, even with this reorganization of the party system, the INC still
remained the only party able to garner support from a plurality of national
regions. This was exemplified by the landslide victory in 1984—after the
assassination of Indira Gandhi—that solidified the party's new approach
to development. Rajiv Gandhi had a viable electoral mandate to pursue
economic reforms that complicated intraparty relations within the Congress
organization.[26] The newly elected prime minister now had a "delegative
advantage" among voters, yet he chose to modify his style of linkage with
voters and with democratic institutions. Checks on power and legislative
approval were regularized under Rajiv Gandhi's executive rule. Unlike his
predecessor, he sought congressional approval when implementing reforms.
However, he was able to rally support through these policies with his direct

appeal to voters and his familial legacy. The national electorate still mobilized under this populist banner, even if it was not used to centralize executive authority.[27]

From 1984 to 1989, Rajiv Gandhi began to implement a liberal economic agenda that expanded India's relationship with the global economy. During this period, regulations on the industrial sector were loosened, trade tariffs were decreased or cut, and the Information Technology (IT) sector was tapped into as an important source of national revenue.[28] While Rajiv Gandhi's brand of populist linkage was comparatively "limited" to that of his predecessor's, intraparty split within the INC worsened, as traditionally socialist sectors grew displeased with the liberal economic policies being generated. Much like Modi's current platform, Rajiv Gandhi governed under the mantra of modernization and a breakaway from the old guard tactics to patronage politics practiced during the initial decades after independence. However, this included an ideological pivot away from socialism, which caused a split among leftist INC legislators.[29]

The INC's fracture culminated in the loss of power for Rajiv Gandhi during the 1989 general elections. Dissident cabinet member, Vishwanath P. Singh, used support from his old guard wing of the party to stage an electoral coup and win the prime ministership. This resulted in the formation of a new opposition coalition, the Janata Dal, and the further dispersion of the party system. Political representation was becoming closely associated with ethnic and regional identity, opposed to the social democratic composition of Indian democracy under Nehru and Indira Gandhi.[30] Throughout the 1990s, this trend grew more prevalent, as the prominence of the Congress Party eroded to bare minorities in the legislature.

The plebiscitarian style of governing was severely curtailed during the 1990s with the initiation of structural adjustment policies. In the midst of an economic crisis, Indian politicians aligned themselves with the policies of international financial organizations. On one hand, this afforded them legitimacy with Western finance to bring investment into the country that would improve growth. On the other, it also allowed the political class to elude personal accountability for the adverse effects caused by liberalization. This new political strategy eventually damaged the INC's credibility and gave legitimacy to opposition groups, like the BJP. The leadership of Rao (1991–1996) was characterized by harsh adherence to fiscal programs constructed by the International Monetary Fund (IMF) and the reliance of broad "centrist" appeals. By the turn of the century, the support base of the Congress Party had been scattered, and the party system took the form of large coalitional groups. Presently, these groups remain the only way to gain an electoral and parliamentary majority.

1990S–2014: UPA (CONGRESS), NDA (BJP), AND CONSOLIDATION OF COALITION POLITICS

In 1989, the dominance of the Congress Party, which was threatened in 1977, was once again shaken by a coalition led by Vishwanath P. Singh. By 1990, coalition politics, struggling for stability and longevity, became commonplace in the Indian political dynamics. Between 1989 and 1999, there were five general elections at the federal level. This period marked the emergence of coalitions and a series of attempts at formation of government, which were of short duration than the five-year parliamentary cycle. In the 1996 elections, the right-wing Hindu BJP secured 20 percent of the votes, but could not garner the alliances needed to form a government, leading to quick dissolution. The intervening United Front coalition was short lasting, giving way to yet another election in two years' time. In 1998, BJP won 25 percent of the votes, but still short of absolute majority. The BJP, the major challenger to the Congress Party, formed a coalition with regional and state parties and, in the 1999 elections, formed the NDA. This time, its alliance with coalition partners from the regional parties proved to be stronger and more stable.[31]

This frequent change of government party affiliations did not and should not indicate instability leading to institutional decay but to an adaptation through deinstitutionalization, the absence of which could be debilitating to democratic stability and cohesion. In fact, in terms of institutionalization, this phase of coalition building can be said to contribute to a new pattern of politics in which the dominant party ideology and personality gives way to a more accommodating, pragmatic one. It is interesting to examine the growth of coalition parties in this phase against the backdrop of India's economic, social, and political challenges.

Starting with the five-year plans that were instituted during the Nehru era, and their subsequent emphases of development priorities, it can be surmised that development priorities in India in the past did go hand in hand with ideological bent of political parties. With coalition politics, the challenges are a bit more complex. For one, depending on the coalition partners, especially with the regional and state parties, both the United Progressive Alliance (UPA) and NDA have had to work through those networks and their aspirations and expectations. Furthermore, immediate and pressing national level economic challenges involving economic growth, employment, and allocation of resources, needed to be addressed. Finally, the support base of the major coalition partners and their ideological or communal ties had to be recognized.

In short, in this context, there has emerged a consensus around the UPA and NDA in terms of addressing the aspirations and expectations of a diverse citizenry. The strategies and priorities of these two umbrella coalitions are different, but the fundamental, underlying phenomenon of giving voice to the economic and cultural needs of diverse groups has become the norm, leading to resilience to the Indian democracy. In recent decades especially, the erosion of party dominance and fluidity of coalitions, despite signifying chaos, have ironically lent resilience and a mechanism to work with political institutions and diverse groups within the citizenry. As Subrata K. Mitra writes:

> Governments make policies; policies give coherence, structure and legitimacy to government . . . . Seen from a distance, and over time, political transactions have taken manifold forms ranging between voting and lobbying to protest movements and ultimately, violent conflict. These in turn have produced knowledge of what leads to violence, instilling in the process greater understanding and accommodation of cultural and religious differences. Castes, religious communities and ethnic groups are all impregnated by the spirit of transaction and coalition building.[32]

While Mitra primarily focuses on India's parliamentary system, federalism, and the judiciary with lending much stability and coherence to the process of managing adversarial politics, there is much to be said about the way in which India's major political parties and coalitions have shaped policies when they were at the helm, and what the outcome has been, by and large. An examination of at least three areas of impact will help shed some light of how this deinstitutionalization has shaped in the past two decades, amid a complex political and economic reality. These areas include coalition leaders and their regional party affiliations with their bargaining chips, economic liberalization, and finally, the ideological and support base of the coalitions.

Even though the BJP's main identity and appeal in previous elections and governments had been the promotion of right-wing Hindu principles embedded in the ideological perspective of *Hindutva*, by the second time it contested in the late 1990s, there was a shift in its strategy. The earlier winning mantra of *Hindutva* was not on the front burner; its primary strategy was alliance building, especially with parties that had severed their ties with the Congress and the erstwhile popular Janata Dal. It managed to secure one-third of the seats as a single party, but overall, the difference with Congress was very narrow, and the government collapsed, necessitating another election the following year, when its more comprehensive alliance structure started taking shape. Earlier, it had managed to ally with a major party from the South, the *Telegu Desam* party (TDP). Even though Congress did well in this election in winning a larger percentage of the vote overall than the NDA (28%, as opposed to the latter's 24%), the BJP won 182 seats while Congress won only 114.[33]

Geographically, the NDA's coalitions spanned much of the country, reaching out to regions that hitherto were not part of the coalition, lending more stability. Between 1989 and 1991, the BJP had focused on the Hindi speaking belt in northern India, also its bastion of the *Hindutva* ideology. In the second phase, it focused on the western states of Maharashtra and Gujarat capitalizing on the partnership of the former's *Shiv Sena* party, also strong on promoting Hindu nationalist values, and victory in the assembly elections of the latter. In the north, it allied with parties such as the *Shiromani Akali Dal* in the Punjab and others in Haryana and Bihar. Since 1998, it was successful in entering into alliances with regional parties in states such as Orissa (*Biju Janata Dal*) and West Bengal (*Trinamool Congress*). In the South, the BJP's alliances continued beyond the TDP and added the *All India Anna Dravida Munetra Kazhagam* (AIADMK) and *Dravida Munetra Khazagam* (DMK). Thus, the BJP carefully created and managed to sustain coalitions of regional parties. This, in turn, provided stability in the central government, which was a rare occurrence for both the Indian federation under coalition government and the BJP.

By the 2004 elections, belying expectations and predictions, the NIC, along with its coalition partners, were victorious. Out of 539 Lok Sabha seats, UPA wrested 217 as opposed to the NDA's 186. Analysts argue that the performance of regional parties contributed somewhat to the overall outcome, but the victory of the Congress Party in 2004 and 2009 did not signify a huge swing in people's mandate. Moreover, in many states, due the high percentage of voters, more votes meant more seats. Therefore, the Congress Party was able to reap the benefits in many states, which were heavily populated. This was coupled by poor performance by the BJP and its allies, who, in 2004, were able to win only 51 seats, whereas they had managed to win 118 in 1999. The southern allies, DMK and AIADMK in Tamil Nadu also contributed to NDA's corrosion of strength. This process was repeated again in the 2009 elections when the Congress Party improved its election performance, winning 206 seats, with a slightly higher percentage of the votes than in 2004.[34]

Successful coalition building was a key aspect of the stability of the BJP-led NDA coalition. The NDA also performed well in terms of its promise of an India shining, and promises to make India a global power. Moreover, it was also widening the gap between those who found new employment in the service-based urban economy, and the larger poorer masses in rural and semiurban areas. The INC, with the promise of more equitable growth, which was an underlying promise of Nehruvian socialism, did better in many parts of India.

At a time when there was lingering desire for a growth-based political economy and the priorities it dictated, there was understandable nervousness at the defeat of the NDA. Meanwhile, with the erosion of populist politics also came a new economic thinking that gradually replaced state supremacy, complementing it, if not replacing it, with free market principles. It was no accident that from the 1990s onward, the dominance of market priorities interfered and took precedence over state power or even party strength. Within the Congress-led coalition of the UPA, the centrality that Manmohan Singh, who had previously served as finance minister and ushered in a period of economic liberalization, received within the Congress Party, and eventually became prime minister, was symptomatic of this shift toward a market-driven economy.

Prime Minister Singh was fortunate to be at the helm when India's growth hovered around an impressive 9 percent rate prior to the 2008 global recession and managing to stay at 6 percent in the face of that global market turmoil. The global commodity boom helped keep agricultural sector, employing about 60 percent of the Indian population, at a steady and profitable growth. The government also launched programs to help the rural poor, including the National Rural Employment Guarantee Act (NREGA), debt forgiveness for small farmers, and other initiatives to give incentive to employment and welfare in both rural and urban areas. Thus, the Singh government tried to avert the debacle of the previous promises of economic growth, which benefited the urban areas mostly.[35]

The return of the Congress-led government in 2004 and 2009 in no way signifies a return to one-party dominant system, nor to India's fascination with the Nehru-Gandhi family. It reveals India's cultural hesitance to accept a national identity based on *Hindutva* wholeheartedly or widely.[36] This is borne out by the fact that even though Sonia Gandhi and Rahul Gandhi were voluntary king makers as opposed to contenders within the party, the country was more comfortable with a bureaucrat with experience in the IMF and World Bank. It also helped that his acumen and the ethos of the Nehruvian era of socialistic pattern of growth might have resonated somewhat. To Singh's credit, he was forward thinking in removing barriers to business left over from the License Raj, but was also mindful of India's economic and other aspects of diversity. Even though India's markets operate on a model that is relatively free of state control and more market based than earlier decades, global financial crises have not affected it drastically, given its limited reliance on global finance and trade.[37]

Finally, the deinstitutionalization process also included a process of cultivation of an inclusive culture of citizenship by both the UPA and NDA. It is this complex but discernible trend of the coalition-led governments for much of India's political economy since the 1980s and in particular since the late 1990s into the 2009 elections, which provided much of the resilience to both the Congress Party and BJP-led coalitions. Each of them led coalition governments, whereby the state acted as a broker between competing interests related to central and regional and state parties, diverse economic groups, rural and urban priorities, and cultural and religious identities, particularly in the BJP-led coalition. If economic liberalization and its successes as well as electoral maneuvers in heavily populated states, and a notion of inclusive development spelled success for the Congress Party and its allies, the success of the NDA, as alluded to, lay in careful, pragmatic overtures. These included measured reliance on *Hindutva*, which led to their political gains in the 1990s until 2004.

To reiterate, the UPA was successful in cultivating this culture by incorporating a series of programs and policies that sought to alleviate the challenges of the weaker sections of the population. They included access to affordable and skill-based education, welfare of women and minorities, employment opportunities through NREGA, and other policies that led to empowering citizens to strengthen civil society through measures such as the Right to Information Act. Amid large-scale illiteracy and poverty, such policies and moves created an environment of inclusivity of citizens who came from different socioeconomic and ethnic groups.[38] Hence, UPA was able to carefully become a mouthpiece for a wider section of the population, beyond those that were direct beneficiaries of the hitherto trend of urban centered IT-based growth that was the flagship of the years preceding the UPA-led government of 2004. These measures clearly show that the New Congress Party, even when in office for two successive election cycles, did not revert to populism or even the Nehru-Gandhi dynasty.

In comparison, the record of the NDA and the BJP in particular, in terms of creating a culture of citizenship is more complicated and hinges on the fulcrum of its fundamental premise of promoting *Hindutva*. Even so, the BJP's moves and policy priorities have been affected by its desire and need to bring in alliances from all parts of the country. These, in turn, meant modifying its push for Hindu nationalism and rallying the masses that worked in the early 1990s, including its support for the destruction of the *Babri Masjid* in Ayodhya in 1992. Perhaps it was India's deep-seated tolerance for secular culture that resulted in waning of support for the BJP in the aftermath of the Ajodhya incident.

Predictably, the BJP tried to institutionalize its commitment to Hindu nationalism through various measures. These included an initiative for textbook revisions by altering the historical narrative of the coexistence of Hindu–Muslim relations in India's history, a move that the UPA government later denounced. Its other attempts toward antisecular measures did not materialize due to its allegiance to a wider coalition base and the cultural complexity and diversity of the Indian polity.[39]

In sum, then, regional party affiliations, including those based on caste considerations, the polemics of the pull between secular culture and Hindu nationalism, and the impetus to spread the fruits of economic liberalization and growth to a wider section of the India populace rallied toward strengthening a complex and wider basis of citizenship. It seemed that coalition politics was in India to stay, ushering in a new phase, a move away from both, a one-party dominant system, as well as party based on personality cult. This was also a sort of redefining the plebiscitary politics, meaning that now the coalition leaders had to accommodate a plurality of constituents and priorities, forcing them to modify the deinstitutionalization process.

2014–2019: ELECTION OF NARENDRA MODI AND PORTENDS OF THE FUTURE

In May 2014, the BJP, led by Narendra Modi, won a major election victory, securing 282 of the 543 seats in parliament. While it is too early to predict the trajectory of Modi's government, his past record as well as the current platform present intriguing questions and interesting analysis of the process of development and deinstitutionalization.

As governor of the state of Gujarat since 2001, Modi was successful in attracting investments to the state. In the face of declining rate economic growth and growing political corruption, voters rejected the Congress Party. Whether this mandate is also a rejection of the Congress Party's commitment to sharing the wealth of the country among all sections, especially the weaker ones, and a rural centric development priority, remains to be seen. In 2004, the Indian electorate had welcomed the Congress Party in a call for moving away from urban centric growth. In 2014, the mandate suggested that Modi's message and record of growth based on manufacturing and anticorruption resonated with the electorate. The lackadaisical performance of the Congress Party in the years preceding the 2014 elections notwithstanding, the personal narrative and political leadership of Modi is compelling. A self-made man, hailing from humble ranks in society, Modi has served as a loyal party member for the Hindu nationalist party and its predecessor, the *Rashtriya Swayamsevak Sangh*. His appeal seems to rest on his success as the leader of Gujarat, a state that has seen much prosperity as well as his style of direct and straight talk, his commitment to remove corruption, and the status quo.[40]

It seemed that the Indian voter had demonstrated not only a need for accountability, but also aspiration for entry into the rising and shining India. Even though the message of the Congress Party and the Congress-led coalition had resonated with the rural poor, amid a rising India, many of them and their neighbors aspire to become part of the new economic miracle, the glitz of shopping malls, personal transportation, and an urban lifestyle. Even though the Congress Party and its affiliates undertook welfare programs and policies geared toward poverty alleviation, the elites surrounding the Nehru-Gandhi family failed to continue the allegiance. Both Nehru, and particularly Indira Gandhi, appealed to the masses. Sonia Gandhi, and in particular, her son and "heir apparent" to the Congress Party, grew alienated from them over the past decade. It seems that this disenchantment was so predominant that voters have also, even if temporarily, looked beyond the questions surrounding the violent conflict between Muslims and Hindus under his watch as chief minister of Gujarat in 2002.

Derived from data on public opinion polls, analysts find that the BJP was able to forge a coalition uniting social and economic conservatives. First, there was a clear "rightward" shift among voters who preferred a minimized role of the state in managing the economy. Second, even though the UPA government had put in place several initiatives, administrative corruption of that coalition swayed voters away from it. Such was the dual impact of this negative benefit (meaning the weakness of UPA), and mobilization of the social and economic conservatives, which Prime Minister Modi was able to pivot away from the 2002 pogrom narrative to the administrative genius of a chief minister who was the architect of Gujarat's shining economy.[41]

By the time Prime Minister Modi faced his reelection in 2019, India's party system was clearly turning away from reliance on coalition politics, and strengthening populist appeal, in this case, of the Prime Minister. Interestingly, accountability, which has been a mainstay of the democratic fervor of India, seemed to also be waning. A look into some of the outcomes of domestic policy decisions and their outcomes will make this point clearer. The image of Prime Minister Modi as an architect of economic revival was seriously questioned and tarnished by the country's poor economic performance under his leadership. At best, there were clear indications of economic decline even prior to the 2019 elections, but the messaging was carefully orchestrated by officials who successfully managed to steer a clear and overwhelming victory for the BJP. One analysis has put it thus: "India's unemployment rate is as high as 6.1 percent. (Modi has refused to release the official figures.) An abrupt demonetization in 2016 took as much as 86 percent of all currency out of circulation, causing extraordinary hardship for the vast majority of the population. And a goods and services tax that the government haphazardly rolled out in 2017 wreaked havoc on small businesses."[42] If the economic miracle that was the promise of 2014 did not happen, what explains the huge mandate that Modi and his party, the BJP, obtained in 2019?

Interestingly, rather than a victory of alliances building based on party strength, BJP's victory seemed to use some strategies that were previously anathema to India's democratic culture. One such idea was that of secularism. Prime Minister Modi's charisma, and the party's effective use of social media aside, it became apparent that the party was able to successfully garner majoritarian support in a state that had thrived on tolerance for all religions by slowly but surely pivoting toward majoritarian politics, favored by a majority in a nation that is primarily Hindu. This narrative could also be corroborated by the one that India's political parties in the past had catered to, even pandered to, minority sentiments to use them as vote banks. While the latter might be true, Modi's move indicates a deeper cultural shift away from India's brand of secularism that may have resonance with the majority of the voters, but come at a dear price for the country's long-standing democratic ethos. "Under Modi's tutelage, the party has come to embrace a parochial vision of Hinduism. In this vision, Muslims are considered only quasi-citizens, since they have putative homes in the Muslim-majority nations of Bangladesh and Pakistan."[43] This vision, which the BJP and its more rightist followers have been aiming for since the 1990s, is slowly becoming institutionalized under Modi, and is being aligned with a notion of Hindu nationalism. That this wave of *Hindutva* or formulating a Hindu nation was "profoundly religious and profoundly, even aggressively, political form of militant nationalism are clear."[44] Furthermore, Modi and his followers have also successfully aligned this idea with nationalism to garner more political mileage. Reflecting on the 2019 elections, noted expert on Indian politics, Pratap Bhanu Mehta, concludes, "What was striking about this campaign was that the two things which dominated it were nationalism and a nod-nod-wink-wink gesture toward majoritarianism—consistently."[45] Given these trends of popular appeal of Prime Minister Modi and his deft use of charisma aligned with Hindu nationalism, it is difficult to equate the success of the BJP in terms of its strength as a political party in the strict sense of a vehicle to serve as a receptacle of pluralistic democratic views.

The Modi government has not only used anti-Muslim and anti-minority sentiments as a rhetorical tool. Utilizing "the National Register of Citizens, [it] excluded significant numbers of minorities from the electoral rolls in the border state of Assam. Such moves are indicative of the BJP's exclusionary national vision."[46] In fact, many decisions, including demonetization, goods and service taxes, and citizenship bill that discriminates on the basis of religion, have not been the result of extensive vetting or democratic decision-making. They have been rather swift decisions meted out by the central government, sometimes with little warning or lead time. Even the government's decision to impose nationwide lockdown to prevent the spread of the coronavirus as a public threat was taken hastily, giving a two-day notice for millions of people, many of them migrant laborers, to return to their villages, while simultaneously shutting down major transportation systems was symptomatic of that trend. A combination of this style of personality-based leadership and sloganeering initiatives such as "Swacch Bharat Abhiyan" or the "Clean India Mission," "Make in India and Skill India," and also giving

80 percent of the people a bank account, 100 million toilets, and other appealing initiatives seemed to have paled the deeper problem in the economy, such as lack of job creation and 6 percent unemployment rate that was at a forty-five-year high.[47] Clearly, the BJP success rests on a combination of all of the above factors and weakness of any veritable opposition, namely from the Congress Party.

CONCLUSION: SHIFTS IN PARTY SYSTEM, RISE OF POPULISM, AND FUTURE OF DEMOCRACY IN INDIA

In analyzing the historical shift of the Indian party system, one can view its effects on democracy from varied perspectives. While much of the literature explains populism as the result of weak institutions and poorly consolidated democracy, the decentralization of the Indian party system raises questions on the strength of democratic norms. This phenomenon from 1980 onward can be viewed as the strengthening of Indian democracy through inclusivity. India's diversity has been incorporated into the political system by the emergence of regional coalitions and factional parties. Although Indian democracy remains complicated, the break from a dominant party apparatus and the threat of democratic suspension have insulated stable elections. The dispersion of interests has also forced the state to be responsive to the needs of groups that fall out of the central voting bloc. Political groups that would traditionally use subversive means to participate in the democratic system can now expect their electoral support to be crucial for the large party establishments, like the INC or BJP, respectively.

At the same time, India still struggles with what Khilnani calls "paradoxical" democratic success:

> The unstoppable rise of popular engagement in electoral politics, the fact that in a national study conducted in 1996 more than 70 percent of the electorate rejected the suggestion that India would be better governed without political parties and elections, attests to the authority of the democratic idea. Yet the meaning of democracy has been menacingly narrowed to signify only elections. The compulsion to win power publicly and legitimately has provoked unpicturesque illegalities.[48]

Khilnani's assessment asserts that Indian democracy falls within the bounds of a minimalist, Schumpeterian framework. The benefits of popular incorporation have created a system in which democratic accountability is measured primarily by an electoral mandate and not on programmatic policy output. This is evident in the governments of Rajiv Gandhi, Vishwanath P.

Singh, and Rao throughout the 1980s and 1990s. Although all three adminis-
trations were elected popularly, they failed to initiate any meaningful political change through neoliberal reforms. The dispersed nature of party politics
generally empowers weak executives to rise through coalition building rather
than substantive policy platforms.

This incorporative political structure is a characteristic of a modern Indian
democracy, one that is distinctive from the Nehruvian or Gandhian forms
throughout the years following independence. The growing prevalence of
elections has contributed to the importance of regional interests on political
outcomes and decisions. India's democratic legacy remains divided between
a strong interplay of democratic norms, in the form of elections, and the lack
of executive accountability once the mechanisms of democracy have been
executed. The lack of a firm ideological platform and strong party foundation
make this a difficult trend to escape. Moreover, at the same time, it is this
fluidity that lends resilience to India's democracy. As one commentator has
concluded, "In the final analysis, the inter-party consensus on the institutional
arrangement and political transaction underpinning party competition is an
explanation of the resilience and buoyancy of India's parliamentary democratic system."[49] It is this perplexing mix of tradition and modernity, development and disparity, why the party system has to accommodate a vibrant,
aspirational, diverse electorate.

This analysis has shown that the party system has modified itself at several
turning points in India's democratic history since 1950 and provided resilience. Ganguly assesses that the verdict portends a new future for India, as
a plurality of voters, not just Hindu nationalists, has chosen a conservative
leader to deliver on the economic promise of a brighter future. But given
India's plurality, it also means that the BJP cannot revert to its agenda of
promoting Hindu nationalism.[50] Hinduism, as most Indians will agree, in
being a way of life rather than solely a religious pursuit, itself is plural. As
renowned Bengali Hindu ascetic, Ramakrishna, preached, "Jata Maat, Tata
Path," (There are as many ways as there are opinions and beliefs).

However, as recent months since the 2019 elections have revealed, much
rests on India's current prime minister, to "Modi-fy" the BJP's agenda, fulfill
and manage aspirations of more than billions of people, many of whom want
to trade Nehruvian socialism with individual-centric development policies
and ascertain accountability in governance. Alongside, gender violence and
equity, religious plurality, and stubborn, large-scale poverty will need to be
addressed to remove the uncertainties of millions of people in this apparent
glorious time for India and its democracy. Promotion of *Hindutva* and marginalization of religious minorities challenge the core of India's secularist
pillar of a pluralist democracy. Much of Modi's success so far has been associated with his charisma and personal attributes. Will they be successfully

combined with institutional efficiency and efficacy so that India does not return to a period of plebiscitary politics, or worse?

DISCUSSION QUESTIONS

1. What are some of the strengths of India's democratic system?
2. Did India's one-party system strengthen or weaken India's democracy?
3. What have you learned from this chapter about coalition politics in India?
4. What is the meaning and impact of deinstitutionalization on India's democracy?
5. What is "plebiscitary" politics? Discuss with examples.
6. The rise of the BJP is actually due to the decline of the Congress Party. Analyze this statement thoroughly.
7. Although representing markedly different political ideologies, India's current prime minister Narendra Modi's use of charisma in politics is reminiscent of Indira Gandhi. Explain.
8. India is considered the largest democracy in the world, but is actually lagging behind on many of the indicators of democracy that are outlined in chapter 1. Explain where it is lagging.

NOTES

1. Joseph, Sarah, "Neoliberal Reforms and Democracy in India." *Economic and Political Weekly* 42, no. 31 (2007): 3213–3218.

2. The data and concepts presented in this section are derived from Jean Dreze and Amartya Sen, *An Uncertain Glory: India and Its Contradictions* (Princeton, NJ: Princeton University Press, 2013), Chapter 1.

3. V. Bijukumar, "Economic Reforms, Populism and Party Politics in India." *The Indian Journal of Political Science* 65, no. 2 (2004): 161–180.

4. Stephan Haggard, *Pathways from the Periphery: The Politics of Growth in the Newly Industrializing Countries* (Ithaca, NY: Cornell University Press, 1990).

5. Samuel P. Huntington, *Political Order in Changing Societies* (New Haven, CT: Yale University Press, 1968).

6. Steven Levitsky, "Institutionalization and Peronism: The Concept, the Case and the Case for Unpacking the Concept." *Party Politics* 4, no. 1 (1998): 77–92. Also relevant is Vicky Randall and Lars Svåsand, "Party Institutionalization in New Democracies." *Party Politics* 8, no. 1 (2002): 5–29.

7. Richard Sisson and William Vanderbok, "Mapping the Indian Electorate II: Patterns of Weakness in the Indian Party System." *Asian Survey* 24, no. 10 (1984): 1086–1097.

8. Sunil Khilnani, *The Idea of India* (New York, NY: Farrar, Straus, and Giroux, 1999), 26.

9. Aditi Dey Sharma, "The Party System: National." In *Politics India: The State-Society Interface*, ed. Rakhahari Chatterji (New Delhi: South Asian Publishers, 2009), 58–59.

10. Ibid.

11. Ibid.

12. Rajni Kothari, "The Congress 'System' in India." *Asian Survey* 4, no. 12 (December 1964): 1171.

13. Ibid., 1170–1171.

14. Ibid., 1170.

15. Sharma, "The Party System," 60.

16. Ibid., 60–61.

17. Vicky Randall and Lars Svåsand, "Party Institutionalization in New Democracies." *Party Politics* 8, no. 1 (2002): 22.

18. Sharma, "The Party System," 61.

19. Atul Kohli, "Introduction." In *The Success of India's Democracy*, ed. Atul Kohli (Cambridge: Cambridge University Press, 2001), 8.

20. Ibid.

21. Khilnani, *The Idea of India*, 49.

22. Ibid., 54.

23. Kohli, "Introduction," 8.

24. Lloyd I. Rudoplh and Susanne Hoeber Rudolph, "Transformation of Congress Party: Why 1980 Was Not a Restoration." *Economic and Political Weekly* 16, no. 18 (1981): 811.

25. Khilnani, *The Idea of India*, 56.

26. Sharma, "The Party System," 64.

27. Khilnani, *The Idea of India*, 56–57.

28. Sumit Ganguly and Rahul Mukherjee, *India Since 1980* (Cambridge: Cambridge University Press, 2011), 70–74.

29. Bijukumar, "Economic Reforms," 168–170.

30. Khilnani, *The Idea of India*, 58.

31. Ganguly and Mukherjee, *India Since 1980*, 131.

32. Subrata K. Mitra, "Adversarial Politics and Policy Continuity: The UPA, NDA and the Resilience of Democracy in India." *Contemporary South Asia* 19, no. 2 (June 2011): 182.

33. These observations and data are drawn from Eswaran Sridharan, "Coalitions and Party Strategies in India's Parliamentary Federation." *Publius: The Journal of Federalism* 33, no. 4 (Fall 2003): 136–152.

34. Ganguly and Mukherjee, *India Since 1980*, 134–135.

35. Shalendra Singh, "India in 2009: Global Financial Crisis and Congress Revival." *Asian Survey* 50, no. 1 (January/February 2010): 139–156.

36. Ibid., 128.

37. Ibid., 149.

38. For details of such programs, see Mitra, "Adversarial Politics," 178–180.

39. For a fuller discussion of the programs and policies, and the complex situation that the NDS faced during this period, see Ganguly and Mukherjee, *India Since 1980* and Mitra, "Adversarial Politics."

40. Ellen Barry, "Narendra Modi's Ambitious Agenda Will Face Difficult Obstacles." *The New York Times*, May 16, 2014. http://www.nytimes.com/2014/05 /17/world/asia/india-elections.html on November 2, 2014.

41. Pradeep Chibber and Rahul Verma, "The BJPs 2014 'Modi Wave': An Ideological Consolidation of the Right." *Economic and Political Weekly* 49, no. 39 (September 2014): 50–56.

42. Sumit Ganguly, Himanshu Jha, and Rahul Mukherji, "India's Poor Economic Performance Should Have Hurt the Prime Minister at the Polls. Instead, Appeals to Nationalism Won Him the Vote." *Foreign Policy*, May 25, 2019. https://foreignpolic y.com/2019/05/25/the-modi-mystery/.

43. Ibid.

44. Robert E. Frykenberg, "Hindutva as a Political Religion: A Historical Perspective." In *The Sacred in Twentieth Century Politics*, eds. Roger Griffin, Robert Mallette, and John Tortorice (London: Palgrave Macmillan, 2008), 178.

45. Pratap Bhanu Mehta's phone interview, as edited and noted by Isaac Chotiner, "An Indian Political Theorist on the Triumph of Narendra Modi's Hindu Nationalism." *The New Yorker*, May 24, 2019. https://www.newyorker.com/news/q-and-a/an-indian -political-theorist-on-the-triumph-of-narendra-modis-hindu-nationalism.

46. Ganguly et al., "India's Poor Economic Performance."

47. Akshara Baru, *Modi's Second Term Economic Development Roadmap*. Asia Policy Institute, January 13, 2020. https://asiasociety.org/policy-institute/modis-sec ond-term-economic-development-roadmap.

48. Khilnani, *The Idea of India*, 58.

49. Mitra, "Adversarial Politics," 184.

50. Sumit Ganguly, "India's Missing Right-Wing: What BJP's Victory Says About India's Politics." *Foreign Affairs*, June 3, 2014. http://www.foreignaffairs .com/articles/141514/sumit-ganguly/indias-missing-right.

FURTHER READING

Brass, Paul R. *Caste, Faction and Party in Indian Politics*, Vol. 2. New Delhi: Chanakya, 1985.

Datta, Rekha. *Contemporary India*. London: Routledge, 2017.

Datta, Rekha. "Hindu Nationalism or Pragmatic Party Politics? A Study of India's Hindu Party." *International Journal of Politics, Culture, and Society* 12 (1999): 573–588. doi:10.1023/A:1025938125870.

Gould, Harold A. and Ganguly, Sumit, eds. *India Votes: Alliance Politics and Minority Governments in the Ninth and Tenth General Elections*. Boulder, CO: Westview, 1993.

Kohli, Atul. *India's Democracy: An Analysis of State–Society Relations*. Princeton, NJ: Princeton University Press, 1988.

Kohli, Atul and Singh, Prerna. *Routledge Handbook of Indian Politics*. London and New York, NY: Routledge, 2013.

Kothari, Rajni. *State Against Democracy: In Search of Humane Governance*. New Delhi: Ajanta Publications, 1998.

Manor, James, ed. *Nehru to the Nineties: The Changing Office of Prime Minister in India*. London: Hurst & Company, 1994.

Rudolph, Lloyd and Rudolph, Susanne Hoeber. *Explaining Indian Democracy: A Fifty Year Perspective – 1956–2006*. New Delhi: Oxford University Press, 2008.

Thakur, Ramesh. *Government and Politics of India*. New York, NY: St. Martin's Press, 1995.

Weiner, Myron. *India at the Polls: The Parliamentary Elections of 1977*. Washington, DC: American Enterprise Institute, 1978.

Chapter 8

Digital Authoritarianism in the People's Republic of China

Peter W. Liu and Justin M. Liu

The People's Republic of China (PRC) is a digital authoritarian state under the rule of the Chinese Communist Party (CCP). It is able to spy on its 1.4 billion people by using a variety of surveillance technologies. In the battle against Covid-19, for example, China has increased the deployment of such technologies, including apps monitoring people in quarantine or tracking apps, advanced facial recognition software, artificial intelligence-enabled fever detection systems, and thermal camera-equipped drones. Obviously, such governmental practices, when they are taken to extreme or when they become permanent, harm privacy and civil liberties. This phenomenon is not new to China's past and present.

CHINA: A MODEL OF AUTHORITARIAN GOVERNMENT

The CCP, which took control in 1949, is a continuation of the 2000-year history of Chinese totalitarian system, which is characterized by a centralized imperial rule that controlled all aspects of individual life through coercion and suppression. For imperial rulers and the CCP leaders, free thinking and free speech by the people are the most formidable threats to their ruling. Chinese authoritarian regimes especially underscored speech censorship—suppressing dissident opinions on political affairs. Confucianism, prevalent for over 2000 years, has influenced the Chinese government, emphasizing obedience to authority.[1] An ancient and extreme example of censorship was the burning of books and burying of 460 scholars alive during the Qin Dynasty (221–210 BC) by the First Emperor Qin Shihuangdi due to his paranoia over opposition and dissent.[2]

When the Internet and personal computer became a new way of communication in the early 1990s, the Chinese people had a great dream that the strict
government censorship would become obsolete and the freedom of online
speech would ultimately lead to the new nation of democracy. What everyone
did not realize is that with a technological tweak the traditional authoritarian
regime has changed into a digital authoritarian state. Realizing the trend of
liberal democracy, which was an initial result of an open Internet, the CCP
has defined the sphere of ideology and identified major concerns that may
threaten the authoritarian leadership in Document 9: Communiqué on the
Current State of the Ideological Sphere. To deal with the problems, the CCP
demands the following:

> Historical experience has proven that failures in the economic sphere can result
> in major disorder, and failure in the ideological sphere can result in major disor-
> ders as well. Confronting the very real threat of Western anti-China forces and
> their attempt at carrying out Westernization, splitting, and "Color Revolutions,"
> and facing the severe challenge of today's ideological sphere, all levels of
> Party and Government, especially key leaders, must pay close attention to their
> work in the ideological sphere and firmly seize their leadership authority and
> dominance.[3]

Strengthen Leadership in the Ideological Sphere

Party members and governments of all levels must become fully aware that
struggles in the ideological sphere are perpetual, complex, and excruciating;
you must strengthen awareness of the current political situation, big picture,
responsibility, and risks. Leaders at all levels of government must strengthen
their sense of responsibility—make work in the ideological sphere a high priority in their daily agenda, routinely analyze and study new developments in
the ideological sphere, react swiftly and effectively, and preemptively resolve
all problems in the ideological sphere.

Guide Our Party Members and Leaders to
Distinguish Between True and False Theories

Forcefully resist influential and harmful false tides of thoughts, help people
distinguish between truth and falsehood, and solidify their understanding.
Party members, especially high-level leaders, must become adept at tackling
problems from political, big-picture, strategic, and theoretical perspective.
They must clearly recognize the essence of false ideas and viewpoints, both
their theoretical falsehood and the practical political harm they can cause.
We must have a firm approach and clear-cut stance toward major political

principles, issues of right and wrong, what to support and what to oppose. We must uphold strict and clear discipline, maintaining a high-level unity with the Party Central Committee under the leadership of General Secretary Xi Jinping in thought, political stance, and action. We must not permit the dissemination of opinions that oppose the Party's theory or political line, the publication of views contrary to decisions that represent the central leadership's views, or the spread of political rumors that defame the image of the Party or the nation.

Adhere Unwaveringly to the Principle of the Party's Control of Media

The [principle of the Party's control of media] stems from our political system and the nature of our media. We must maintain the correct political direction. We must firmly hold fast to the principle of the media's Party spirit and social responsibility, and that in political matters it must be of one heart and mind with the Party. We must persist in correct guidance of public opinion, insisting that the correct political orientation suffuse every domain and process in political engagement, form, substance, and technology. We must give high priority to building both the leadership and rank and file in the sphere of media work. We need to strengthen education on the Marxist perspective of media to ensure that the media leadership is always firmly controlled by someone who maintains an identical ideology with the Party's Central Committee, under General Secretary Xi Jinping's leadership.

Conscientiously Strengthen Management of the Ideological Battlefield

When facing sensitive events and complex puzzles in the ideological sphere, we should implement the principle that the people in charge assume responsibility and use territorial management.

We must reinforce our management of all types and levels of propaganda on the cultural front, perfect and carry out related administrative systems, and allow absolutely no opportunity or outlets for incorrect thinking or viewpoints to spread. Conscientiously implement the "Decision of the Standing Committee of the National People's Congress on Strengthening Information Protection on Networks," strengthen guidance of public opinion on the Internet, purify the environment of public opinion on the Internet. Improve and innovate our management strategies and methods to achieve our goals in a legal, scientific, and effective way.

Document 9 did not hide the CCP's ambition to build a society of digital authoritarianism, which refers to the use of digital information technology by authoritarian regimes to surveil, repress, and manipulate domestic and foreign populations.[4] The goal of the CCP's digital authoritarianism is to build a real-time, nationwide surveillance network, a national system that can aggregate bank data, hospital records, real-world movements, online activity, and other records into a single "trustworthiness" score; a system that will "allow the trustworthy to roam everywhere under heaven while making it hard for the discredited to take a single step."[5] The CCP's digital authoritarianism is not limited within China's territory; it is also part of its global vision. First, it demands that foreign companies that obtain data from the Chinese market must store the Chinese data within China's borders, where the information can be accessed by security agencies.[6] Second, the CCP exports digital authoritarianism through the Belt and Road Initiative (BRI) in order to control a large part of the world to offset the world of liberal democracy led by the United States. By exporting elements of China's digital surveillance and technology of information connectivity, the BRI strategy envisions a more connected world brought together by a web of Chinese-funded physical and digital infrastructure.[7] (The CCP's global version of digital authoritarianism will not be discussed in this chapter.)

China began to transform from a traditional authoritarian regime to a digital one in the 1990s. There are three major components of the digital authoritarianism. First, in the name of upholding "cyber sovereignty," the CCP initiated the Golden Shield Project in 1997 and the project has evolved into a massive Internet censorship system that contains several forms—(1) using the Great Firewall (GFW) to block the population's access to foreign Internet services; (2) forcing Internet service providers and users to self-censor the contents on their platforms (exampled later with the case of WeChat); (3) misinforming the public by using an Internet troll army called the 50 Cent Army or 50 Cent Party. Second, the government controls and manages the society by creating a social credit system (SCT) so everyone must conform and contribute to the state capitalism. And third, the government surveils the society by using the Skynet so no one can step out of the boundaries defined by the CCP.

First, the Government Enforces the Internet
Censorship, Which Contains Several Forms

By claiming "cyber sovereignty," the CCP initiated "The GFW of China" in 1997.[8] China continues to control the Internet. For instance, in 2010 alone, the central government enacted 20 laws and directives to regulate public and private activities on the Internet.[9] State Council Order No. 195 explicitly brought the Internet under state control. More than sixty government agencies are involved in enforcing those laws and directives.[10] In the early days, according to Amnesty International, around 30,000–50,000 Internet police were employed by the Chinese government to enforce Internet laws.[11] The Ordinance for Security Protection of Computer Information Systems of 1994 gave the responsibility of Internet protection to the Ministry of Public Security.[12] In this criminal Ordinance, the following Internet behaviors are illegal and violations are subject to punishment.

1. Inciting to resist or obstruct the implementation of the constitution, legislation, or administrative regulations;
2. Inciting to overthrow the government or the socialist system;
3. Inciting division of the country, harming national unification;
4. Inciting hatred or discrimination among ethnic groups or harming the unity of ethnic groups;
5. Fabricating or distorting the truth, spreading rumors, destroying the order of society;
6. Promoting feudal superstitions, obscenity, pornography, gambling, violence, murder, and terrorism or encouraging criminal activity;
7. Publicly insulting or distorting the truth to slander other people;
8. Defaming state organizations;
9. Other activities against the constitution, legislation, and administrative regulations.

In a confidential internal document issued by the CCP leadership in 2013, known as Document No. 9, the Communist Party leader Xi Jinping listed seven problems in the sphere of the Chinese Internet:[13]

1. Promoting Western Constitutional Democracy: An attempt to undermine the current leadership and the "socialism with Chinese characteristics" system of governance. (Included are the separation of powers, the multiparty system, general elections, and independent judiciaries.)
2. Promoting "universal values" in an attempt to weaken the theoretical foundations of the Party's leadership (i.e., "the West's values are the prevailing norm for all human civilization," that "only when China accepts Western values will it have a future.")
3. Promoting civil society in an attempt to dismantle the ruling party's social foundation (i.e., individual rights are paramount and ought to be immune to obstruction by the state.)
4. Promoting neoliberalism, attempting to change China's basic economic system (i.e., unrestrained economic liberalization, complete privatization, and total marketization.)
5. Promoting the West's idea of journalism, challenging China's principle that the media and publishing system should be subject to Party discipline.

6. Promoting historical nihilism, trying to undermine the history of the CPC and of New China (e.g., to deny the scientific and guiding value of Mao Zedong thought.)
7. Questioning Reform and Opening and the socialist nature of socialism with Chinese characteristics (e.g., saying "We have deviated from our Socialist orientation.")

To fight against the above listed problems, the CCP enhanced its weapon of Internet censorship through the GFW and self-censorship by the service providers. This form of digital authoritarianism has become a way for the CCP to control the Chinese people through technology, capsizing the original idea of the Internet as social drive for human liberation. The GFW is the combination of legislative actions and technologies enforced by the government to regulate the Internet domestically. Its purpose is to block access to selected foreign websites and foreign Internet tools (e.g., Google search, Facebook, Twitter, Wikipedia, and others) and mobile apps.[14] The GFW has effectively brainwashed the Chinese population because only the communist propaganda is available on the Internet when it comes to political, economic, historical, moral, religious, and social issues. It is a strong method for the CCP to maintain its authoritarian goals. As a result, many controversial issues in China have become unarguable facts. For example, Taiwan, Xinjiang, and Tibet are part of China since ancient times; the 1989 Tiananmen Square massacre did not happen; Falun Gong is an antihumanity cult and must be banned; Hong Kong protesters are terrorists; all prodemocracy organizations and individuals are Anti-China enemies; the CCP is the guardian of the nation and patriotism means the love of the Party and its leaders, and so forth.

Second, the Government Controls and Manages the Society by Creating a Social Credit System

The second effort of building a digital authoritarian society in China is to create an information-based SCT where every citizen's behavior is constantly evaluated and adjusted by the state and by her or him. The U.S. Vice President Mike Pence describes the SCT as "an Orwellian system premised on controlling virtually every facet of human life."[15]

Since its founding, the regime of Communist China has established systems of hard copy personal records (*dang'an*) and household registration recodes (*hukou*) on every citizen and every family. Society's mobilization was strictly limited prior to the 1980s because one must show a travel permission (*jieshaoxin*) issued by government agencies to purchase train or airline tickets. When citizens drew attention from the authority (could be in either a good or bad way), their personal history of actions and thoughts would be examined to determine their degree of trustworthiness. The systems of manual record keeping in later days were deemed to be ineffective due to the fact that massive amounts of bookkeeping work required accurate and rapid feedback but simple human labor could not fulfill the task effectively. As a result, since the 1990s an integrated electronic record keeping system came into being.[16] Personal records became digital, and the vast databases built upon them allowed further data aggregation and analysis.

Since 2009, the Communist regime in China has begun a new and proactive way of personal data collection, restoration, aggregation, and utilization. The government launched a SCT, which centralizes and unifies the credit scores for all individuals and institutes.[17] The system consists of big data technology and a mass surveillance system that includes facial recognition technology. It is estimated that more than 200 million of monitoring CCTVs are in use in 2019 and the number is expected to reach 600 million in 2020 when the SCT becomes fully in force.[18]

As of November 2019, in addition to dishonest and fraudulent financial behavior, other behaviors that some cities have officially listed as negative factors of credit ratings include:

> playing loud music, eating in rapid transits, violating traffic rules such as jaywalking and red-light violations, failure to appear at a doctor or dentist's appointment, missing a job interview, missing restaurant reservation without notice, missing hotel reservation without making notification to cancel, failure to comply with the waste sorting rules, fraudulently using other people's public transportation identity document (ID) cards, failure to use the DiDi Chuxing transportation service after it is booked, cheat or rude behavior in video games, malicious comments on internet services in order to bring down their review points, fraud on Internet sales, failure to pay utility bills, failure to pay cell phone services, participating in indirect sale network, failure to pay credit card on time, having sleeping credit cards, fraudulent educational degree, losing personal ID or internet passwords, failure to pay insurances on time, engaging in derogative behavior on social media, frequently using products of intellectual property theft, using incorrect mailing address, uncivil behaviors when traveling, failure to visit elderly family members, cheating on examinations, violating drinking and driving rules, and failure to register dogs with the government or keep dogs on a leash.

However, behavior listed as positive factors of credit ratings includes donating blood, donating to charity, and volunteering for community services.[19] People with high credit ratings may receive rewards such as less waiting time at hospitals and governmental agencies, discounts at hotels, and greater likelihood of receiving employment offers.

According to the report by the National Development and Reform Commission of China, 26.82 million air tickets and 5.96 million high-speed rail tickets have been denied to people who were deemed untrustworthy, and 4.37 million untrustworthy people have acted to fulfill their duties to remedy their behaviors required by the law.[20] While still in the preliminary stages, the system has also started to ban people and their children from entering certain schools, prevent low scorers from renting hotels and using credit cards, and disallow blacklisted individuals from being able to procure employment.[21] The system has also been used to rate individuals on their Internet habits (excessive online gaming reduces one's score), personal shopping habits, and a variety of other personal and wholly innocuous acts that have no impact on the wider community.[22]

As a punishment, public shaming in Chinese culture is a particularly effective deterrence. Certain personal information of blacklisted people is deliberately made accessible by the society and is displayed online as well as at various public venues such as movie theaters and buses. For example, names, home addresses, and redacted ID numbers of twelve people who were on the blacklist of debtors in Xinchang County, Zhejiang Province were exposed in local movie theaters in July 2019.[23]

Researchers argued that the credit system will be part of the government's plan to automate their authoritarian rule over the Chinese population.[24],[25],[26] Professor Genia Kostka of Free University of Berlin stated that "if successful in [their] effort, the Communist Party will possess a powerful means of quelling dissent, one that is comparatively low cost and which does not require the overt (and unpopular) use of coercion by the state."[27]

Third, the Government Surveils the Society by Using the Skynet so no One Can Step Out of the Boundary Defined by the CCP

Mass surveillance has been a major class struggle tool for the CCP since 1949. In the early years, every "bad element" in the society—namely the former Nationalist government employees, the counter-revolutionaries, the upper- and middle-class property owners in cities, the landlords in countryside, the intellectuals who criticized the CCP and its government, and anyone who disrespected the CCP leader Chairman Mao—was surveilled and punished. Millions of class enemies were killed during the class struggle movements. Prior to the 1990s when technology was relatively undeveloped in China, mass surveillance was done through human network organized by the government and through disseminating information by word of mouth. The Chinese people were required to keep a watchful eye on one another and report inappropriate behaviors that infringed upon the Communist ideology and CCP policies.[28]

Since the 1990s, computer and Internet technology had become popular in China. The government took advantage of the technology research and development (R&D) and made the mass surveillance project called Skynet a priority for R&D. The most notable mechanisms today are mass camera surveillance on the streets, Internet surveillance, and newly invented surveillance methods based on social credit and identity.[29] The system is equipped with all the latest technologies, including facial recognition, artificial intelligence, Global Positioning System tracking, surveillance drones, and big data analysis.[30]

Informal surveillance system has been implemented through various mobile phone apps. Local governments launched mobile apps for national security purposes and to allow citizens to report violations, "which is a way for residents to conduct social supervision," according to a commentary in the state-run newspaper *Global Times*.[31]

The Skynet system has proven to be very effective in identifying and apprehending individual citizens. Last year, British Broadcasting Corporation journalist John Sudworth visited one of China's local police control rooms. To demonstrate the system, police took a mugshot of him before he started to "escape." It took police just seven minutes to find him. Four months later, a Chinese college student who was writing a thesis on Skynet decided to take on the same challenge in Hunan. A police officer tracked him down just a little over five minutes after he was given 10 minutes to "escape."[32]

In the area of general population control, the surveillance network allows the government to again use public shaming as an extremely effective mechanism. For example, when the police were unable to stop the problems of jaywalking or speeding at a street intersection, they used Skynet system to capture images of people who had violated rules. The personal information such as names, ages, gender, and redacted ID numbers are shown on a large display screen live at the intersection. Because the Chinese people are afraid of losing face in the eyes of their acquaintances—their neighbors and colleagues may see their picture online in a negative context, therefore they desire to behave in accordance with the government requirements.[33]

The CCP is essentially building a society of fear and blind obedience. From the beginning of their lives, the Chinese people are trained to be afraid of being exposed by public cameras or being caught doing anything incorrect so their social credit scores would be affected. Eventually, such a society of digital authoritarianism will create extremely obedient and fearful modern slaves who comply with all orders due to paranoia.

WECHAT: A CASE STUDY OF
DIGITAL AUTHORITARIANISM

Fearing the free flow of information on the Internet, the CCP has banned all foreign Internet services in China and built the GFW to deny the Chinese people's access to the online sources from outside. As a result, social media services such as Facebook, Twitter, YouTube, and other service such as Google, Wikipedia, and Amazon are not available. China has developed its own domestic Internet and affiliated services. WeChat is a smartphone app developed in China, "boasting over 1.1 billion users."[34] Released by the state-sponsored company Tencent in 2011, it originally started out as a simple messaging app. However, hand in hand with its popularity, WeChat quickly grew into a "megaplatform," boasting a massive number of practical features.[35] The list of uses includes public social media, ordering food delivery, Uber/Lyft-like functionality, sending money to friends, making doctor's appointments, paying off bills, communicating in the business world, and even using government services.[36] As its monopoly continues to expand, the app has become more and more indispensable in Chinese citizen's lives. Though it may sound like an exaggeration to someone who has not used the app before, "leaving WeChat means leaving [social] life in China," not to mention missing out on the convenience of all of its other functions.[37] Beyond its surface-level ease and accessibility, however, is a darker side, a side strictly monitored and regulated by the CCP: censorship. Explored by cybersecurity journalist Patrick O'Neill's 2019 MIT *Technology Review* article, Beijing heavily pressures Tencent to implement effective real-time censorship of not only text, but also images posted to users' moments (analogous to Facebook's timelines) and even in group chats and one-on-one conversations. What follows will focus on the social dimension of WeChat that has allowed this social media giant to become a powerful weapon in tightening censorship and state control in China. Analysis will mainly rely upon censorship theories and other articles on modern events regarding China's media suppression.

As mentioned previously, censorship has had a long and unfortunate history in China. Two millennia of emperors, wars, revolutions, and bloodshed after Qin Shihuangdi, General Secretary Xi Jinping sits at the head of the CCP. Under his leadership, both traditional and newer Internet media are being tightly regulated in order to avoid "potential subversion of authority," going as far as jailing dissenting "journalists, bloggers, and activists."[38] Despite its constitution stating that Chinese citizens have free speech, by keeping its definition of "state secrets" vague, anthropologist Beina Xu argues that authorities are able to "crack down" on any information under the pretext of exposing state secrets. With the emergence of WeChat, the CCP has a new medium with cooperative developers in order to maintain their stranglehold on the availability of information. Despite WeChat defining its mission to "improve the quality of life through internet value-added services," in reality its work is to "reflect the party's will, safeguard the party's authority, and safeguard the party's unity."[39],[40] This is legally echoed in WeChat's privacy policy, which offers no protection against government surveillance.[41]

Despite political science Professor Langdon Winner's ideas in "Do Artifacts Have Politics?" being developed before the popularization of the Internet, WeChat's model fits his outline of an authoritarian technology very well, being "system centered" and "immensely powerful," a technology that leads society toward authoritarianism.[42] This is made evident by WeChat's unprecedented rise and the ways that it censors information. As a point of emphasis, WeChat is everything in today's China. However, it has not become a backbone of Chinese lifestyle simply from its usefulness; as long as it continues to align with the CCP's values, it will receive plenty of help from the government. On top of granting subsidies to Tencent, Beijing has globally banned or heavily handicapped virtually all of WeChat's foreign competitors, making it the only logical choice for practical use.[43]

This rise from service platform to infrastructure has allowed WeChat to become an easy one-stop shop for a large portion of the government's censorship, fulfilling its role as an authoritarian technology. As the publishing platform of virtually all media outlets in China as well as the newsfeed provider of most citizens, information flow can be strictly controlled with ease, effectively making WeChat a propaganda machine of the state. This is accomplished by Tencent's censorship algorithms, ever-improving due to stress from Beijing such as monitoring by government agencies in "special operations."[44] Beyond simply blacklisting words and phrases, the real-time censorship technologies have even been improved to recognize images and any text that may be contained in those pictures, using a self-reinforcing machine learning approach to generate dynamic blacklists.[45] According to the article "Technology: Emergence of a Hazardous Concept," technology becomes hazardous when it becomes the driving force of society due to people's complete dependence on machines.[46] The sticky nature of WeChat has not only enforced complete dependence by enhancing its users' addictive behaviors, but taken the hazard one step further by creating an intimate and dangerous one-way relationship with China's central government through its censorship technologies.[47]

As a specific example, in the Hong Kong protests in which its people opposed the extradition law passed by the central government, WeChat played a prominent role in keeping mainland citizens out of the know. As a bit of background, Hong Kong holds a special classification different from the rest of China due to its previous status as colony of the United Kingdom. It was returned to China in 1997 under the principle of "one country, two systems," in which Hong Kong would enjoy "a high degree of autonomy" for fifty years.[48] However, in June 2019, just twenty-two years later, plans of an extradition from Hong Kong to mainland China sparked protests in Hong Kong that have now grown to encompass more general arguments for democratic reform.[49] Early in the protests, CNBC concluded that searching for the Hong Kong demonstrations on WeChat did not return any relevant results, and that images of the protests sent in one-on-one conversations did not go through.[50] Not only has information availability been limited, but WeChat has also been the root of the spread of misinformation. *The Guardian*'s Lily Kuo recently reported that on WeChat's newsfeeds, prior peaceful movement was described as "riots," protesters were portrayed as "radicals" and "thugs" "lured by the evil winds of foreign agents," and the United States was accused of being the "black hand" behind the protests. By painting radicals or other nations as the instigator, the narrative in mainland China has been shifted toward a nationalist sentiment in which the protestor's arguments are the minority, while the rest of Hong Kong's citizens just want to live their lives peacefully under the CCP's rule.[51] As tensions continue to increase, Beijing can maintain its control over the rhetoric and keep its citizens in blissful ignorance by implementation of their nearly omnipotent authoritarian technology.

Meanwhile, WeChat has also begun its conquest of Tibet, a far-west region in China. Ever since Dalai Lama's failed uprising against the PRC in 1959, activists have maintained a government-in-exile, claiming that "Tibet is an independent state under unlawful occupation."[52] However, as smartphone usage rises in the region, WeChat has invaded the lives of over 70 percent of the Tibetan population.[53] As one would predict, Dalai Lama's spiritual messages are heavily censored by Tencent and the CCP, and users with dissenting political viewpoints are cut off from the Internet by removing them from the app, effectively silencing activism.[54] Rates of restrictions, fines, and arrests doled out have also been increasing, with recent news stating that Tibetans could face up to eight years of prison time for sharing information on WeChat about politically sensitive current events like Hong Kong's protests.[55] In this remote region over 1,500 miles away from Beijing, previous insurrection has been crushed and new information is being censored easily through WeChat and looming punishments.

One final striking example of WeChat's role as an extension of state control is in the introduction of China's relatively new SCT. This system is a way for the CCP to monitor, shame, and punish 1.4 billion Chinese citizens, separating the trustworthy from the disobedient. Just like a personal credit score, one's social credit score can fluctuate depending on good behavior (e.g., paying bills on time) and bad behavior (e.g., smoking in a non-smoking zone), and those with low scores may be placed on blacklists in all aspects of life.[56] Tencent and WeChat's role in this topic of unease is its implementation of a system nicknamed the "deadbeat map." This disturbing application will display the full name, court case number, reason they are deemed untrustworthy, and even partial home addresses of anyone with low social credit scores within a user's 500-meter radius, with a radar changing colors as the density of "deadbeats" increases or decreases.[57] This massive infringement of personal privacy by Western standards aims to enhance the repercussions of the SCT by shaming the "deadbeats" and encouraging others to "treat those people as subhuman," effectively making Chinese society a "virtual prison."[58] Without the support of WeChat as a medium, consequences of a low social credit score would obviously still be felt in citizens' daily lives, but not in the same dimension as being publicly exposed and shunned by everyone within 500 meters.

With their willingness to provide users' information, it is no surprise that Tencent's WeChat scored dead last in Amnesty International's ranking of messaging app privacy, achieving a grand total of zero out of 100 points.[59] With the role of media under President Xi Jinping's reign to be supporting "the party's unilateral rule, and nothing less," WeChat has demonstrated its commitment to this philosophy from end to end, helping the CCP move quickly from its role of spectator to authority in today's information age.[60] Without resorting to brute force that would attract the attention of countries around the world, China has ensnared its people in a digital vice grip, filtering and manipulating this grasp as the CCP pleases. By downloading WeChat and clicking on the happy little icon, all that the Chinese citizens wanted was modern convenience. The price: whatever limited social and political freedom they had left, engulfed by the abyss of one of today's most ambitious and successful authoritarian censors.

DISCUSSION QUESTIONS

1. What is digital authoritarianism and what distinguishes it from traditional authoritarianism?
2. What is Chinese digital authoritarianism? What is its goal and main components?
3. Why is it important to distinguish between China, Chinese people, Chinese government, and the CCP? What role does each play in the context of digital authoritarianism?
4. How can one become a "trustworthy" person under the Chinese digital authoritarian regime? What are the benefits and costs to become such a person? Conversely, how can one become an "untrustworthy" person, and what are the consequences to be such a person?
5. What is the GFW of China? How does it contribute to Chinese digital authoritarianism?

6. What is the Skynet in China and what role does it play in the Chinese digital authoritarian regime? How would you feel as a foreign traveler if you were aware that you are always surveilled everywhere you go in China? How would you feel if you were a Chinese citizen?

7. What is WeChat? Why is it popular among the Chinese population throughout the world? How does WeChat create a personal dependency on the Chinese authority? How does WeChat censor everyone's communication?

NOTES

1. Sor-Hoon Tan, "Authoritative Master Kong (Confucius) in an Authoritarian Age." *Dao* 9, no. 2 (2010): 137–149. doi:10.1007/s11712-010-9157-2.

2. Anthony Barbieri-Low, *Burning the Books and Killing the Scholars: Representing the Atrocities of the First Emperor of China*. US-China Institute, 2008. https://china.usc.edu/calendar/burning-books-and-killing-scholars-representing-atrocities-first-emperor-china.

3. *ChinaFile*, "Document 9: A ChinaFile Translation – How Much Is a Hardline Party Directive Shaping China's Current Political Climate?" November 8, 2013. http://www.chinafile.coms/document-9-chinafile-translation.

4. Alina Polyakova and Chris Meserole, "Exporting Digital Authoritarianism: The Russian and Chinese Models." *Foreign Policy*, August 27, 2019. https://www.brookings.edu/wp-content/uploads/2019/08/FP_20190827_digital_authoritarianism_polyakova_meserole.pdf.

5. Ibid.

6. Freedom House, *Freedom on the Net 2018*, 2018. https://freedomhouse.org/report/freedom-net/freedom-net-2018.

7. Daniel Kliman and Abigail Grace, *Power Play: Addressing China's Belt and Road Strategy*. Center for a New American Security, September 20, 2018. https://s3.amazonaws.com/files.cnas.org/documents/CNASReport-Power-Play-Addressing-Chinas-Belt-and-Road-Strategy.pdf?mtime=20180920093003.

8. Geremie Barme and Sang Ye, "The Great Firewall of China." *Wired*, June 1, 1997. http://www.wired.com/1997/06/china-3/.

9. China Internet Laws, *Central Government Laws for 2010*. http://topics.gmw.cn/node_10213.htm.

10. Polyakova and Meserole, "Exporting Digital Authoritarianism."

11. Amnesty International Australia, *What Is Internet Censorship?* March 28, 2008. https://web.archive.org/web/20150427065800/http://www.amnesty.org.au/china/comments/10926/.

12. "Internet Censorship in China."

13. *ChinaFile*, "Document 9."

14. Xiao Qiang, "How China's Internet Police Control Speech on the Internet." *Radio Free Asia*, November 24, 2008. https://www.rfa.org/english/commentaries/china_internet-11242008134108.html.

15. Jamie Horsley, "China's Orwellian Social Credit Score Isn't Real." *Foreign Policy*, November 19, 2018. https://foreignpolicy.com/2018/11/16/chinas-orwellian-s ocial-credit-score-isnt-real/.

16. Chuncheng Liu, "Multiple Social Credit Systems in China." *Economic Sociology: The European Electronic Newsletter* 21, no. 1 (November 2019): 22–32.

17. Mirjam Meissner, "China's Social Credit System: A Big-Data Enabled Approach to Market Regulation with Broad Implications for Doing Business in China." *Merics*, May 24, 2017. https://www.merics.org/sites/default/files/2017-09/China%20Monitor_39_SOCS_EN.pdf.

18. Coco Feng, "China the Most Surveilled Nation? The US has the Largest Number of CCTV Cameras per Capita." *South China Morning Post*, December 9, 2019. https://www.scmp.com/tech/gear/article/3040974/china-most-surveilled-nation -us-has-largest-number-cctv-cameras-capita.

19. Padraig Moran, "How China's 'social credit' system blocked millions of people from travelling." *Canadian Broadcasting Corporation*, March 7, 2019. https:/ /www.cbc.ca/radio/thecurrent/the-current-for-march-7-2019-1.5046443/how-china-s -social-credit-system-blocked-millions-of-people-from-travelling-1.5046445.

20. *XinhuaNet*, "2682万人次因失信被限制乘机." 2019. http://www.xinhuanet .com/fortune/2019-07/17/c_1124761947.htm.

21. Alexandra Ma, "China Has Started Ranking Citizens with a Creepy 'Social Credit' System – Here's What You Can Do Wrong, and the Embarrassing, Demeaning Ways They Can Punish You." *Business Insider*, October 29, 2018. https ://www.businessinsider.com/china-social-credit-system-punishments-and-rewards-ex plained-2018-4.

22. Maya Wang, "China's Chilling 'Social Credit' Blacklist." *Human Rights Watch*, December 12, 2017. https://www.hrw.org/news/2017/12/12/chinas-chilling -social-credit-blacklist.

23. Xinchang Shi Ting, "加大曝光！这12名"老赖"登上了新昌影院大银幕，最高欠款2000多万元." *Sohu.com*, July 22, 2019. http://www.sohu.com/a/328563042 _678276.

24. Samantha Hoffman, "Programming China: The Communist Party's Autonomic Approach to Managing State Security." *China Monitor*, December 12, 2017. https ://www.merics.org/sites/default/files/2017-12/171212_China_Monitor_44_Progr amming_China_EN__0.pdf.

25. Min Jiang and King-Wa Fu, "Chinese Social Media and Big Data: Big Data, Big Brother, Big Profit?" *Policy & Internet* 10 (December 23, 2018): 372–392. doi:10.1002/poi3.187.

26. Fan Liang, Vishnupriya Das, Nadiya Kostyuk, and Muzammil Hussain, "Constructing a Data-Driven Society: China's Social Credit System as a State Surveillance Infrastructure." *Policy & Internet* 10, no. 4 (December 23, 2018): 415–453, doi:10.1002/poi3.183. ISSN:1944-2866.

27. Genia Kostka, "China's Social Credit Systems and Public Opinion: Explaining High Levels of Approval." *New Media & Society* 21, no. 7 (2019): 1565–1593. doi:10.1177/1461444819826402. ISSN:1461-4448.

28. Jung Chang, *Wild Swans: Three Daughters of China* (UK: HarperPress, 2012).

29. Paul Mozur, "Inside China's Dystopian Dreams: A.I., Shame and Lots of Cameras." *The New York Times*, July 8, 2018. https://www.nytimes.com/2018/07/08/business/china-surveillance-technology.html.

30. Ibid.

31. Liu Xin, "Reporting Apps Allow Chinese To Take Part In National Governance: Experts." *Global Times*, January 2, 2018. http://www.globaltimes.cn/content/108305 1.shtml.

32. Xinmei Shen, *Skynet, China's Massive Video Surveillance Network*, October 4, 2018. https://www.abacusnews.com/who-what/skynet-chinas-massive-video-s urveillance-network/article/2166938.

33. Vision Times, "China's Skynet Surveillance System Is a Disaster Waiting to Happen." *Vision Times*, September 4, 2018. http://www.visiontimes.com/2018/09/04 /chinas-skynet-surveillance-system-is-a-disaster-waiting-to-happen.html.

34. Patrick Howell O'Neill, "How WeChat Censors Private Conversations, Automatically in Real Time." *MIT Technology Review*, July 15, 2019. https://ww w.technologyreview.com/s/613962/how-wechat-censors-private-conversations-au tomatically-in-real-time/.

35. Yujie Chen et al., *Super Sticky WeChat and Chinese Society* (UK: Emerald Publishing, 2018).

36. O'Neill, "How WeChat Censors."

37. Chen et al., *Super Sticky WeChat*.

38. Beina Xu, *Media Censorship in China*. Council on Foreign Relations, 2017. https://www.cfr.org/backgrounder/media-censorship-china.

39. Tencent, *Tencent*, 2019. https://www.tencent.com/en-us/abouttencent.html.

40. Xu, *Media Censorship in China*.

41. Emma Lee, "Updated: WeChat's Privacy Policy Update Draws Attention to Information Shared with the Government TechNode." *TechNode* (blog), September 19, 2017. https://technode.com/2017/09/19/now-its-official-wechat-is-watching -you-1/.

42. Langdon Winner, "Modern Technology: Problem or Opportunity?" *Daedalus* 109, no. 1 (Winter 1980): 121–136.

43. Tenzin Dalha, *How WeChat Conquered Tibet*, 2019. https://thediplomat.com /2019/07/how-wechat-conquered-tibet./.

44. Chuin-Wei Yap, "Smartphone Messaging Apps Face New Pressure in China." *Wall Street Journal*, May 27, 2014, sec. Tech. https://www.wsj.com/articles/smartp hone-messaging-apps-face-new-pressure-in-china-1401191388.

45. O'Neill, "How WeChat Censors."

46. Leo Marx, "Technology: Emergence of a Hazardous Concept." *Technology and Culture* 51, no. 3 (July 2010): 561–577. *Project MUSE*. doi:10.1353/ tech.2010.0009.

47. Chen et al., *Super Sticky WeChat*.

48. Matthew Campbell, "What Happens to Hong Kong When 'One Country, Two Systems' Expires in 2047." *Bloomberg.com*, August 27, 2019. https://www .bloomberg.com/news/articles/2019-08-27/countdown-to-2047-what-will-happen-to -hong-kong-quicktake.

49. Helier Cheung and Roland Hughes, "The Background You Need on the Hong Kong Protests." *BBC News*, September 4, 2019, sec. China. https://www.bbc.com/news/world-asia-china-48607723.

50. Arjun Kharpal, "How Social Media Is Shaping What People Know – And Don't Know – About the Hong Kong Protests." *CNBC*, June 13, 2019. https://www.cnbc.com/2019/06/13/hong-kong-protests-role-of-technology-and-china-censorship.html.

51. Lily Kuo, "Beijing's New Weapon to Muffle Hong Kong Protests: Fake News." *The Observer*, August 11, 2019, sec. *World News*. https://www.theguardian.com/world/2019/aug/11/hong-kong-china-unrest-beijing-media-response.

52. Walt van Pragg, *The Legal Status of Tibet*, 2010. https://www.culturalsurvival.org/publications/cultural-survival-quarterly/legal-status-tibet.

53. Dalha, *How WeChat Conquered Tibet.*

54. Ibid.

55. "Tibetan WeChat Users Could Face Eight Years in Prison for Sharing News about Hong Kong." *Free Tibet*, September 5, 2019. https://freetibet.org/news-media/na/tibetan-wechat-users-could-face-eight-years-prison-sharing-news-about-hong-kong.

56. Ma, "China Has Started Ranking."

57. Erin Handley, "'Deadbeat Map': China Opens up Social Credit Scores to Social Media Platform WeChat." Text. *ABC News*, January 24, 2019. https://www.abc.net.au/news/2019-01-24/new-wechat-app-maps-deadbeat-debtors-in-china/10739016.

58. Ibid.

59. Angus Grigg, "WeChat's Privacy Issues Mean You Should Delete China's No. 1 Messaging App." *Australian Financial Review*, February 21, 2018. https://www.afr.com/world/asia/wechats-privacy-issues-mean-you-should-delete-chinas-no1-messaging-app-20180221-h0wgct.

60. Bob Dietz, *In China, Mainstream Media as Well as Dissidents under Increasing Pressure*, October 7, 2014. https://cpj.org/blog/2014/12/China-mainstream-media-as-well-as-dissidents-under-incre.php and Phillip Bennett, "21st-Century Censorship." *Columbia Journalism Review*, 2015. http://www.cjr.org/cover_story/21st_century_censorship.php.

FURTHER READING

Campbell, Charlie. "How China Is Using 'Social Credit Scores' to Reward and Punish Its Citizens." *Time*, January 16, 2019. https://time.com/collection/davos-2019/5502592/china-social-credit-score/.

Chen, Yujie et al. *Super Sticky WeChat and Chinese Society.* UK: Emerald Publishing, 2018.

ChinaFile. "Document 9: A ChinaFile Translation – How Much Is a Hardline Party Directive Shaping China's Current Political Climate?" November 8, 2013. http://www.chinafile.com/document-9-chinafile-translation.

Hoffman, Samantha. "Programming China: The Communist Party's Autonomic Approach to Managing State Security." *China Monitor*, December 12, 2017. https ://www.merics.org/sites/default/files/2017-12/171212_China_Monitor_44_Progra mming_China_EN__0.pdf.

Kostka, Genia. "China's Social Credit Systems and Public Opinion: Explaining High Levels of Approval." *New Media & Society* 21, no. 7 (2019): 1565–1593. doi:10.1177/1461444819826402. ISSN:1461-4448.

Liang, Fan, Das, Vishnupriya, Kostyuk, Nadiya, and Hussain, Muzammil M. "Constructing a Data-Driven Society: China's Social Credit System as a State Surveillance Infrastructure." *Policy & Internet* 10, no. 4 (2018): 415–453. doi:10.1002/poi3.183. ISSN:1944-2866.

O'Neill, Patrick Howell. "How WeChat Censors Private Conversations, Automatically in Real Time." *MIT Technology Review*, July 15, 2019. https://www.technolo gyreview.com/s/613962/how-wechat-censors-private-conversations-automatically -in-real-time/.

Polyakova, Alina and Meserole, Chris. "Exporting Digital Authoritarianism: The Russian and Chinese Models." *Foreign Policy*, August 27, 2019. https://www.bro okings.edu/wp-content/uploads/2019/08/FP_20190827_digital_authoritarianism_ polyakova_meserole.pdf.

Vision Times. "China's Skynet Surveillance System Is a Disaster Waiting to Happen." *Vision Times*, September 4, 2018. http://www.visiontimes.com/2018/09/ 04/chinas-skynet-surveillance-system-is-a-disaster-waiting-to-happen.html.

Chapter 9

The Erosion of Democracy in Post-Soviet Russia

A Model for Eurasia

Thomas S. Pearson

More than any other event, the collapse of the Soviet Union in 1989–1991 signaled the end of the Cold War and heralded the triumph of liberal democracy and global capitalism.[1] The Baltic countries of Estonia, Lithuania, and Latvia, according to conventional wisdom, emerged as the most successful of the Soviet successor states in transitioning to liberal democracy.[2] By contrast, Belarus, Turkmenistan, and Uzbekistan intensified their authoritarian regimes. With its orientation to the European Union and a government in which parliament and President Leonid Kuchma shared power, Ukraine found its transition to democracy compromised by economic crises, corruption, and scandal.[3] However, it was in Russia where democracy suffered its greatest setback after 1991. It exemplified the region's growing disillusionment with liberal democratic values and the failure of democratic reform to take root in post-Soviet Eurasia. A combination of economic calamities, political conflicts, and elite corruption delegitimized liberal democracy for most Russians and produced a "Time of Troubles" in the 1990s that enabled Vladimir Putin, beginning in 2000, to curb the democratic freedoms and institutions introduced under Mikhail Gorbachev and Boris Yeltsin. Putin has since reestablished a strong authoritarian state in Russia and disparaged the concept of Western liberal democracy on the world stage.

GORBACHEV, 1987–1991: DEMOCRATIC ASPIRATIONS AND THE END OF THE SOVIET REGIME

When Mikhail Gorbachev became General Secretary of the Communist Party in 1985, with the autocratic authority inherent in his position, few imagined that the Union of Soviet Socialist Republics (USSR) would implode within seven years and that civil society and "grassroots" democratic activists would play a vital role in the process. After all, the Soviet party-state "colonized public life by controlling all public association" and directed people's lives through a planned economy, an official ideology (Marxism-Leninism), and state security forces (above all the Komitet Gosudarstvennoy Bezopasnosti [KGB]). The Communist Party selected the *nomenklatura* (the administrative and cultural elite) who held special privileges and elite status in Soviet society. However, in assuming power, Gorbachev faced three immediate, systemic problems: (1) an inefficient socialist economy that no longer met the needs of Soviet citizens, much less competed in the global economy; (2) the loss of Communist Party control over an inert, corrupt state bureaucracy; and (3) the bankruptcy of Marxism-Leninism as an ideology that mobilized social support for the regime. This was a particularly serious problem with non-Russian nationalities in the USSR (and in the Soviet Bloc in Eastern Europe) that sought autonomy.[4]

Gorbachev's initial plan was to crack down on corruption within the Party and push for the acceleration and democratization (*demokratizatsiia*) of economic production in 1985–1986. When that failed to bring the desired results, he turned to bolder methods aligned with his belief in "socialism with a human face"—an approach that underscored his belief in socialism as a superior system to capitalism but rejected Stalin's coercive methods of Party rule. As the first (and only) Soviet leader of the post-World War II generation, Gorbachev was profoundly influenced by the De-Stalinization program of Nikita Khrushchev (1956–1964) and the Prague Spring of 1968 and Charter 77 movement in Czechoslovakia. He admired the Czech reform movement and its emphasis on freedom, human rights, and the rule of law. Unlike his General Secretary predecessors and other high-ranking Soviet officials, Gorbachev opposed the use of military force to resolve conflicts or protect Soviet spheres of influence. His commitment to humanize the party-state and rekindle people's faith in socialism, while preserving the Party's monopoly on power and keeping the Soviet Union intact, revealed his quixotic, democratic principles but also explained why the USSR and Soviet Bloc would unravel under his rule.[5]

Gorbachev's efforts at democratization faced resistance from the entrenched Soviet bureaucracy at nearly every level and his calls to mobilize workers and interest a new generation of entrepreneurs in the development of cooperatives (as part of his program of *perestroika*) did not yield immediate results. Both groups resented Party control and distrusted the communist and noncommunist intelligentsia and professionals.[6] However, the nuclear explosion at Chernobyl on April 26, 1986, proved to be a game-changer in advancing Gorbachev's agenda of *perestroika* (reform by restructuring) and democratization under the banner of *glasnost* (opening up the Soviet past and present to public criticism). As Gorbachev emphasized,

> Chernobyl shed light on many of the sicknesses of our system as a whole. Everything that had built up over the years converged in this drama: the concealing or hushing up of bad news, irresponsibility and carelessness, slipshod work, wholesale drunkenness. This was one more argument in favor of radical reforms.[7]

Gorbachev's *glasnost* policy brought immediate changes in Soviet censorship and the lives of Soviet citizens. The liberalization of press laws and publication of previously banned literary works such as Alexander Solzhenitsyn's *The Gulag Archipelago*, and the showing of prohibited films like Tengis Abuladze's "Repentance" (made in 1984 but released in 1987) were early signs of Gorbachev's democratization. His liberalization measures in 1987—his policy to "activate the human factor," as he called it—triggered the rise of over 30,000 *neformaly* ("informal" groups not registered with or controlled by the Communist Party) eager to push the limits of free speech and free association. These *neformaly* usually pursued nonpolitical aims, for instance, historic preservation and environmental protection. Their activities raised questions about the Party's claims to have met the needs of the Soviet people.[8] Even more, they exemplified a democratic spirit (*narodovlastie*) that was deeply embedded in a Russian political culture dominated by autocratic rule (*samoderzhavie*). These democratic roots not only included the dissidents who had opposed the tsarist and Soviet regimes (they comprised a small fraction of the population), but also peasants in their village communes (*mir*) who defended their customs against state encroachment, and the local self-governing institutions (*zemstvo*) and voluntary public associations in late imperial Russia that represented a civil society that nearly brought down the monarchy in the 1905 Revolution. The more immediate inspiration for the *neformaly* of the 1980s came from the village prose writers of the 1950s–1960s who criticized the Soviet regime for polluting the environment and destroying the Russian Orthodox Church and rural life by its reckless industrialization.[9]

The growth of the *neformaly*, which by 1989 numbered 60,000 organizations in most republics, Moscow, and Leningrad (now St. Petersburg), resulted from the urbanization and education of Soviet society over the previous six decades. It demonstrated that Soviet citizens had higher expectations of their government.[10] As such, the *neformaly* were potentially a disruptive factor in Gorbachev's strategy to implement democratization from above for two reasons. First, their "informal" activities threatened to turn the more conservative reformers among Gorbachev's colleagues, notably Yegor Ligachev, against *perestroika*. Second, they helped spark the growth of secessionist national movements in the non-Russian Soviet republics, as illustrated by the turmoil in the Baltic states, Georgia, Nagorno-Karabakh, and even Russia itself (for instance, in Chechnya). Gorbachev hoped to steer the independent activity of the *neformaly* into the Soviet political system, under the guise of "socialist pluralism," and use it as leverage against Party officials who opposed opening up the Soviet economy to private cooperatives and other regulated market reforms.[11] When that plan foundered in late 1987 to early 1988 under the attacks of both Party conservatives and radicals (principally Yeltsin, who complained about the slow tempo of *perestroika*), he made the fateful decision to open up the Soviet political system at the Nineteenth Party Conference (June 28 to July 1, 1988).

The Nineteenth Party Conference marked a triumph for Gorbachev and democratization in the USSR. For the first time in Soviet history, Party Conference proceedings were televised for Soviet citizens. They were stunned to see Party luminaries, such as Andrei Gromyko, being dressed down by other delegates for their resistance to change. Andrei Sakharov, the eminent nuclear physicist and human rights champion—and moral inspiration for Russia's democratic activists—emphasized shortly before his death in late 1989 that the televised coverage of the Conference and the ensuing sessions of the Congress of People's Deputies (CPD) provided an invaluable education for Soviet citizens. He also called for reforms in the Soviet constitution that incorporated the language and principles of liberal democracy found in the Preamble to the U.S. Constitution and in the Universal Declaration of Human Rights adopted by the United Nations in December 1948.[12]

Gorbachev on his part persuaded the Conference delegates to approve fundamental constitutional reforms that established a multiparty system in the name of "socialist pluralism" through a three-pronged CPD of 2,250 members (750 in each bloc) that would meet to elect 542 members to the Supreme Soviet. By such means he intended to defeat his political opponents and accelerate *perestroika* by turning up the heat on the Party bureaucracy. The very high voter turnout for the election of the "public organization" bloc of delegates in March 1989 (versus the two other blocs chosen according to population distribution and "national territorial" formations) appeared to vindicate his strategy.[13] The CPD, in turn, approved a law on public associations in 1990 that gave the *neformaly* institutional outlets for political participation—an important step on Russia's path to democracy.[14]

Years later, Gorbachev claimed that the Nineteenth Party Conference was when *perestroika* became "irreversible."[15] More ominously, it was also the moment when "*perestroika* from above" turned into "*perestroika* from below" and he lost control of the democratization process.

"*Perestroika* from below," with its centrifugal forces of "grassroots" democracy and national secession, clashed with Gorbachev's desire to preserve the leading role of the Communist Party and the integrity of the Soviet empire. In 1989, Gorbachev admitted as much. He conceded that the Kremlin could no longer prop up its satellite states in Eastern Europe because of severe economic problems. The Soviet budget deficit stood at 12 percent of gross domestic product (GDP) (by 1991, it was at 30%); store shelves were empty as distribution networks broke down; and coal miners went on strike in the Donbass demanding their pay and the right to organize in private unions. These conditions accounted for Gorbachev's reticence in responding to the fall of the Berlin Wall in November 1989 and the democratic revolutions that followed in Eastern Europe.[16] Moreover, unlike his rival Yeltsin, who was elected president of the Russian Republic by a landslide margin in June 1991, Gorbachev never stood for direct election by the Soviet people to become president of the USSR. Rather, his election in March 1990 by the CPD, acting as a surrogate for Soviet voters, combined with his refusal to step down as Secretary General of the Communist Party, tainted him as a democratic leader.[17]

Although many factors contributed to Gorbachev's failures as Soviet leader and to the establishment of an independent Russia under President Yeltsin following the aborted *putsch* of August 19–21, 1991 by hardline Communist Party officials, Gorbachev ultimately bequeathed a positive legacy for the development of democracy in post-Soviet Russia. Unwilling to perpetuate a Soviet regime based on lies and police repression, he wanted to provide the Soviet people freedom and a better future. Unable to deliver on his vision of "socialism with a human face," Gorbachev nevertheless left behind the fundamental liberal principles to govern a post-communist, independent Russia: the framework for a state based on the rule of law; the codification of civil liberties and universal standards of human rights; private property rights; representative institutions; independent courts of law; a multiparty political system; a free press (by Soviet standards); and independent interest group formation.[18]

YELTSIN: DISILLUSIONMENT WITH DEMOCRACY DURING A "TIME OF TROUBLES" (1992–1999)

With his immense popularity as a national hero who defeated the Communist hardliners in the August 1991 *putsch* and his commitment to freedom, Boris Yeltsin embodied the charismatic leader that many Russians desired to lead Russia's new democracy. The new Russian state also had a parliament chosen by free elections and it enjoyed the political and, in some cases, substantial material support of the Western democracies.[19] At the same time,

Yeltsin and his team of liberal reformers in early 1992 faced the truly herculean task of clearing away the vestiges of the Soviet regime, establishing a market economy, persuading the Russian people to put their faith in a new liberal democratic government with its checks and balances and rule of law, and restraining secessionist challenges from autonomous republics such as Tatarstan and Chechnya. Making matters worse, Yeltsin had little time to introduce these sweeping changes and suffered from serious health problems (a history of coronary artery disease that included several heart attacks). Even though the country had a new name and new institutions, the old interpersonal ties and habits formed during Soviet times remained strong.

Consequently, Yeltsin made the eradication of communism and the communist legacy his foremost priority. His unwavering pursuit of that goal throughout the 1990s largely explains why Russia's democratic opportunities withered away under his leadership, resulting in the authoritarian rule of Putin, Yeltsin's hand-picked successor. Unfortunately, as Yeltsin later acknowledged in his memoirs, he was far stronger in confronting authority (as in August 1991) than in creating an administration to govern Russia. He was a democrat in principles but authoritarian (Bolshevik) by temperament. His unwillingness to form and lead a liberal centrist democratic party was a major blunder that allowed the former Soviet *nomenklatura*, now calling themselves democrats, to fill the vacuum of power and protect their own interests. This hindered Yeltsin's subsequent efforts to get parliamentary support for his political agenda.[20] Even worse, in his preoccupation to eliminate the communists as a political threat, Yeltsin missed a golden opportunity to introduce a new constitution in Russia in 1991–1992, when he had in his hands a draft document prepared by his own constitutional commission (October 1990) and the authority granted by parliament (October 1991) to implement emergency executive decrees for one year. Rather than act decisively, Yeltsin, who preferred to remain above the political fray, allowed his government to drift. In the anxiety and uncertainty of the political transition, he also preserved a number of key Soviet institutions, including the Supreme Soviet and the agencies dealing with the armed forces and state security, most notably the KGB (renamed the FSB or Federal Security Service).[21]

Yeltsin's procrastination proved especially costly in establishing a balance of power between the various branches and levels of government that protected private property and delineated taxation authority between the center and localities, and in implementing his market economy reforms known as "shock therapy" in 1992–1993. According to S. Frederick Starr, in 1994, only 50 percent of the taxes imposed by the federal government were collected, whereas about 93 percent of all local taxes went "for the pet projects of the republics, *oblasts*, and cities, which carry on as if they were sovereign entities."[22] The break-up of the USSR exacerbated the economic difficulties of both Russia and the other successor states (Ukraine, Kazakhstan) that previously did the greatest volume of business with Russia and produced a conflict between Russia and Ukraine over the status of the Russian Black Sea fleet in the Crimea (a May 1997 accord would be nullified by Russia's annexation of the Crimea in 2014).

The "shock therapy" program introduced in January 1992 by Prime Minister Yegor Gaidar was the linchpin of Yeltsin's plan to move Russia to a free market economy. Yeltsin regarded a market economy as a precondition for Russia's development as a democracy. Unfortunately, "shock therapy" was immediately unpopular with Russia's parliament and most consumers. With price subsidies lifted for most commodities (except for main staples like bread and milk), shops were soon full but people could not afford to buy the goods. Inflation rates ballooned, reaching 245 percent in spring 1992. Even though the energy sector with its huge state industries and labor force maintained their massive state subsidies (to prevent widespread unemployment), Yeltsin's reforms came under fire in the CPD. In December 1992, it threatened to impeach the president and forced him to replace Gaidar with Viktor Chernomyrdin, the conservative head of Gazprom, a huge state energy company.

The constitutional crisis in 1993 and the military confrontation between Yeltsin and his CPD opponents, including Russia's Vice President Alexander Rutskoi, on October 3–4, had tragic consequences for Russia's fledgling democracy. The act of Russia's armed forces firing on CPD rebels in the Russian White House—the building that served as headquarters for Yeltsin's resistance against the communist hardliners just two years earlier—struck many Russians as a "minicivil war" and dispelled their illusions about Russia's evolution to a liberal democracy.[23] Yeltsin, however, contended that the confrontation proved the need for a new constitution which voters approved in a referendum conducted in December 1993. Although the 1993 constitution gave all Russian citizens guaranteed rights, codified the new system of government (including the offices of president and prime minister), and established a bicameral legislature (with the State Duma as the lower house and the Federation Council as the upper chamber), its most significant provision was the increase in the president's authority to introduce legislation by executive decree. In the short term, this "superpresidential" system reawakened voter's support for Russia's democracy; but the liabilities of this "delegative democracy"—that is, a government that appears to be democratic but functions solely on the authority of its leader—soon became evident. As M. Steven Fish notes, "In Russia, where the constitution relegates parliament to a subordinate role, parties have had a difficult time winning the loyalty and securing the participation of ordinary voters, whose resources are better spent pressuring agencies and officials in the executive branch."[24]

The political clash between Yeltsin and parliament that arose mainly over the "shock therapy" program created an additional problem for Russia's democratic development. Although the democratization process under Yeltsin saw approximately 50,000 nongovernmental organizations (NGOs) active in 1993 promoting, among other things, the spread of public charity, environmental protection, and the education of Russian citizens in the rule of law and their legal rights, by 1995, these organizations were struggling to find funding in Russia to support their work.[25] Thus, they turned increasingly to Western aid and use of the Internet to find resources. Such links to foreign states and foundations for funding became increasingly problematic for these NGOs, especially over the next decade. The absence of a steady revenue stream also prevented them from developing the organizational and coalition-building skills necessary to serve as a constraint on the behavior of Russia's elites (by forming oppositionist parties and holding officials accountable for their actions).[26]

No episode, however, was as damaging in eroding popular support for democracy in Russia under Yeltsin as the "loans for shares" scandal of 1994–1995, and the alliance between corrupt Russian oligarchs and Yeltsin's team that secured the president's reelection in 1996. Both stemmed from Yeltsin's decision in 1992 to privatize residential space and small businesses, and state industries in 1993–1995, to provide revenue for the government and prevent a return to communism. Marketed as a program that would benefit apartment dwellers and business managers, "the integrity of the privatization of state economic enterprises was undermined when the Yeltsin administration, under political pressure, allowed people with political skills and connections [the new oligarchs] to exploit the process of the distribution of shares in those enterprises to amass assets for their own purposes."[27] Unfortunately, the first round of privatization did not meet the revenue targets in the 1995 state budget. The second stage, which entailed the sale of major state oil and metallurgical companies and coincided with the start of Yeltsin's unpopular war against Chechnya (1995–1996), was an even greater public relations disaster. Certain large banks were each invited to loan the government $800 million and receive, as collateral, shares in twelve major state companies. When the government failed to repay the loans, these banks exercised their rights to auction off their shares in the companies and keep 30 percent of the profits. The banks that ran the auctions and were under the control of Russia's wealthiest oligarchs, for example, Mikhail Khodorkovskii, usually won them with bids just above the starting price. "Loans for shares" amounted to "insider trading" and the process came under blistering attack from the communists and conservatives in the Duma.[28]

Privatization left many Russians feeling tricked into buying vouchers for property that were snapped up by crooked oligarchs. They were quick to associate such corrupt, unscrupulous business practices with Yeltsin and liberal democracy. Worse yet, they observed little evidence of law and order in Russia. By late 1995, 8,000 criminal gangs were active in Russia; violent crime rates were higher in many provinces than in Moscow, and St. Petersburg had the reputation of being the violent crime capital of Russia because of the contract killings and extent of mafia activity in the city. As one scholar observed, Yeltsin's government functioned as a "decentralized kleptocracy with no laws or mechanism of law enforcement."[29] A volatile market economy that benefited oligarchs, pervasive lawlessness, and an infirm president at war with Chechnya and the Russian State Duma explain why Yeltsin's public approval rating plummeted to 3 percent in late 1995.

These conditions also rallied the public behind Gennadi Ziuganov, leader of the Russian Communist Party, who decided to run for president in 1996. Faced with the possibility of a Communist Party return to power, Yeltsin defied the odds and sought reelection. Russia's most powerful oligarchs including Boris Berezovskii and Vladimir Gusinskii, who owned independent television stations, collaborated with Yeltsin's daughter (Tatiana Diachenko) and his advisers to turn the election into a referendum on communism versus democracy. Similar concerns prompted the Clinton Administration and the International Monetary Fund (IMF) to provide public relations consultants and financial resources to Yeltsin's campaign because, as U.S. officials told one executive of Russia's independent media, "Yeltsin is your only democratic institution."[30] Although Yeltsin eventually won reelection, his victory, as Michael McFaul (the U.S. ambassador to Russia in 2012–2014) notes, "did not feel virtuous. He had run a negative campaign, stoking fears about the perils of a communist restoration. He had used state resources to win—not exactly in keeping with "free and fair." And allegations of electoral fraud dampened the celebration about Russian democracy's resilience."[31] In fact, according to an exit poll conducted during the election, only 7 percent of voters approved of the existing state of democracy in Russia. Russian voters generally viewed Yeltsin's reelection as a victory of the oligarchs who had acquired state property by unscrupulous means and stored their profits in offshore accounts, rather than investing their resources in building democratic institutions and political parties in Russia. In assessing Yeltsin's record in 2000, Joseph Stiglitz concluded that "privatization, as it was imposed in Russia, undermined confidence in government, in democracy, and in reform."[32]

Although Yeltsin's reelection averted a return to the Soviet past (and planned economy), his frail health led to his withdrawal from politics and reliance on a small group of confidants surrounding his daughter (including Berezovskii, Anatolii Chubais, and Deputy prime minister Boris Nemtsov). For a brief period, Russia enjoyed a measure of stability and good economic fortune. Voter participation had increased in the 1995 Duma and 1996 presidential elections, reversing the two previous years of decline. Positive economic growth appeared for the first time since 1991 and annual inflation fell from 22 percent in 1996 to 11 percent in 1997. But, in 1998, Yeltsin's luck ran out. A global drop in oil prices led to the loss of more than $1.5 billion in state revenue and a major financial meltdown in Russia. With a budget deficit of $25 billion (over 5% in GDP), the Kremlin announced on August 17, 1998 a mandatory conversion of short-term bonds into longer term issues, a ninty-day moratorium on Russian debts owed to Western commercial banks, and a 30 percent reduction in the value of the Russian ruble. Russians on average lost approximately 60 percent of their wealth in an economic collapse that overnight erased two of Yeltsin's most impor-tant recent economic achievements—low inflation and a stable currency.[33] Adding insult to injury, United States and North Atlantic Treaty Organization (NATO) intervention on behalf of the rebels in Kosovo against the Serbian government of Slobodan Milosevic (an ally of Russia)—in spite of Russia's protests—provided a reminder of her humiliating fall from the ranks of a global superpower. NATO's bombing of Serbia in 1999 and U.S. recognition of Kosovo as an independent state, in violation of international law, infuri-ated Russia's leaders (including Yeltsin and Putin, his new prime minister) and aroused suspicions that NATO was changing its mission from a defensive alliance against the former Soviet Bloc to an instrument that enabled U.S. intervention throughout the world.

As the Duma threatened to impeach the president on charges of corruption and incompetence, Yeltsin changed prime ministers frequently. In August 1999, he appointed Putin, a former KGB official who in the 1990s served under Anatolii Sobchak as Deputy Mayor of St. Petersburg before he became head of the FSB in 1998. What led Yeltsin to appoint Putin as prime minister and designate him as his successor as president? Yeltsin appreciated Putin's career of dedicated state service, especially at a time when he himself was resorting to more authoritarian methods of rule.[34] Putin's lack of charisma and attachment to any specific ideology such as communism appealed to him. But, most of all, Yeltsin valued the loyalty that Putin had shown to his previ-ous bosses, be they KGB chiefs or Sobchak, all the more because he wanted protection against investigations into his own family's affairs.

The elevation of the hitherto obscure Putin as prime minister shocked much of Russian society. Putin quickly had his hands full responding to an attack by Chechen terrorists on neighboring Dagestan in early August 1999 and, according to the Russian state media, their bombing of apartment build-ings in Moscow and several other cities in September, killing more than 300 people. Putin retaliated by starting a second war with Chechnya and ordering massive air strikes on the Chechen capital, Grozny, on September 23. The timing and pro-Kremlin media coverage of these events raised Putin's profile as a future presidential candidate so much that a number of Russian critics and Western scholars have conjectured that the Moscow bombings were an FSB plot to increase the odds of Putin's election.[35] With the strong showing of pro-Kremlin parties in the December 1999 Duma elections, President Yeltsin surprised his compatriots when he suddenly resigned from office on New Year's Eve, designated Putin as his interim successor, and stated that the presidential election would be moved forward to March 2000, a decision that favored Putin's candidacy over several rivals (including Ziuganov and Moscow mayor Yurii Luzhkov) who had announced their intentions to run. Significantly, Putin's first act as Interim President was to grant Yeltsin and his family immunity from prosecution for his past actions—a clear signal that under Putin personal ties (*sviazi*) and loyalty would count for more than the rule of law.[36]

PUTIN 2000–PRESENT: FROM "MANAGED DEMOCRACY" TO THE ASSAULT ON DEMOCRACY

President Putin was quick to depart from Yeltsin's compromised democratic approach in appealing to voters who would determine his fate in the March elections, even as he assured foreign leaders of his democratic inclinations in stating: "History has proven that dictatorships, all authoritarian forms of government are transient. Only democratic systems are intransient."[37] As stated in his autobiography, *First Person*, and his manifesto "Russia on the Threshold of the New Millennium"—both published in late December 1999—Putin's primary goal was to bring stability to Russia by strengthening the authority of the state (*gosudarstvennost*) and restoring the traditional Russian core values of patriotism, collectivism, and great power status (*derzhavnost*). This did not immediately mean a complete break from Western democratic practice; in fact, as Putin noted, "Russia is a very diverse country, but we are part of Western European culture."[38] Yet, he reminded the Russian people that a strong state—a "dictatorship of the law"—was the best guarantor of their freedom.[39] Putin's message resonated with Russian voters. According to a January 2000 opinion poll, 55percent expected Putin to restore Russia's great power status; a much smaller percentage of those polled anticipated closer Russian ties with the West.[40] Meanwhile, many Western leaders and investors were pleased when Putin implemented a flat tax of 13 percent on individuals and lowered the tax on corporate profits from 35 percent to 24 percent (effective January 2002), enacted a new criminal code (2001) that in language echoed Western law codes, and suggested that Russia was willing to explore the possibility of joining NATO. Putin's decision to provide logistical support for the U.S. war in Afghanistan immediately following the 9/11/2001 terrorist attacks on the United States allowed the Bush Administration to overlook the Kremlin's crackdown on Gusinskii's independent television channel, following its broadcast of a program on the eve of the March 2000 presidential election that connected the September apartment bombings to the FSB. Soon after, Putin drove both Gusinskii and Berezovskii into exile and seized their assets, including their independent television stations.[41]

In fact, nearly all of Putin's actions during his first term (2000–2004)—a period of "managed democracy"—adhered to the transition plan "Reform of the Administration of the Russian Federation," prepared for him in December 1999 and "leaked" for publication days before his inauguration as president on May 7, 2000. The document provided a blueprint for dismantling what was left of Yeltsin's democracy by expanding Putin's executive power and allowing him to rule Russia with his chosen elite, the *siloviki* (FSB and business cronies, especially from St. Petersburg). The plan called for Kremlin control of the state and independent media, the Duma (through the United Russia Party), every level of government, and all propaganda on behalf of the president and government of the Russian Federation. It also prescribed the use of covert strategies to undermine political opponents by the security agencies that would report directly to Putin and ensure that "an informational-political barrier" was established between Russia's president and the political opposition.[42]

The key to "managed democracy," a term conceived by Putin's chief political and media strategist, Vladislav Surkov, was the President's mastery of television and other media to create an alternative universe to outside news sources and cultivate support for the Kremlin's point of view. Putin's appreciation for manipulating the media derived from his experience in St. Petersburg under Sobchak, who was also highly talented in this area, and it was reinforced in August 2000 when he was excoriated by the independent media for his failure to carry out the rescue of 130 sailors who drowned in the Kursk submarine tragedy in the Barents Sea. As Putin's close confidant, Sergei Pugachev, emphasized at the time, "He [Putin] understands that the basis of power in Russia is not the army, not the police, it's the television. It's his deepest conviction."[43] Putin demonstrated his grasp of "delegative democracy" and use of the media to expand his executive authority on two occasions during his first term as president. The first was linked to Chechen terrorists seizing hostages in Moscow in 2002 and the second to their attack on the Beslan School (in Northern Ossetia) in September 2004. In both cases, Putin employed military force to end the standoffs, leaving hundreds of innocent hostages dead. Putin was quick to go on television to justify his actions and his decision in September 2004 to abolish elected governorships, make all such appointments, and submit his choices to regional parliaments for ratification.[44]

A more ominous sign for supporters of Russian democracy appeared with the Kremlin's arrest of the billionaire oligarch Khodorkovskii in October 2003. He had defied Putin's warning to oligarchs in 2000 to keep out of politics if they wished to hold on to their fortunes. In 2001 Khodorkovskii created Open Russia, an organization that subsidized political parties that challenged Putin's United Russia Party. In February 2003, he embarrassed Putin in a meeting shown on Russian television by alleging that corruption consumed 25 percent of Russia's annual budget. Khodorkovskii recommended that Russian firms adopt Western accounting procedures. His arrest eight months later on charges of tax evasion and the state's seizure of Khodorkovskii's Yukos Oil assets had all the earmarks of an act of revenge ordered by Putin and it rattled Western governments. Putin, however, did not mince words in December 2003 when foreign journalists questioned him about the erosion of democratic freedoms in Russia. He insisted, "If by democracy, one means the dissolution of the state, then we do not need such democracy. Why is democracy needed? To make people's lives better, to make them free. I don't think there are any people in the world who want democracy that could lead to chaos."[45]

In 2004, Putin easily won reelection in a campaign that had all the signs of a charade—he received 71 percent of the vote in an election that featured Kremlin-picked rival candidates and many reports of electoral fraud. Yet, it was several events that occurred outside Russia that disturbed Putin and have led to his attacks on Western liberal democracy in the past decade. First, the personal bond that he had developed with President George W. Bush after the 9/11 attacks unraveled when the latter ignored Putin's warnings and invaded Iraq in 2003. Putin complained that such a brazen attempt to oust Saddam Hussein promised even greater instability in the Middle East and that the false claim that Iraq had weapons of mass destruction showed the disrespect of the United States for the United Nations Security Council and Russia. It magnified his earlier suspicions that the United States intended to use its power to fashion a global order in America's image.[46] Even worse, the "Rose Revolution" in Georgia that put the pro-American Mikheil Saakashvili in power in January 2004, coupled with NATO's admission of Estonia, Latvia, and Lithuania in 2004, prompted Putin to challenge NATO's eastward expansion. His strategy to use Russia's natural gas exports as leverage to get Ukrainians to support his candidate, Viktor Yanukovych, as president in November 2004, backfired when Ukraine's high court nullified Yanukovych's election because of massive evidence of electoral fraud. In December, with Kiev's "Orange Revolution" in full swing, Ukrainians elected Viktor Yushchenko, a pro-Western candidate, as president. The spontaneous nature of these "color revolutions" reinforced Putin's determination to support authoritarian dictators challenged by such "democratic" upheavals.

He declared his opposition to the "freedom agenda" of the United States in his speech to the Munich Security Conference on February 10, 2007. By then, Putin had established a reactive, unwieldy authoritarian regime in Russia with little more than his personal leadership holding it together. Nonetheless, the Russian state continued to adhere to the 1993 constitution as there were no mass arrests, martial law, or cancellation of national elections.[47]

Prior to 2011, Putin's increasingly authoritarian actions faced little overt opposition, even as the Kremlin imposed tighter controls on NGOs and journalist critics who were arrested or, as in the case of Anna Politkovskaya and others, assassinated. Two factors explain this paradox. First, Russians credited Putin for Russia's remarkable economic recovery from 2001 to 2007 that saw income levels for nearly all increase on average 6.6 percent each year. By mid-2008, Russia also had $570 billion in hard currency reserves that cushioned the country against the 2009 global recession. Second, as Russia's relations with the West deteriorated, Putin amplified his message of Russia's exceptionalism to citizens at home and his supporters abroad. He emphasized Russia's unique Eurasian identity and exalted the virtues of a strong Russian state that upheld traditional Christian values against the agnostic, multicultural West. Inherent in the message was Putin's contention that Russia was a "besieged fortress" that required her citizens to support the state and celebrate its glorious past (most notably, Russia's victory over Nazi Germany in World War II). In this vein, Putin began a propaganda campaign that has largely whitewashed Stalin's reputation as a Soviet totalitarian tyrant and instead glorified him as a heroic Russian state leader.[48]

The 1993 constitution prevented Putin from serving a third consecutive term as president. Consequently, in 2008, United Russia nominated Dmitrii Medvedev, Putin's prime minister, as president. Based on a prearranged plan, Putin became Medvedev's prime minister. Many of Russia's Western-oriented intelligentsia hoped that the election of the younger, more technologically savvy Medvedev would bring Russia into the high-tech global economy and liberalize the political climate at home. Newly elected U.S. President Barack Obama shared this view and, in 2009, initiated a "Reset" strategy designed to improve Russian-American relations and revitalize prodemocracy forces in Russia. But, it quickly became clear that Putin remained the power in Russia and he was not interested in any "Reset" with the United States. On the contrary, the Obama's Administration's support for street protesters using social media to coordinate efforts to bring down such dictators as Egypt's President Hosni Mubarak during the Arab Spring in 2011 alarmed Putin. He was indignant when the United Nations authorized a NATO bombing campaign that led to the overthrow and execution of Libyan despot Muammar Qaddafi in October 2011.[49]

Fall 2011 brought Putin greater problems at home when he announced his intention to seek a third (now six-year) term as president, in essence trading places with Medvedev. This cynical arrangement insulted many younger, urban middle-class voters, coming at a time when economic growth had slowed in Russia.[50] When Russian demonstrators went online and into the streets of Moscow to protest the voter fraud and falsification by United Russia in the Duma elections in December, Putin lashed out and attributed the demonstrations—the largest of their kind since 1991—to the Obama Administration. He specifically charged Secretary of State Hillary Clinton with orchestrating the protests as part of a U.S. conspiracy to effect regime change without offering hard evidence to support his allegations. In spring 2012, demonstrations against Putin's presidential campaign intensified with political activists such as Alexei Navalny attacking United Russia as the "party of swindlers and thieves" and calling for a "Russia without Putin." Harsh Kremlin crackdowns followed Putin's election in March 2012 and his inauguration two months later. Russia's police arrested many peaceful demonstrators and state-run television, in full "besieged fortress" mode, assailed the West as the haven of evil, and "labeled liberals, gays, and recipients of foreign grants [NGOs and certain cultural organizations] as 'Western agents'"—rhetoric that recalled the paranoia of Stalin's terror.[51]

More than anything else, these demonstrations and the Kremlin's perceptions of their causes explain what has transpired under Putin as president since 2012: the heavy-handed and arbitrary arrests of regime critics; Russia's annexation of the Crimea and intervention on behalf of pro-Russian rebels in the civil war in Ukraine, beginning in 2014; and recent Russian-sponsored strategies to delegitimize liberal democracy in Europe and the U.S. by supporting neo-populist parties and cyberattacks on elections outside Russia. The most notorious example of Russia's influence campaign occurred in the 2016 U.S. presidential election as Kremlin proxies used various tactics to undermine the electability of Hillary Clinton and assist Donald Trump's election. Putin has denied any responsibility for these actions, even as he has acknowledged his preference for candidate Trump in 2016. Even though crippling Western economic sanctions remain in place against Russia because of its annexation of the Crimea, the reduction in United States support for NATO and the Atlantic Alliance under Trump is a significant return on the Kremlin's investment in his election.[52]

In sum, Russia's transition from Soviet rule to liberal democracy and a market economy within one generation faced nearly insurmountable obstacles, given the comprehensive changes in institutions and people's mindset required. The inclination of Russia's state leaders and elites (oligarchs and *siloviki*) to put their self-interests ahead of investment in reforming the political and economic infrastructure of their country, especially under Putin, undermined

even those slight prospects. By most of the conventional measures—freedom to form and join organizations, freedom of expression, rule of law,
protection of minorities and individual liberties, free and fair elections, and
political accountability—Russia today falls far short of being a democracy.[53]
Nonetheless, Putin's Russia is not a totalitarian state with all of the controls
over public and private life that totalitarianism entails.[54] It is rather an autocratic state in need of substantial structural reforms, especially in the economy,
to improve living standards in Russia and raise public morale. To date, Putin
and his *siloviki* have shown little will to make such changes and reduce the levels of corruption and the increasing bifurcation of wealth in Russia that point
to a bleak future.[55] Public approval of Putin himself, which reached 85 percent
following Russia's annexation of the Crimea, dropped to 64 percent after he
signed an unpopular pension reform bill in 2018. As of summer 2019, increasing numbers of Russians are participating in public demonstrations against the
Kremlin's efforts to prevent independent candidates from competing for positions on Moscow's City Council and the ham-fisted actions of Russia's law
enforcement agencies against Kremlin critics.[56] While such developments so
far do not portend an imminent overthrow of the Kremlin leadership—in fact,
they more likely reveal anxiety about what will happen when Putin's current
term ends in 2024—they show that Russians continue to hold the democratic
belief that their government remains accountable to the people.

DISCUSSION QUESTIONS

1. What does democracy mean in Russia's political culture?
2. Were political conflicts between Yeltsin and Russia's parliament, or
   economic problems, more significant in disillusioning the Russian people
   with liberal democracy?
3. How has Vladimir Putin redefined the concept of democracy during his
   years in power?
4. Have Putin's leadership and attacks on Western liberal democracy
   brought benefits to Russia and its people?

NOTES

1. Alfred B. Evans, "The Failure of Democratization: A Comparative Perspective."
Journal of Eurasian Studies 2, no. 1 (2011): 40–43, cites the work of Francis
Fukayama and Samuel Huntington, among others, on the bright prospects for liberal
democracy in the early 1990s.
2. See Anders Aslund, *How Capitalism Was Built: The Transformation of
Central and Eastern Europe, Russia, and Central Asia* (Cambridge: Cambridge
University Press, 2007), 306–307.

3. Serhii Plokhy, *The Gates of Europe: A History of Ukraine* (New York, NY: Basic Books, 2015), 328–332.

4. Marcia A. Weigle, *Russia's Liberal Project: State-Society Relations in the Transition from Communism* (University Park, PA: Pennsylvania State University Press, 2000), 75–76, 348–349.

5. Mikhail Gorbachev, *Memoirs* (New York, NY: Doubleday, 1995), 81–83, 482–483; Archie Brown, *The Gorbachev Factor* (Oxford: Oxford University Press, 1997), 28–31, 41; and John L. H. Keep, *The Last of the Empires: A History of the Soviet Union, 1945–1991* (Oxford: Oxford University Press, 1995), 332.

6. Weigle, *Russia's Liberal Project*, 117–118, 125.

7. Quoted from Gorbachev, *Memoirs*, 193. In Werner Herzog and Andre Singer's documentary, "Meeting Gorbachev" (2019), Gorbachev reiterates the enormous significance of the Chernobyl disaster in not only accelerating *perestroika* but also in bringing about nuclear disarmament by the U.S. and USSR and ending the Cold War. He observes: "Chernobyl was a Lesson, a Big Lesson, and it is Still Relevant Today."

8. Weigle, *Russia's Liberal Project*, 77–79.

9. See Nicolai N. Petro, *The Rebirth of Russian Democracy: An Interpretation of Political Culture* (Cambridge, MA: Harvard University Press, 1995), 2–3, 22–24, 43–47, who calls these groups democratic forces that "constrained" autocracy.

10. In 1974, six times as many people percentage-wise lived in Soviet cities than in 1924. Valerie A. Kivelson and Ronald Grigor Suny, *Russia's Empires* (Oxford: Oxford University Press, 2016), 346.

11. Weigle, *Russia's Liberal Project*, 96–100, 127; Brown, *The Gorbachev Factor*, 169–172.

12. See Sakharov's interview with *Ogonyok* correspondent Grigorii Tsitriniak in June 1989, reprinted in Andrei Sakharov, "Dimensions of Freedom." In *Perils of Perestroika: Viewpoints from the Soviet Press*, ed. Isaac J. Tarasulo (Wilmington, DE: SR Books, 1992), 338–339.

13. The elections for "public organization" delegates produced a turnout of 89.8 percent of all eligible voters in the USSR. The Communist Party leaders in Leningrad, Kiev, and Minsk were voted out and Yeltsin, fired by Gorbachev in late 1987 as Moscow Party chief for his attacks on Party conservatives, won a seat to represent Moscow in the CPD with 89.4 percent of the vote. See Brown, *The Gorbachev Factor*, 188–205; and M. Steven Fish, *Democracy from Scratch: Opposition and Regime in the New Russian Revolution* (Princeton, NJ: Princeton University Press, 1996), 35–47.

14. Weigle, *Russia's Liberal Project*, 104. Nonetheless, the "informal" groups and associations found it difficult to organize their members to support specific political parties.

15. Gorbachev, *Memoirs*, 237.

16. Daniel Treisman, *The Return: Russia's Journey from Gorbachev to Medvedev* (New York, NY: Free Press, 2012), 28–31; Gale Stokes, *The Walls Came Tumbling Down: Collapse and Rebirth in Eastern Europe*, 2nd edition (Oxford: Oxford University Press, 2011), 162–168; and Stephen Kotkin (with Jan Gross), *Uncivil Society: 1989 and the Implosion of the Communist Establishment* (New York, NY: The Modern Library, 2010), xiii–xviii, 136–144, who argue that the mistakes of

communist leaders were more important than the demonstrations of civil society in bringing down communist rule in the USSR and Eastern Europe.

17. Keep, *The Last of the Empires*, 354–358, 373–379; and Gorbachev, *Memoirs*, 317–323.

18. Weigle, *Russia's Liberal Project*, 81. Even after his fall from power Gorbachev reaffirmed his faith in socialism based on democratic and humanistic principles as beneficial for Russia and a post-Cold War world. Mikhail Gorbachev, "No Time for Stereotypes." (Op-Ed), *The New York Times*, February 24, 1992, A19. In the film "Meeting Gorbachev" the last Soviet leader again expresses regret for the collapse of the USSR and acknowledges that he should have given the republics more rights and autonomy earlier. He blames both the putschists and politicians like Yeltsin (i.e., Yeltsin) for their rush to grab power.

19. Timothy Snyder, *The Road to Unfreedom: Russia–Europe–America* (New York, NY: Tim Duggan Books, 2018), 42. Germany was the most active in providing financial support.

20. Petro, *Rebirth of Russian Democracy*, 151. Ironically, in an interview he had given to *Ogonyok* in March 1991, Yeltsin emphasized that "a powerful, well-organized party of the left based on the democratic platform and other democratic movements" was necessary to prevail over the Communist Party. However, he showed no inclination to lead the formation of such a party. Boris Yeltsin, "There Won't Be a Civil War." *Perils of Perestroika*, 315.

21. Michael McFaul, *From Cold War to Hot Peace: An American Ambassador in Putin's Russia* (Boston, MA: Houghton Mifflin Harcourt, 2018), 32.

22. Quoted from S. Frederick Starr, "The Paradox of Yeltsin's Russia." *The Wilson Quarterly* 19, no. 3 (Summer 1995): 69.

23. McFaul, *From Cold War*, 36.

24. M. Steven Fish, *Democracy Derailed in Russia: The Failure of Open Politics* (Cambridge: Cambridge University Press, 2005), 248–249. See also Archie Brown, "Evaluating Russia's Democratization." In *Contemporary Russian Politics: A Reader*, ed. Archie Brown (Oxford: Oxford University Press, 2001), 557. The Duma elections of December 1993 raised another red flag for Russia's democracy as Vladimir Zhirinovskii, leader of Russia's fascist-oriented and misnamed Liberal Democratic Party, won almost 25 percent of the seats in the new state Duma.

25. Weigle, *Russia's Liberal Project*, 353–355.

26. See Maxwell Votey's synopsis of the presentation of Danielle Lussier to the Kennan Institute for Advanced Russian Studies on September 11, 2012, under the title *The Failure of Democracy in Post-Soviet Russia*, https://www.wilsoncenter.org/publication/the-failure-democracy-post-soviet-eurasia.

27. Quoted from Evans, "The Failure of Democratization," 44.

28. According to Treisman, in 1994 workers owned around 50 percent of Russia's enterprises; by 1999 their shares had dropped to 36 percent, whereas during the same period shares held by outside private investors increased from 15 percent to 47 percent. Treisman, *The Return*, 224.

29. On Yeltsin's kleptocracy see Stefan Hedlund's presentation to the Kennan Institute on December 12, 1995, as discussed in Thomas Porter and Thomas

Pearson, "Historical Legacies and Democratic Prospects: The Emergence of a Civil Society in Twentieth-Century Russia." *The Soviet and Post-Soviet Review* 23, no. 1 (1996): 61–62. Comparisons of Yeltsin's Russia with developing countries in Latin America are discussed in K. G. Kholodkovskii, "Demokratiia i Reform v Rossii." In *Grazhdanskoe obshchestvo v Rossii: Zapadnaia paradigma i Rossiiskaia realnost'* (Moscow: IMEMO, 1996), 138. According to Anders Aslund the Russian public today blames many of their economic and political problems on the privatization of large state enterprises in the 1990s: "Many see [this] as the 'original sin'," because the superrich oligarchs who purchased them were disinterested in the welfare of the people and the nation. Anders Aslund, *Russia's Crony Capitalism: The Path from the Market Economy to Kleptocracy* (New Haven, CT: Yale University Press, 2019), 253.

30. Quoted in Arkady Ostrovsky, *The Invention of Russia: From Gorbachev's Freedom to Putin's War* (New York, NY: Viking, 2015), 190. According to Andrew Wilson, the value of American consultants in guiding Yeltsin in running a sophisticated media campaign has been vastly overrated; Yeltsin's associates were already highly knowledgeable in the arts of "dirty politics and black PR." See Andrew Wilson, *Virtual Politics: Faking Democracy in the Post-Soviet World* (New Haven, CT: Yale University Press, 2005), 50.

31. Quoted from McFaul, *From Cold War*, 47.

32. Quoted from Evans, "The Failure of Democratization," 45. On the political costs of the oligarchs' corruption, see J. E. Stiglitz, *Globalization and its Discontents* (New York, NY: W. W. Norton, 2002), 159–160.

33. McFaul, *From Cold War*, 49.

34. Timothy J. Colton, *Yeltsin: A Life* (New York, NY: Basic Books, 2008), 431.

35. See, for example, Snyder, *Road to Unfreedom*, 45; and Karen Dawisha, *Putin's Kleptocracy: Who Owns Russia?* (New York, NY: Simon & Schuster, 2014), 208–209.

36. Brown, "Evaluating Russia's Democratization," 563.

37. Putin, as quoted in Snyder, *Road to Unfreedom*, 37.

38. Quoted from Vladimir Putin, *First Person: An Astonishingly Frank Self-Portrait by Russia's President*, with Nataliya Gevorkyan, Nataliya Timakova, and Andrei Kolesnikov, trans. Catherine A. Fitzpatrick (New York, NY: Public Affairs, 2000), 169.

39. Dawisha, *Putin's Kleptocracy*, 237.

40. Ostrovsky, *The Invention of Russia*, 265.

41. On these events see Steven Lee Myers, *The New Tsar: The Rise and Reign of Vladimir Putin* (New York, NY: Alfred A. Knopf, 2015), 193; Peter Solomon, Jr., "The Criminal Procedure Code of 2001: Will It Make Russian Justice More Fair?" In *Ruling Russia: Law, Crime, and Justice in a Changing Society*, ed. William Alex Pridemore (Lanham, MD: Rowman & Littlefield Publishers, Inc., 2005), 77–98; and Putin, *First Person*, 177.

42. Dawisha, *Putin's Kleptocracy*, 2–3, 8–9, 251–255; and Aslund, *Russia's Crony Capitalism*, 152, who emphasizes that Putin's Russia "is not an oligarchy," as the president correctly claims. "It is something much worse, an authoritarian kleptocracy," in which Putin relies on a few close *silovik* friends from St. Petersburg

and manipulates various state organs (the FSB) to amass personal wealth and reign supreme.

43. Quoted in Myers, *The New Tsar*, 202.

44. Snyder, *Road to Unfreedom*, and Wilson, *Virtual Politics*, 39, who emphasizes that Putin has only perfected techniques that "were already common under Yeltsin, and already common elsewhere in the former USSR." Putin restored a modified election system for governors after he won his third term as president in 2012.

45. Quoted in Roxanne Easley, Mark Davis Kuss, and Thomas Pearson, *A History of Modern Russia*, preliminary edition (San Diego, CA: Cognella Academic Publishing, 2019), 306. Fish, like Dawisha, argues that Putin's motive for arresting Khodorkovskii and seizing the assets of Yukos may have been to provide rewards for his loyal *silovik* supporters. See Fish, *Democracy Derailed*, 259–262; and Dawisha, *Putin's Kleptocracy*, 324.

46. McFaul, *From Cold War*, 67; Myers, *The New Tsar*, 251.

47. McFaul, *From Cold War*, 68–69. See also Andrew Wilson, *Ukraine Crisis: What It Means for the West* (New Haven, CT: Yale University Press, 2014), 38–39.

48. See Ostrovsky, *The Invention of Russia*, 308; and Angela Stent, *Putin's World: Russia Against the West and with the Rest* (New York, NY: Twelve, 2019), 33–37. According to Timothy Snyder, Putin's views on Russia's exceptionalism adhere closely to the ideas of Ivan Ilyin, an anti-Soviet White counterrevolutionary who from the 1920s to 1940s advocated a return to Russia's traditional culture of autocracy, orthodoxy, and Russian nationality. See Snyder, *Road to Unfreedom*, 19–34. According to a poll published by the independent Levada Center on April 3, 2019, 70 percent of Russians agree that Stalin has a positive role in Russian history, a sharp increase from his 10 percent public approval rating in 1988. In addition, the share of Russians polled who agreed that Stalin's crimes were unjustified has declined from 60 percent in 2008 to 45 percent in 2019. See "Stalin's Approval Rating Among Russians Hits Record High – Poll." *The Moscow Times*, April 3, 2019. http://www.themoscowtimes.com, April 16, 2019; and for the 1988 poll results, Hedrick Smith, *The New Russians* (New York, NY: Avon Books, 1990), 133.

49. McFaul, *From Cold War*, 224–226.

50. Ibid., 246 and Ostrovsky, *The Invention of Russia*, 308–309.

51. Maria Lipman, "How Putin Silences Dissent: Inside the Kremlin's Crackdown." *Foreign Affairs* 95, no. 3 (May–June 2016): 41–42; McFaul, *From Cold War*, 243–245. McFaul makes the point that even with all of the voter manipulation, United Russia won only 49.3 percent of the vote in the 2011 Duma election, a sharp drop from its 64.3 percent showing four years earlier.

52. Stent, *Putin's World*, 311–323, 326–335, 343–344; and *Putin's Asymmetric Assault on Democracy in Russia and Europe: Implications for U.S. Security* with an introduction by Chris Sampson (Washington, DC: Skyhorse Publishing, 2018), 2–4.

53. On the prerequisites for democracy see Brown, "Evaluating Russia's Democratization," 546; and Sheri Berman, *Democracy and Dictatorship in Europe: From the Ancien Regime to the Present Day* (Oxford: Oxford University Press, 2019), 6.

54. For a different assessment see Masha Gessen, *The Future Is History: How Totalitarianism Reclaimed Russia* (New York, NY: Riverhead Books, 2017).

55. According to Transparency International's Corruption Perception Index, Russia ranked 138 out of 180 countries in terms of corruption in 2018 (Denmark ranked as the least corrupt—1/180 according to the same survey). For the Transparency International 2018 CPI, see www.transparency.org.

56. Sergei Vedyashkin, "Disapproval with the Country's Course Hits 12-Year High in Russia Poll." *The Moscow Times*, February 1, 2019. www.themoscowtimes .com; and Ivan Nechepurenko, "Moscow Police Arrest More Than 1,300 During an Election Protest." *The New York Times*, July 28, 2019, A12. Aslund, quoting Lev Gudkov of the Levada Center, contends that Putin lost the support of the urban middle class in the larger Russian cities in 2011 and has abandoned his hopes of winning back the elites. Aslund, *Russia's Crony Capitalism*, 243.

FURTHER READING

Aslund, Anders. *Russia's Crony Capitalism: The Path from Market Economy to Kleptocracy.* New Haven, CT: Yale University Press, 2019.

Myers, Steven Lee. *The New Tsar: The Rise and Reign of Vladimir Putin.* New York, NY: Alfred A. Knopf, 2015.

Stent, Angela. *Putin's World: Russia Against the West and With the Rest.* New York, NY: Twelve, 2019.

Treisman, Daniel. *The Return: Russia's Journey from Gorbachev to Medvedev.* New York, NY: Free Press, 2011.

Wilson, Andrew. *Virtual Politics: Faking Democracy in the Post-Soviet World.* New Haven, CT: Yale University Press, 2005.

Chapter 10

The Challenges of American Democracy

Joseph Patten

The election of President Donald J. Trump in 2016 was a result of a race that was unlike any other in modern American history in many ways. While presidential politics has long been a blood sport, the partisan divisions were much wider and deeper than in previous elections, and the political acrimony has only intensified throughout President Trump's first term in office. Perhaps the only shared values uniting the electorate in 2016 was the anger it held toward the leaders of its political parties, and the dislike Trump and Hillary Clinton supporters felt toward one another.

POLITICAL POPULISM AND AMERICAN DEMOCRACY

Rather than simply addressing disagreements over tax rates or health-care policy, customary in campaigns, politics has become exceedingly personal and vindictive, and is now polarized into bifurcated camps of citizens who are extremely distrustful of one another. One recent study on political polarization found that because our divisions are now so deeply rooted in conflicting cultural worldviews, it has caused the "politicization of everything," from the type of car we drive (Prius vs. pickups), the coffee we drink (Starbucks vs. Dunkin Donuts), the pets we keep (cats vs. dogs), to our parenting philosophy (self-reliance vs. obedience).[1] Identifying the causes of our political divide is simple, but bridging these divisions in our democracy will be much more challenging, as roughly half of all Republicans and Democrats now view each other as immoral as well as wrong-headed.[2]

Political polarization has thus seeped from our political system into our personal relationships, with one study finding families that are politically divided over the Trump presidency now spend one hour less together on

Thanksgiving than politically unified families.[3] Even worse, another study found that political polarization might be harming some people's love life, given that 22 percent of college-aged students claim to have broken up with someone over clashing political viewpoints.[4] Much of the political rancor that exists in American democracy today can be partly traced to the negative side effects of political populism, currently raging throughout Europe and the United States.

DEFINING POLITICAL POPULISM

During the 2020 presidential primary season, Senator Bernie Sanders (Democrat-Vermont), Senator Elizabeth Warren (Democrat-Massachusetts) and President Trump were all angling to be viewed as the true populist candidate. But how can candidates who appear to be polar opposites of one another all be considered political populists? Sanders and Warren are liberal Senators who railed against corporate greed, called for a Medicare-for-all health-care system, and advocated for the decriminalization of illegal border crossings. Donald Trump is a billionaire real estate tycoon who lowered the corporate tax rate from 35 percent to 21 percent and implemented a zero-tolerance immigration policy that resulted in a family separation policy on the southern border. Trump's presidential campaign announcement in 2015 was also historically different in that he coupled his criticism of U.S. immigration policy with an ethnic smear against Mexicans, by saying: "When Mexico sends its people, they're not sending their best . . . . They're bringing drugs. They're bringing crime. They're rapists."[5] So if political opposites like Sanders/Warren and Trump are all labeled as political populists, can populism even be defined in a meaningful way, let alone be blamed for fueling our political divisions?

One groundbreaking work titled, *The Populist Zeitgeist*, defines populism as the framing of politics as a Manichean struggle between "the pure people versus the corrupt elite."[6] In this sense, Sanders/Warren and Trump can be labeled as populists as they share a proclivity to frame American politics as a rigged system that pits corrupt political elites against their powerless supporters. But there is really nothing new about candidates running campaigns from an anti-elitist perspective. Presidential candidates have branded themselves as political outsiders fighting for the people as far back as President Andrew Jackson's election in 1828, when his populist campaign attacked political elites for conspiring against him in a corrupt bargain in the election of 1824. A more corrosive feature of modern populists is their tendency to use anti-pluralist tactics by claiming "only some of the people are really the people."[7] Rather than adopting unifying rhetoric that brings together the potpourri of groups that exists in our pluralistic society, populists instead use

divisive rhetoric that attracts some groups of voters by intentionally alienat-
ing others. For example, in one of his campaign speeches, Trump once said
"The only important thing is the unification of the people—because the other
people don't mean anything."[8] When populist candidates refer to the people,
they are usually only referring to the people who support them, not the people
favoring other candidates. Populist candidates are also particularly skillful at
appealing to disgruntled segments of society because their rhetoric aims at the
"gut feelings of people," and they tend to offer "simple solutions" to complicated problems, and try to "buy" voter support by pandering to their deepest
fears.[9] It is for these reasons that another political scientist defines populism
as a "conflict between elites that are becoming increasingly suspicious of
democracy and angry publics that are becoming increasingly illiberal."[10]

Where populist candidates like Sanders/Warren and Trump disagree is how
they define corrupt political elites, and the ways in which their supporters
have been negatively impacted by them. Left-wing populists, like Warren,
tend to highlight socioeconomic concerns by emphasizing growing levels of
income inequality and the outsized influence the wealthy and well-connected
have over the government. The Occupy Wall Street movement in 2011 was an
example of a left-wing populist movement that took to the streets in order to
call attention to corporate greed and the corrupt influences of the wealthiest 1
percent of Americans. Economic inequality in the United States has widened
considerably since the 1980s, fueled by a restructured tax policy under which
the 47 percent tax rate paid by the wealthiest Americans in the 1980s was cut
in half to only 23 percent today, which is lower than the average 24.2 percent
rate now paid by the bottom half of American earners.[11] Left-wing populists,
like Warren, point out that the wealthiest 1 percent of Americans now control
42 percent of the nation's wealth.[12] Her campaign called for shrinking economic inequality levels by placing a new wealth tax on Americans holding
more than $50 million in assets. In rolling out her wealth tax proposal, she
argued she was "fighting for an economy and a government that works for all
of us, not just the wealthy and well-connected . . . wealthy donors don't get
to buy this process."[13]

Right-wing populists also highlight socioeconomic concerns, but tend to
give greater emphasis to sociocultural and nationalistic themes. President
Trump's 2016 campaign slogan "Make America Great Again" tapped into
cultural anxieties held by his supporters that the country's greatness was being
diluted through the forces of globalism, unfair trade agreements, and shifting
demographics within the country. Trump's political rallies were renowned
for his ability to whip supporters into a frenzy with his signature campaign
promise to build a 2,000-mile wall across the southern border with Mexico.
Trump successfully tapped into white grievance, where more than half of
white Americans viewed themselves as victims of reverse discrimination.[14]

One recent study on white identity politics found that a significant percentage of white voters identify with their whiteness as something important to them.[15] The study also found that voters who identify with their whiteness can be further divided into two distinct groups, including white voters who hold negative views toward non-whites and white voters who do not hold negative views toward non-whites, but rather fear losing their status as members of a dominant culture.[16] Focusing on the immigration issue proved successful for Trump because it appealed to both of these groups of white voters, those with negative prejudices against non-whites and those fearing cultural displacement. Table 10.1 shows that fears of white cultural displacement are being driven by the shifting demographics of American society. In the 2020 presidential election, non-white voters will make up 33.3 percent of the national electorate, which is up from 23.6 percent of the electorate twenty years ago. Most of the growth of non-white voters comes from the Hispanic community, which has almost doubled from 7.4 percent of the electorate in 2000 to 13.3 percent of the electorate in 2020. The U.S. census projects whites will lose majority status in 2045, when they will drop to 49.7 percent of the U.S. population and when Hispanics are projected to increase to 24.6 percent of the population.[17]

What makes the shifting demographics in the United States particularly menacing to American democracy is the emergence of identity politics, where political allegiances are increasingly forming along racial and ethnic lines, rather than along traditional issue-based party politics. Table 10.2 reveals that in the 2016 presidential election, Trump won the white vote by 20 percentage points (5–37%), but lost the African American vote by 80 percentage points (89% to 8%) and the Hispanic vote by almost 40 points (66–28%). One study titled, *Political Tribes*, argues that identity politics is "tearing the United States apart" because it has "seized the American left and right in an especially dangerous, racially infected way. In America today, every group feels threatened: whites and blacks, Latinos and Asians, men and women, liberals and conservatives."[18]

This chapter highlights the evolution of American democracy from the colonial period to the modern era. It begins with a discussion of how the

Table 10.1   Percentage of Total Vote in 2000 and 2020 by Race and Ethnicity

2000 Electorate as Percentage of Total Vote By Race and Ethnicity (%)	*2020 Electorate as Percentage of Total Vote by Race and Ethnicity (%)*
Hispanics: 7.4	Hispanics: 13.3
African Americans: 11.5	African Americans: 12.5
Asians: 2.5	Asians: 4.7
Caucasians: 76.4	Caucasians: 66.7

Source: Cillufa, Anthony and Richard Fry. 2019. "An Early Look at the 2020 Electorate" Pew Research Center. Retrieved from https://www.pewsocialtrends.org/essay/an-early-look-at-the-2020-electorate/.

Table 10.2 Voting Behavior in Presidential Elections Based on Race and Ethnicity, 2004–2016

Year	Presidential Candidates	Caucasian (%)	African American (%)	Hispanic (%)	Other (%)
2016	Donald Trump (R)	57	8	28	36
	Hillary Clinton (D)	37	89	66	56
2012	Barack Obama (D)	39	93	71	58
	Mitt Romney (R)	59	6	27	38
2008	Barack Obama (D)	43	95	67	66
	John McCain (R)	55	4	31	31
2004	George W. Bush (R)	58	11	44	54
	John Kerry (D)	41	88	53	40

Source: Roper Center for Public Opinion Research. "How Groups Voted in 2016." Retrieved from http://ropercenter.cornell.edu/how-groups-voted-2016.

American government was shaped by previous populist movements, such as the Boston Tea Party, Shays' Rebellion, and the era of Jacksonian democracy. It spotlights how the American government was originally designed to limit the negative effects of populist movements through federalism and the system of representative democracy. Populist movements were further checked by non-constitutional influences with the emergence of political parties during George Washington's administration, where a new class of political elites (i.e., party bosses) came to serve as political intermediaries between government and the people by recruiting, vetting, and funding mainly mainstream candidates, most of whom promoted shared values and pluralistic ideals. This chapter argues that today's populist movement has been enabled by recent political reforms that have removed safeguards intended to check the excesses of populist movements. More specifically, this chapter maintains that political reforms to our presidential nomination system (i.e., primary system) and campaign finance system (i.e., Citizens United) have weakened political parties and crippled the important role parties have played in limiting the negative effects of populist movements.

AMERICAN DEMOCRACY AND THE ANCIENT GREEKS

Most of the framers of the U. S. Constitution viewed the term *democracy* in a negative light because it conjured up images of political anarchy and mob rule. John Adams once said a "Democracy never lasts long. It soon wastes exhausts and murders itself. There was never a Democracy yet that did not commit suicide."[19] Many of the delegates at the Constitutional Convention

shared this negative view of democracy and believed only the most enlightened members of society should assume public positions. Ancient Greek
philosopher Plato categorized democracies as one of the worst forms of
government in *The Republic* because he believed they tend to be ruled by
uninformed mobs who advocate for their own self-interest, rather than the
public good. For Plato, the fatal flaw of democracies relates to how they
wrongfully assume that all opinions are equally valid, giving both ignorant
and knowledgeable voices an equal say in decision-making. In *The Republic*,
he explained it in this way: "Democracy is a charming form of government,
full of variety and disorder, and dispensing a sort of equality to equals and
unequals alike."[20] Democratic "man" is not qualified to rule, according to
Plato, because his "life is subject to no order or restraint, and he has no wish
to change an existence which he calls pleasant, free, and happy."[21] Plato
argued that allowing the unenlightened masses to rule over powerless minorities would eventually lead to political ruin, because oppressed minorities
were prone to rise up in insurrection against tyrannical majorities.

IS AMERICA A DEMOCRACY OR A REPUBLIC?

In part because of the writings of ancient Greek philosophers, the word
"democracy" was viewed as a pejorative to the delegates at the Constitutional
Convention, which is why it was not included in either the Declaration of
Independence or the Constitution. James Madison instead referred to the
American system of government as a "republic" to avoid the negative trap-
pings associated with the term democracy. So how is a republic different from
a democracy? And does this mean we are wrong to refer to the United States
as a democracy today? Madison explained that a republic is different from
a democracy in the "delegation of the government . . . to a smaller number
of citizens elected by the rest."[22] It is important to note that when theorists
such as Plato and Madison referred to a democracy, they were speaking of
a direct democracy, where all citizens would vote directly on public laws.
They were speaking of the type of direct democracy that existed in ancient
Greece over 2,500 years ago. It was in 508 BC that the Athenian leader
Cleisthenes created the world's first democratic system, then referred to as a
"demokratia," which translates to "rule by the people." We can now barely
fathom what it would be like to live in the type of direct democracy that
existed in ancient Greece. In that system, all nonslave adult males who completed military training were eligible to participate directly in governmental
decision-making. That means over 30,000 Athenian men were eligible to
serve in the lower assembly, which met approximately forty times a year on
a hilltop and enacted laws with majority votes.[23] Greek scholars estimate that

only 5,000 of the eligible 30,000 Athenian men actually participated in these legislative sessions, because many were preoccupied with military or other responsibilities.[24] But compare the assembly that existed in ancient Greece with today's U.S. House of Representatives. The United States functions as a representative democracy in which citizens vote for members of Congress, who then vote on their behalf in the House of Representatives. Today, each of the 435 members of the House represents congressional districts that each includes approximately 750,000 residents. Only India's lower parliamentary body Lok Sabha currently has larger legislative districts than the House of Representatives, with 545 members representing 1.3 billion people.[25] So when Madison referred to the American government as a republic, he meant the United States is a representative democracy and not the type of direct democracy that existed in ancient Greece.

AMERICAN DEMOCRACY AND
THE REVOLUTIONARY WAR WITH GREAT BRITAIN

To assess the impact of populism on American democracy today, it is essential to understand the original intent of the framers of the U.S. Constitution. The very concept of the United States was first realized with the signing of the Declaration of Independence from Britain in 1776. British colonization of the eastern seaboard of the United States first began in the founding of Jamestown, Virginia in 1607. And Britain ruled over the American colonies in relative tranquility for 170 years, which, for some perspective, is the same number of years spanned by George Washington and Dwight D. Eisenhower's presidencies. What sparked discontent in the colonies was Britain's decision to tax them without first gaining the approval of the colonial legislature. While Britain was ultimately victorious against France in the Seven Years War (1756–1763), the expense of waging a war on multiple continents caused the doubling of its national debt. Desperate for revenue, the British Parliament passed the Stamp Act of 1765, which required colonists to pay a tax on each piece of printed paper. A couple of years later in 1767, the Townshend Revenue Act placed taxes on other items, such as glass, lead, and paints. The Townshend Act was named after British House of Commons member Charles Townshend, the leading advocate of using tax revenue from the American colonies to solve Britain's financial problems. Famed Anglo-Irish political philosopher and statesman Edmund Burke once recounted how Townsend captivated British House of Commons members "with the image of a revenue to be raised in America."[26] And it was after the Tea Act of 1773 was passed that Samuel Adams led a group of colonists called the Sons of Liberty to rise up in an act of civil disobedience by storming three British ships before throwing 92,000 pounds of tea into the Boston Harbor, an event that later came to be known as the Boston Tea Party.[27] Britain responded to what could arguably be referred to as America's first populist movement with the Coercive Acts, which closed Boston Harbor and replaced elected officials with pro-British appointees, and with the Quartering Act, which permitted the British military to stay in colonial housing without the consent of property holders. These events inspired the Revolutionary War against British rule.

AMERICA'S FIRST GOVERNMENT: THE FAILURE OF THE ARTICLES OF CONFEDERATION

To fight the Revolutionary War with Great Britain, the thirteen states formed the first American government, known as the Articles of Confederation (1781–1789), whose design reflected the prevailing philosophy of pre-revolutionary states' rights advocates. This first national government was exceedingly weak in that it did not have the power to tax, did not include an executive or judicial branch, and conferred most powers on the original thirteen states. The articles placed so much emphasis on states' rights that the framers felt it necessary to remind the signers that they were in fact entering a "firm league of friendship" with other states in order to "perpetuate mutual friendship and intercourse."[28] One of the most lasting contributions of the articles is the placement of Congress at the center of the national government, granting it important war and foreign policy powers that were later mostly cut and pasted into the U.S. Constitution. However, it soon became clear that this loose association of states was not up to the task of governing; it was unable to create a national currency or ensure that colonial troops received needed military supplies during the Revolutionary War.

THE ANNAPOLIS CONVENTION AND SHAYS' REBELLION

The failure of the articles was made obvious by two high-profile events in 1786: the Annapolis Convention and Shays' Rebellion. In 1786, the State of Virginia called a meeting in Annapolis to discuss problems associated with war funding efforts and other issues related to national commerce. However, collective action obstacles became apparent when only five of the thirteen states even bothered to send representatives to Annapolis. Fearful that the association of states was falling apart, Alexander Hamilton organized the Constitutional Convention the following year in Philadelphia and stressed the need for states to consider the "Articles of Confederation and to propose such changes therein as might render them adequate to the exigencies of the union."[29] Unlike at Annapolis, the Philadelphia Convention took on an air of importance across the colonies, perhaps because the revered George Washington agreed to chair the Convention. Washington is one of the few figures in history who was as large in life as he became in death. Though Washington only spoke once during the Constitutional Convention when asking the body to support the motion that granted states one representative for every 30,000 residents instead of every 40,000 residents, his mere presence drew enough delegates to Philadelphia to ensure a quorum.[30] And, of course, it was at this Constitutional Convention that the framers abolished the Articles of Confederation altogether and created an entirely new system of government, as outlined in the Constitution.

Shays' Rebellion could be referred to as America's second populist movement. It began in Northampton, Massachusetts, on August 29, 1786, when a group of farmers seized the local courthouse to prevent judges from foreclosing on their farms. Led by Daniel Shays, who fought at Bunker Hill, the insurrection spread throughout the state of Massachusetts and lasted several months.[31] Many people across Massachusetts either hoped or feared the 1,000 or so insurgents were aiming to topple the state government and replace it with either a monarchy or a direct democracy system of government.[32] While the insurrection was ultimately defeated, the national government's clumsy and slow-footed reaction caused some of the framers to believe that the Articles of Confederation would need to be replaced. In a letter to Richard Lee, Washington reacted to Shays' Rebellion by saying, "I am mortified beyond expression when I view the clouds that have spread over the brightest morn in any country."[33]

THREE PRINCIPLES OF THE CONSTITUTION: SEPARATION OF POWERS, CHECKS AND BALANCES, AND FEDERALISM

Shays' Rebellion made a major impact on the mind-sets of the fifty-five delegates who travelled to Philadelphia to participate in the Constitutional Convention in 1787. Prior to Shays' Rebellion, there was near consensus among the framers that the new government should be relatively weak so as not to draw comparisons with the British Monarchy against which they were rebelling. After the rebellion, however, some framers and their supporters came to believe that it was not enough to build a government that did not tyrannize over the people; a central government should also be strong enough to withstand the excesses of populist movements. In Federalist Paper #51, Madison or Hamilton (author unknown) explained it in this way: "In framing a government which is to be administered by men over men, the great difficulty lies in this: You must first enable the government to control the governed, and in the next place oblige it to control itself."[34] And, at the Constitutional Convention, the framers designed a national government that it believed was strong enough to limit the negative impact of populism, with a chief executive empowered with the authority to enforce democratic pluralism.

IF MEN WERE ANGELS: WHY POLITICAL ELITES
(AND NOT PEOPLE) GOVERN BEST

The three fundamental principles of the Constitution include separation of powers, checks and balances, and federalism. While the term "separation of powers" is not explicitly stated in the U.S. Constitution, the document itself divides the legislative branch, the executive branch, and the judiciary branch of government in the document's first three articles. In separating the three branches of government, the framers were influenced by Montesquieu's *The Spirit of Laws,* published a few years earlier in 1748. Madison highlighted a famous passage from Montesquieu's work in Federalist Paper #47 in asserting that "when the legislative and executive powers are united in the same person, or in the same body of magistrates, there can be no liberty."[35] But Madison and Hamilton did not believe liberty could be gained by simply separating the three branches of government. Although Thomas Jefferson, while writing the Declaration of Independence, was influenced by the English philosopher John Locke in assuming human nature was mostly cooperative and guided by natural law, Madison and Hamilton held a much darker view of our nature. Federalist Paper #51, for example, paints a more Hobbesian view of human nature, asserting that "if men were angels, no government would be necessary. If angels were to govern men, neither external nor internal controls on government would be necessary."[36] The implication is that it is not enough to simply separate branches of government, because power-seeking impulses can lead one branch of government to dominate over the others. These institutional power debates are still going on today; some believe the American presidency has taken on "imperial" qualities since the United States assumed a hegemonic role in world affairs in the 1950s, and others believe increased populism and increased political partisanship have transformed the U.S. Congress into a "broken branch" of government.[37] In structuring the three branches of government, the framer's goal was to make it so the "ambition" of one branch would "counteract" the ambition of the other two to prevent any one of the three branches from becoming dominant.[38] So, in practice, the power of Congress to enact laws is checked by the president's power to veto Congress and the Supreme Court's power to invalidate laws by declaring them unconstitutional (see figure 10.1 for a more complete summary of the ways branches check each other).

Perhaps America's greatest contribution to the canon of democratic thought can be found in Madison's Federalist Paper #10. The Federalist Papers are a collection of eighty-five essays written by Madison, Hamilton, and John Jay that were published in New York newspapers from October 1787 to May 1788. The papers were published under the pseudonym "Publius," as a tribute to Publius Valerius, a Roman statesman who helped create the Roman Republic after Rome's last King Tarquin the Proud was toppled by its own populist movement in 509 BC.[39] The eight-five articles were published to explain the original intent behind the U.S. Constitution and to quell criticisms spread by opponents of the constitution's ratification. Important anti-Federalist state's rights advocates such as Massachusetts's Patrick Henry opposed the Constitution's ratification. Some feared the new government would dominate over the states, while others, like New York's Governor George Clinton, argued against presidential powers, and still others emphasized the need for a Bill of Rights.

HOW THE AMERICAN GOVERNMENT WAS STRUCTURED TO WEAKEN POPULISM

Federalist Paper #10 is the most important of the eighty-five essays because it is here that James Madison explains how safeguards can be built into

Separation of Powers in the Federal Government	Executive Branch: Executes Laws	Legislative Branch: Enacts Laws	Judicial Branch: Interprets Laws
	Can Veto Congressional Statutes	Can Override Presidential Veto with two-third vote	Has Power of Judicial Review
	Appoints Federal Judges	Senate Confirms Judicial Appointments	Can Declare Presidential Acts Unconstitutional
	Can Adjourn Congress	Can Impeach President and Federal Judges	Can Declare Legislative Action as Unconstitutional

Figure 10.1   Examples of Checks and Balances in Action.

governmental structures so that systems based on majority rule can also uphold minority rights. He sets out to challenge commonly cited critiques that democracy is nothing more than "two wolves and a lamb voting on what to have for dinner," or that "democracy is nothing more than mob rule, where 51 percent of the people may take away the rights of the other forty-nine."[40] In designing the U.S. government, Madison was primarily concerned with devising a political system that made it difficult for populist movements to dominate over political minorities. The first way he sought to do this was through federalism, which he believed would make it difficult for populist movements to take hold in the first place. Madison viewed society as a collection of groups, referring to them as factions. We can think of our modern society as a collection of groups, too. Some of us identify with racial and/or ethnic groups, such as African Americans, Hispanics, Asians, Italians, Irish, and/or Mexicans, to name but a few. People also belong to certain socioeconomic groups, including the upper class, the middle class, or the lower class. Others belong to occupational groups, such as carpenters, teachers, waitresses, and lawyers; and still others form groups that advocate for particular policy positions, such as the National Rifle Association or the Sierra Club. Madison defined a faction as a "majority or a minority of the whole, who are united and actuated by some common impulse of passion, or of interest, adversed to the rights of other citizens."[41] Because minority factions will be checked by majority factions, Madison was primarily concerned with making it difficult for populist movements to grow into political majorities. To build a stable political system, it was critical, in Madison's view, to create a framework whereby coalitions of groups could form temporarily and then continually shift and realign, depending upon the public issue. Madison envisioned a society in which a loose alliance of groups might form to advocate for a particular policy, then scramble and form an entirely new alliance of groups to advocate for another policy. In the modern era, American political scientist Hugh Heclo makes a similar argument that each public policy has a separate group of issue networks that influences how policies are made.[42] The issue networks of people who influence gun control policy, for example, are different from the issue networks of people who influence health-care policy. It was vital for Madison to build a political system that promoted pluralism, so that that all groups felt as if their interests were at least sometimes reflected in public decisions, ensuring that society did not bifurcate into two groups of permanent winners and permanent losers. Madison's chief goal was to build a system of government that promoted pluralism, because permanently marginalized groups tend to instigate political rebellions.

Madison reasoned that we can never remove the cause of factions, because they form naturally when like-minded people are free to form group associations. This sentiment is best captured when he asserts, "Liberty is to faction what air is to fire," meaning that just as we should neither try to eliminate air in order to avoid unwanted fires, nor should we eliminate liberty to escape the negative effects of factions.[43] Madison instead advocates "controlling the effects" of political factions through federalism and representative democracy.

Through federalism, power is divided between the federal government and the states, and then again between the states and local governments. Because factions form at the local level, the hierarchal structure of federalism makes it difficult for populist movements to grow into political majorities. For example, suppose a group formed in your hometown that discriminated against the rights of Roman-Catholic voters. That group might be able to form a majority in your town, but in order to grow, the group would have to move up the political ladder from your town to your county, and then from your county to your state, and then once again from your state to the national government. Madison reasoned that it is more likely for factions to grow weaker rather than stronger as they move up the political ladder of federalism because it is easier to destroy political movements than to grow them. This sentiment is captured in the quote from former U.S. Speaker of the House Sam Rayburn, who said, "Any jackass can kick down a barn, but it takes a good carpenter to build one."[44] Accordingly, Madison reasoned that the "influence of factious leaders may kindle a flame within their particular states, but will be unable to spread a general conflagration through the other states."[45] And then Madison conjectured that even if a populist movement is able to scale the political ladder and grow into a political majority, the negative effects of the majority can be mitigated through a representative democracy system. Rather than trust public decision-making to rank-and-file citizens, as is the direct democracy model, Madison instead advocated for selecting representatives who would most likely "possess the most attractive merit and the most diffusive and established characters."[46] These leaders would most likely be the most enlightened members of society and would look to advance the larger public interest rather than impose its will on minority groups. This is why it is dangerous to American democracy when political leaders adopt anti-pluralistic agendas and embrace divisive rhetoric and policies rather than helping to unify the wide range of divergent groups represented in the country today.

LIMITED VOTING RIGHTS IN EARLY AMERICA

It is therefore imperative to acknowledge that the original intent of the framers was to empower political elites so that they, and not the people, controlled public decision-making. Popular elections were not at all popular in the late eighteenth century. In fact, the U.S. Constitution did not confer the right to vote upon any group of Americans until the fifteenth Amendment prohibited states from denying the right to vote based on race in 1870. During Washington's presidency, the only federal officials who were popularly elected were members of the House of Representatives, and even then, only 6 percent of Americans were eligible to vote.[47] Washington was unanimously appointed president by Electoral College members without any citizen involvement, senators were appointed by state legislatures until the seventeenth Amendment was ratified in 1913, and all federal judges were appointed by the president and confirmed by the Senate. And in elections for House members in the eighteenth century, most states required voters to be 21-year-old, white, property-holding men. And seven of the thirteen colonies required voters to own a certain amount of acreage to vote. South Carolina's Constitution of 1790, for example, outlined a voting standard that required citizens to own "five hundred acres and ten negroes."[48] Five colonies denied voting rights to Catholics and four denied them to Jews.[49] John Adams, in a letter to a friend, argued against decoupling property ownership from voting standards by saying:

> Depend upon it, sir, it is dangerous to open so fruitfull a Source of Controversy and Altercation, as would be opened by attempting to alter the Qualifications of Voters. There will be no End of it. New Claims will arise. Women will demand a Vote. Lads from 12 to 21 will think their Rights not enough attended to, and every Man, who has not a Farthing, will demand an equal Voice with any other in all Acts of State.[50]

NON-CONSTITUTIONAL CHECKS ON POPULIST MOVEMENTS: THE EMERGENCE OF POLITICAL PARTIES

And, in the late eighteenth century and throughout the nineteenth century, the American system of government came to include political parties that established an even wider array of political checks against populist movements. Political party leaders weakened populist movements by serving as "political middlemen," standing between the voters and the government.[51] Party bosses came to serve a vital role in recruiting and vetting political candidates and mostly controlled the selection of candidates from which voters were permitted to choose. A new political class of party officials, political consultants, think tanks, and lobbyists took root in the federal and state capitals and largely managed our political system for over 150 years. Lawmaking became complicated, causing nineteenth-century American poet John Godfrey Saxe I to remark that "Laws, like sausages, cease to inspire respect in proportion as we know how they are made."[52]

THE ROLE OF POLITICAL PARTIES IN
THE PRESIDENTIAL SELECTION PROCESS

The delegates at the Constitutional Convention never foresaw the emergence of political parties, and so they naturally never included them in their examination of our government. Many of the framers were astonished to see the weighty influence of parties over our political system a mere ten years after the Constitution's ratification.[53] Political parties emerged during Washington's presidency that forever changed our system of government, with some of the most dramatic changes taking root in our presidential selection process. While the Constitution established an appointed slate of Electoral College members to handpick the chief executive, it was silent on how presidential nominees would be recruited and chosen. In 1789, the Electoral College served the dual purpose of nominating and selecting George Washington as our nation's first president.[54] But the process changed dramatically with the development of political parties in subsequent elections. Since then, there have been three distinct presidential nomination systems, including: the King Caucus system (1796–1824), the convention system (1828–1968), and our current primary system (1972–present). Over the past 200 years, the most dramatic change in the presidential nomination system has been in the way control over the nomination process has shifted from political elites to voters. The transfer of power from political elites to the people has helped to supercharge the populist movement that led to Donald Trump's 2016 electoral victory.

KING CAUCUS NOMINATING SYSTEM (1796–1824)

In the first King Caucus system, presidential nominees were chosen by members of Congress who caucused together with fellow party members, just as congressional Democrats and Republicans caucus separately today to select the Speaker of the House and the Minority Leader. It is somewhat logical that members of Congress initially selected nominees, given that they were in the best position to determine the qualifications of presidential candidates, and Congress represented the only national institution where leaders from across the country could gather to debate national issues. However, the King Caucus system only lasted until 1824, in large part due to concerns that it violated Montesquieu's dictum to separate the three branches of government. John Quincy Adams was one of the fiercest critics of the caucus, claiming it was a "practice which places the president in a state of undue subservience to the members of the legislature."[55]

Table 10.3 Presidential Election of 1824

Candidate	Party	Electoral Votes	Popular Votes
Andrew Jackson	Democratic–Republican	99	153,544
John Quincy Adams	Democratic–Republicans	84	108,740
William H. Crawford	Democratic–Republican	41	40,856
Henry Clay	Democratic–Republican	37	47,531

Source: Retrieved from https://www.270towin.com/1824_Election/ on March 27, 2020.

THE CORRUPT BARGAIN AND THE EMERGENCE OF JACKSONIAN DEMOCRACY

Perhaps the death knell for the King Caucus system occurred in 1824 when only one-fourth of the 261 congressional Democratic-Republicans were present to nominate Treasury Secretary William Crawford. Crawford was later mockingly dubbed the "King Caucus" candidate by presidential opponents Andrew Jackson, John Quincy Adams, and Henry Clay.[56] The election of 1824 is regarded as one of the most controversial elections in American history. It also triggered the era of Jacksonian democracy, which expanded popular elections across the country, particularly in the western states being incorporated into the United States at the time. As Table 10.3 indicates, although Jackson received the plurality of popular and electoral votes, he did not receive the majority of electoral votes needed to win the election. And the Constitution stipulates that the House of Representatives selects the president when no candidate receives a majority of electoral votes, which had happened once before in Jefferson's election in 1800. Jackson became enraged after an anonymous letter appeared in a Philadelphia newspaper claiming the presidential vote in the House was sealed by a "corrupt bargain" between John Quincy Adams and House Speaker Henry Clay, where Adams allegedly promised to nominate Clay Secretary of State in exchange for Clay's support in the House vote.[57] After the House vote, Adams was declared the victor and Clay did in fact go on to serve as his Secretary of State. Jackson went to his grave enraged by the corrupt bargain charge and weaponized relevant populist messaging in his successful presidential bid four years later in 1828.

PRESIDENTIAL NOMINATING CONVENTIONS (1928–1968)

This new era of Jacksonian democracy can be viewed as America's third populist movement, in that it ushered in a more democratic method for selecting presidential nominees. Rather than allowing members of Congress to select party nominees, the process switched to empowering political parties to select presidential nominees themselves in nominating conventions. Nominating systems were more democratic than congressional caucuses in that they permitted input from a wider array of party activists across the nation. Famed American political scientist V.O. Key, Jr. said conventions provided a "mechanism through which party leaders, dispersed over a nation of continental proportions, could negotiate sufficient agreement to maintain parties capable of governing through the presidential system."[58] Nomination conventions, however, were also mostly controlled by political elites, as convention delegates were typically appointed by state and county party bosses.[59] By 1917, however, nominating conventions became more democratic, with forty-five of forty-seven states using rank-and-file voters to select convention delegates, rather than party bosses.

TAKING IT TO THE STREETS:
THE PRESIDENTIAL ELECTION OF 1968

Our existing presidential nominating system emerged after the controversial 1968 Democratic convention. Mired in the Vietnam War, President Lyndon B. Johnson shocked the world in a nationally televised address when he said, "I shall not seek, and I will not accept, the nomination of my party for another term as your president."[60] The political vacuum in the Democratic Party created by Johnson's abdication was quickly filled by Bobby Kennedy, Eugene McCarthy, and Hubert Humphrey. Unlike any other national convention, the 1968 Democratic Convention in Chicago was overshadowed by rioting and massive street demonstrations. Prior to the Convention the country was sent reeling from the Tet Offensive in Vietnam in January 1968, Martin Luther King, Jr.'s assassination in March 1968, and Kennedy's assassination on the campaign trail a month later in April 1968.[61] Protesters were further enraged when Vice President Humphrey was selected as the Democratic nominee at the Convention over antiwar candidate Eugene McCarthy even though Humphrey did not participate in any of the state primary elections. Primary elections prior to 1972 were referred to as beauty contests, because although elections or caucuses were held throughout the states, the results were non-binding and could be overturned by party elites at nominating conventions. Candidates typically entered political primaries to prove to party bosses they had the support of the people as a way to persuade party bosses to support them in the nominating conventions. Protesters took to the street in bloody confrontations with the police after Humphrey was nominated, incensed that primary vote results were being overturned by party bosses. In a reaction to the mass protests, the presidential nomination process was reformed by the McGovern-Fraser Commission, which shifted the control over the nomination system from party bosses to rank-and-file voters.[62]

SOWING THE SEEDS OF POPULISM: THE PRIMARY NOMINATING SYSTEM (1972–PRESENT)

Political parties and party bosses today have almost no influence over the presidential nominating system. Registered voters in state primary elections and caucuses, rather than party bosses in national conventions, control the process. During the 2016 Republican nomination, for example, Donald Trump won the nomination over sixteen other Republican nominees, even though he was opposed by most of the party establishment. Trump was initially viewed as a rogue antiestablishment populist candidate and was not at all supported by party elites. Trump's racially overt messaging ran counter to the Republican National Committee's widely circulated report that called on mainstream Republicans to build support with Hispanic voters by supporting immigration reform. The "autopsy," as the report came to be known, highlighted the growing nonwhite voting population and blamed Mitt Romney's inability to attract non-white voters as the cause of his defeat to President Barack Obama in 2012.[63] The Republican Party's establishment candidate was Jeb Bush, in part because party leaders believed he would attract Hispanic voters, because he speaks Spanish and his wife is Mexican American. Bush referred to Trump as "unhinged" and after one of the debates said Trump was a "chaos candidate . . . and he'd be a chaos president."[64] The voters in the Republican primaries and caucuses disagreed with their party's leadership and instead supported Trump and his anti-immigration agenda. And unlike the King Caucus system or the Nominating Convention system, party leaders had no power to check the will of the people. It is inconceivable that an anti-pluralistic political outsider candidate like Trump would have emerged victorious in the presidential nominating systems that existed from 1796 to 1972.

WEAKENING POLITICAL PARTIES FURTHER THROUGH CAMPAIGN FINANCE LAWS

In the late nineteenth century, Senator Marcus Hanna (R-OH) said, "There are two things that are important in Politics. The first is money and I can't remember what the second one is."[65] Political parties have not only been weakened in recruiting and selecting party nominees, the parties are also no longer playing the leading role they once played in raising campaign funds for candidates. Major donors now give millions to super political action committees (PACs) rather than political parties. Super PACs have also fueled populism by advocating for politically extreme positions. For example, the largest super PAC contributor has been Sheldon Adelson, who has contributed almost $300 million since 2010, including $20 million to Trump's super PAC in 2016.[66] Adelson has been a driving force behind President Trump's Middle Eastern policy, particularly as it relates to the U.S. pulling out of the Iranian Nuclear Treaty and to the provocative U.S. decision to move its Embassy from Tel Aviv to Jerusalem.[67] The second leading donor is Tom Steyer, a billionaire liberal activist who has spent the last few years and millions of dollars trying to get President Trump impeached and removed from office.

Money in federal elections was first regulated by the Tillman Act of 1907, banning corporations from contributing to federal campaigns. In his 1905 State of the Union Address, President Theodore Roosevelt said that "all contributions by corporations to any political committee or for any political purpose should be forbidden by law."[68] Decades later, and in response to the Watergate scandal, Congress enacted the Federal Election Campaign Act (1974), which further weakened the influence of wealthy donors by limiting the amount of money an individual may contribute to any federal campaign to $1,000 (now $2,700). Because it was believed contribution limits were hampering the ability of political parties to engage in party-building measures, Congress attempted to strengthen parties in the Federal Election Campaign Act (1979) by creating a two-tiered campaign finance system for "hard money" (i.e., money given directly to candidates) and "soft money" (i.e., money given to political parties). Contribution limits remained in place for funds donated directly to candidates (i.e., hard money) but were removed for contributions to political parties (i.e., soft money). Soft money strengthened political parties, allowing them to raise and spend unlimited amounts of money, including spending party funds to run political advertisements that benefited political candidates. This strengthened the role of party leaders to recruit and help elect mainstream party nominees. However, Congress later banned soft money to political parties in the Bipartisan Campaign Reform Act (2002), better known as the McCain-Feingold Act. Critics claimed that soft money was being used as a loophole for big money donors, in that donations that were supposed to be used for party-building efforts were instead finding their way to political campaigns.[69] But McCain-Feingold had its own loophole that "replaced one problem with another," in that while it prohibited donors from giving millions of dollars to political parties, it did nothing to regulate contributions to other tax-exempt organizations.[70] Big money donors stopped giving millions to political parties and instead gave millions to advocacy groups such as 527 groups, which raise funds for political activities, or 501(c)(3) tax-exempt organizations that are supposed to advocate for charitable or educational causes.[71]

In 2010, two federal court rulings provided the legal foundation for supercharging PACs into super PACs. The U.S. Supreme Court in Citizens United overturned the 100-year-old ban on corporate political spending that had been in effect since the Tillman Act of 1907. The Court in Citizens United also ruled that it was a violation of free speech to limit contributions to political organizations that do not coordinate with political campaigns. And in the *SpeechNow* case, another federal court ruled that it was unconstitutional to limit how much these same organizations are permitted to receive.[72] These two cases provided the one-two punch that radically changed campaign finance, because now there are no limits on how much individuals are permitted to give (i.e., Citizens United) and no limits on how much organizations are permitted to receive (i.e., SpeechNow) from any particular donor. Supreme Court Justice Ruth Bader Ginsburg once said, "If there was one decision I would overrule, it would be Citizens United. I think the notion that we have all the democracy that money can buy strays so far from what our democracy is supposed to be."[73] The difference between traditional PACs and super PACs is that conventional PACs are only allowed to receive a maximum of $5,000 from individual donors, whereas super PACs may receive unlimited funding. Freed from contribution limits, super PACs quickly overtook political parties as top spenders in political campaigns. Super PACs are playing the traditional role of political parties in campaign fundraising and are now referred by some as "shadow parties."[74]

Helping to fuel political populism is the fact that more than half of the political money spent by outside organizations (i.e., $539 million) in the 2018 election cycle did not disclose its donors.[75] The term "dark money" is used to describe political spending by unknown sources. Dark money is dangerous to democracy because it allows foreign countries or groups to contribute money to influence U.S. elections, which is a violation of federal law. Because 501(c)(4) tax-exempt social welfare organizations such as the National Rifle Association or the Sierra Club are not required to disclose their donors, these organizations can receive foreign contributions and then contribute those same funds to political organizations, without anyone knowing the original source of the funding. The National Rifle Association, for example, contributed $419 million in the 2016 election, and as a tax exempt 501(c)(3) organization, they were not required to disclose the identities of donors.

On February 16, 2018, thirteen individual Russians and three Russian organizations were indicted in the United States for interfering in the 2016 U.S. presidential election. The indictment alleges that Russia sought to "sow discord in the U.S. political system, including the 2016 presidential election . . . and made various expenditures to carry out these activities, including buying political advertisements on social media in the names of U.S. persons or entities."[76] Facebook alone received $350 million in political advertising during the 2018 midterm congressional election. Dark money has been increasingly used in digital advertising, in part because internet political advertising has become the "wild west" of campaign financing, mostly because it is exceedingly difficult to regulate.[77] A Kremlin-linked group called the Internet Research Agency exploited populist and racial divisions during the 2016 presidential election by "weaponizing" racially polarizing advertisements, including one featuring Beyoncé who microtargeted nonwhite groups, urging them to boycott voting in the election.[78] Another report issued by the British Parliament highlights how political cleavages associated with populist movements are exploited in internet advertising through a "relentless targeting of hyperpartisan views, which plays to the fears and prejudices of people, in order to influence their voting plans and their behavior."[79]

CONCLUSION

The number of populist leaders across the globe has more than doubled over the past twenty years.[80] Populism is not only flourishing in the United States, but also in countries like Venezuela, Mexico, Italy, Hungary, the United Kingdom, India, and in almost every country across the globe. Populism at the grassroots level is healthy for democracies in that it helps to fortify the social contract between the government and the governed. However, populist leaders can be dangerous for democracies because they have a tendency to use divisive rhetoric that accentuates differences rather than creating unity through the promotion of shared social values. And populism is already having a particularly negative effect on young people. One recent study shows that young Americans are becoming particularly disillusioned about the importance of democracy. Today, only one-third of millennials believe that the promotion of civil rights is vital to American society, and a quarter of millennials no longer believe free elections are essential. The breakdown of shared social values, such as free speech and freedom of the press, and the emergence of ethnic political tribalism in the United States, should be viewed as warning signs toward a potential slide into authoritarianism. This chapter argues these dangerous political trends have been fueled in part by the weakening of the political party's role in selecting presidential nominees and in the funding of federal campaigns.

DISCUSSION QUESTIONS

1. Have political differences caused a strain in any of your relationships with family or friends?
2. Do you favor direct democratic systems of government or representative systems of government and why?
3. What is the difference between left-wing populism and right-wing populism?
4. Which social identities are important to you (e.g., race, ethnicity, religion, sexual orientation) and how does that help shape your view of politics?
5. Are political parties good or bad for American democracy?
6. Should party elites play a role in selecting party nominees in the presidential selection process?
7. Should individuals be permitted to contribute unlimited amounts of money to political campaigns or should there be limits on how much individuals may contribute?

NOTES

1. Marc Hetherington and Jonathan Weiler. *Prius or Pickup?: How the Answers to Four Simple Questions Explain America's Great Divide* (Boston, MA: Houghton Mifflin Harcourt, 2018).
2. Pew Research Center. *Partisan Antipathy is More Intense, More Personal,* October 10, 2019. https://www.people-press.org/2019/10/10/partisan-antipathy-more -intense-more-personal/.
3. Matt McGrath. "Trump Election Shortens U.S. Thanksgiving Family Dinners." *BBC News.* https://www.bbc.com/news/science-environment-44320026.
4. Wakefield Research. *Till Trump Do Us Part: The President's Effect on U.S. Marriages,* February 13, 2018. https://www.wakefieldresearch.com/blog/2017/05/10/ new-wakefield-research-study-trump-effect-american-relationships.
5. Donald Trump. "Full Text: Donald Trump Announces a Presidential Bid." *The Washington Post,* June 16, 2015. https://www.washingtonpost.com/news/post-poli tics/wp/2015/06/16/full-text-donald-trump-announces-a-presidential-bid/.
6. Cas Mudde. "The Populist Zeitgeist." *Government and Opposition,* Vol. 39, No. 4 (2004): 541–563.
7. Jan-Werner Muller. *What is Populism?* (Philadelphia, PA: University of Pennsylvania Press, 2016), 21.
8. Jan-Werner Muller. "Donald Trump's Use of the Term 'The People' is a Warning Sign." *The Guardian,* January 24, 2017.
9. Ibid.
10. Ivan Kasten. "The Populist Moment." *Eurozine,* September 18, 2007. https:// www.eurozine.com/the-populist-moment/.

11. Ibid.

12. Institute on Taxation and Economic Policy. *The U.S. Needs a Wealth Tax*, January 23, 2019. https://itep.org/the-u-s-needs-a-federal-wealth-tax/.

13. Edward Helmore. "Elizabeth Warren Rips into Billionaires who Oppose Wealth Tax in Scathing Ad." *The Guardian*, November 14, 2019. https://www.theguardian.com/us-news/2019/nov/14/elizabeth-warren-wealth-tax-campaign-ad-billionaires.

14. Don Gonyea. "Majority of White Americans Say they Believe Whites Face Discrimination." *National Public Radio*, October 24, 2017. https://www.npr.org/2017/10/24/559604836/majority-of-white-americans-think-theyre-discriminated-against.

15. Ashley Jardina. *White Identity Politics* (Cambridge: Cambridge University Press, 2019).

16. Ibid.

17. William Frey. *The US Will Become 'Minority White' in 2045, Census Projects.* Brookings Institute, March 14, 2018. https://www.brookings.edu/blog/the-avenue/2018/03/14/the-us-will-become-minority-white-in-2045-census-projects/.

18. Amy Chua. *Political Tribes: Group Instinct and the Fate of Nations* (New York, NY: Random House Large Print, 2018).

19. John Adams. *Letter from John Adams to John Taylor*, December 17, 1814. https://founders.archives.gov/documents/Adams/99-02-02-6371.

20. Plato. *The Republic, Chapter VIII.* http://classics.mit.edu/Plato/republic.9.viii.html.

21. Jennifer Tolbert Roberts. *Athens of Trial: The Antidemocratic Tradition in Western Thought* (Princeton, NJ: Princeton University Press, 1997), 80.

22. James Madison. *Federalist 10*, 1787. https://billofrightsinstitute.org/founding-documents/primary-source-documents/the-federalist-papers/federalist-papers-no-10/.

23. Josiah Ober, Kurt A. Raaflaub, and Robert Wallace. *Origins of Democracy in Ancient Greece* (Berkeley, CA: University of California Press, 2004), 4.

24. Ibid.

25. Milan Vaishnav and Jamie Hintson. *The World's Largest Election, Explained.* Carnegie Endowment for International Peace. https://carnegieendowment.org/publications/interactive/india-elects-2019.

26. Edmund Burke. In *Selected Writing and Speeches on America*, edited by Thomas H. D. Mahoney (Indianapolis, IN: Bobbs-Merrill Company, Incorporated, a subsidiary of Howard W. Sams & Company, Incorporated Publishers, 1964), 106.

27. Benjamin L. Carp. *Defiance of The Patriots: The Boston Tea Party and the Making of America* (New Haven, CT: Yale University Press, 2010).

28. Donald S. Lutz. "The Articles of Confederation as the Background to the Federal Republic." *Publius: The Journal of Federalism*, Vol. 20, No. 1 (Winter 1990): 55–70.

29. Charles A. Beard. "Framing the Constitution." In *American Government: Readings and Cases*, edited by Peter Woll, 11th edition (New York, NY: Harper Collins, 1993).

30. G. A. Phelps. "George Washington and the Paradox of Party." *Presidential Studies Quarterly*, Vol. 19, No. 4 (Fall 1989): 733–745.

31. Joseph Parker Warren. "The Confederation and the Shays' Rebellion." *The American Historical Review*, Vol. 11, No. 1 (October 1905): 67.

32. Ibid.

33. George Washington. *Letter to Richard Lee, October 1786*. https://founders.arc hives.gov/documents/Washington/04-04-02-0286.

34. James Madison and Alexander Hamilton. *Federalist 51*. https://billofrights institute.org/founding-documents/primary-source-documents/the-federalist-papers/f ederalist-papers-no-51/.

35. James Madison. *Federalist 47*. https://avalon.law.yale.edu/18th_century/fed4 7.asp.

36. Madison and Hamilton, *Federalist 51*.

37. See Arthur Schlesinger. *The Imperial Presidency* (Boston, MA: Houghton Mifflin, 1973). Also Thomas E. Mann and Norman Ornstein. *The Broken Branch: How Congress is Failing America and How to get it Back on Track* (New York, NY: Oxford University Press, 2008).

38. Madison and Hamilton, *Federalist 51*.

39. Alexander Hamilton, et al. *The Federalist Papers*. https://books.google.com/ books?hl=en&lr=&id=xWhLIXWKh-0C&oi=fnd&pg=PR7&dq=The+Federalist+P apers&ots=K-gb-Iwgem&sig=2y7VyJ2yhNr7P5F_utute3tyaEQ#v=onepage&q=The %20Federalist%20Papers&f=false, IX.

40. The first quote is sometimes attributed to Benjamin Franklin, but is not found in any of his writings. The second quote is sometimes attributed to Thomas Jefferson, but has not been located in any of his writings. The authors of both of these quotes are of unknown origins.

41. Madison, *Federalist 10*.

42. Hugh Heclo. "Issue Networks and the Executive Establishment." In *The New American Political System* (Washington, DC: American Enterprise Institute for Public Policy Research, 1978), 87–124.

43. Ibid.

44. Craig Volden and Alan E. Wiseman. *Legislative Effectiveness in the United States Congress: The Lawmakers* (Cambridge: Cambridge University Press, 2014).

45. Ibid.

46. Ibid.

47. Jill Lepore. "Rock, Paper, Scissors: How We Used to Vote." *The New Yorker*, October 6, 2008.

48. James Schouler. "Evolution of the American Voter." *The American Historical Review*, Vol. 2, No. 4 (July 1897): 665–674.

49. Alexander Keyssar. *The Right to Vote: The Contested History of Democracy in the United States* (New York, NY: Basic Books, 2000).

50. John Adams. *Letter from John Adams to James Sullivan, 1776*. https://founder s.archives.gov/documents/Adams/06-04-02-0091.

51. Jonathan Rauch. "How American Politics Went Insane." *The Atlantic*, July/ August 2016.

52. John Godfrey Saxe. "Quote Comparing Lawmaking to Sausages is thought to First Appear." *Daily Cleveland Herald*, March 29, 1869.

53. Noble Cunningham, Jr. *The Jeffersonian Republicans: The Formation of Party Organization, 1789–1801* (Chapel Hill, NC: University of North Carolina Press, for Institute of Early American Culture, 1958).

54. Rhodes Cook. *The Presidential Nomination Process* (Lanham, MD: Rowman & Littlefield Publishers, 2004), 12.

55. William G. Morgan. "The Origin and Development of the Congressional Nominating Caucus." *Proceedings of the American Philosophical Society*, Vol. 113, No. 2 (April 1969): 184–196.

56. Cook, *The Presidential Nomination*, 14.

57. William G. Morgan. "John Quincy Adams Versus Andrew Jackson: Their Biographers and the 'Corrupt Bargain' Charge." *Tennessee Historical Quarterly*, Vol. 26, No. 1 (1967): 45.

58. V. O. Key Jr. *Politics, Parties & Pressure Groups* (New York City, NY: Thomas Y. Cromwell Company, 1964), 398.

59. Cook, *The Presidential Nomination*, 18.

60. James R. Jones. "Why LBJ Bowed Out." *Los Angeles Times*, March 30, 2008.

61. Mark Kurlansky. *1968: The Year That Rocked the World* (New York, NY: Random House Trade Paperbacks, 2005).

62. Cook, *The Presidential Nomination*, 44.

63. Kyle Cheney. "Trump Kills GOP Autopsy." *Politico*, March 4, 2016. https://www.politico.com/story/2016/03/donald-trump-gop-party-reform-220222.

64. Jeb Bush. *Excerpt from Presidential Debate*. https://abcnews.go.com/Politics/jeb-bush-donald-trump-chaos-candidate-hed-chaos/story?id=35788736.

65. Ted Nace. *Gangs of America: The Rise of Corporate Power and the Disabling of Democracy* (San Francisco, CA: Berrett-Koehler Publishers, 2003), 147.

66. Michelle Lee and Ye Hee. "Eleven Donors have Plowed $1 Billion into Super PACs Since They Were Created." *The Washington Post*, October 26, 2018. https://www.washingtonpost.com/politics/eleven-donors-plowed-1-billion-into-super-pacs-since-2010/2018/10/26/31a07510-d70a-11e8-aeb7-ddcad4a0a54e_story.html.

67. Chris McGreal. "Sheldon Adelson: The Casino Mogul Driving Trump's Middle East Policy." *The Guardian*, June 8, 2018.

68. Theodore Roosevelt. *President Theodore Roosevelt's State of the Union Address on December 5, 1905*. https://www.infoplease.com/primary-sources/government/presidential-speeches/state-union-address-theodore-roosevelt-december-5-1905.

69. Kaitlin Washburn. "The Legacy and Impact of McCain-Feingold." *Open Secrets*, August 28, 2018. https://www.opensecrets.org/news/2018/08/the-legacy-of-mccain-feingold/.

70. Center for Public Integrity. *McCain-Feingold Fails to Solve Campaign Finance Problems*, 2014. https://publicintegrity.org/federal-politics/mccain-feingold-fails-to-solve-campaign-finance-problem/.

71. Open Secrets. *Types of Advocacy Groups*. https://www.opensecrets.org/527s/types.php.

72. Paige L. Whitaker. *Campaign Finance Law: An Analysis of Key Issues, Recent Developments, and Constitutional Considerations for Legislation.* Congressional Research Service, September 24, 2018, R45320.

73. Adam Lamparello and Cynthia Swann. *The United States Supreme Court's Assault on the Constitution, Democracy, and the Rule of Law* (UK: Routledge Publishing, 2017).

74. Ian Vandewalker. *The Rise of Shadow Parties.* The Brennan Center, October 22, 2018. https://www.brennancenter.org/our-work/analysis-opinion/rise-shadow-pa rties?utm_source=facebook&utm_medium=socialmedia.

75. Anna Maggolia. "State of Money in Politics: Billion-Dollar 'Dark Money' Spending is Just the Tip of the Iceberg." *Open Secrets*, February 21, 2019. https:/ /www.opensecrets.org/news/2019/02/somp3-billion-dollar-dark-money-tip-of-the-i ceberg/.

76. U.S. House of Representatives Permanent Select Committee on Intelligence. *Exposing Russia's Effort to Sow Discord Online: The Internet Research Agency and Advertisements.* https://intelligence.house.gov/social-media-content/.

77. Maggolia, "State of Money in Politics."

78. Natasha Singer. "'Weaponized Ad Technology': Facebook's Moneymaker gets a Critical Eye." *The New York Times*, August 16 2018. https://www.nytimes.com /2018/08/16/technology/facebook-microtargeting-advertising.html.

79. Jim Waterson. "Democracy at Risk Due to Fake News and Data Misuse." *The Guardian*, July 27, 2018. https://www.theguardian.com/technology/2018/jul/27/fake -news-inquiry-data-misuse-deomcracy-at-risk-mps-conclude.

80. Paul Lewis, Caelainn Barr, Sean Clarke, Antonio Voce, Cath Levett, and Pablo Gutierrez. "Revealed: The Rise and Rise of Populist Rhetoric." *The Guardian*, March 6, 2019.

FURTHER READING

Chua, Amy. *Political Tribes: Group Instinct and the Fate of Nations.* New York, NY: Random House Large Print, 2018.

Hetherington, Marc and Jonathan Weiler. *Prius or Pickup?: How the Answers to Four Simple Questions Explain America's Great Divide.* Boston, MA: Houghton Mifflin Harcourt, 2018.

Jardina, Ashley. *White Identity Politics.* Cambridge: Cambridge University Press, 2019.

Muller, Jan-Werner. *What is Populism?* Philadelphia, PA: University of Pennsylvania Press, 2016.

Wood, Gordon S. *The Creation of the American Republic, 1776–1787.* Chapel Hill, NC: The University of North Carolina Press, 2011.

Chapter 11

Comparisons of Measures of Democracy

Stephen J. Chapman

Throughout this book, readers have been offered a wide-ranging view of the historical and institutional characteristics of democracies across time and space. In this concluding chapter, we return to where we started with measuring democracy to compare four of the measures discussed in chapter 1, including Polity, Freedom House, V-Dem, and the EIU.[1] Essentially, the goal here is to understand how closely related some of the measures of democracy are as well as where they diverge. In addition, we analyze how these four measures operate within the distinct regions covered throughout this book as well as the four country case studies included. While many of the previous chapters have analyzed democracy in different settings, it is useful to keep in mind this chapter employs the most recently available measures and does not consider historical trends in democratic shifts.

COMPARING MEASURES OF DEMOCRACY

There are two reasons as to why these four measures were chosen for the current chapter. First, the four measures included have easily quantifiable indices to make comparisons somewhat straightforward. Second, the main unit of analysis is the country, again making for uniform comparison. The two measures not included in this chapter, but are discussed in chapter 1, are the Democracy Barometer and the World Values Survey. The Democracy Barometer dataset includes numerous and individualized facets of democracy. The data are broken up into nine distinct categories, with eighteen underlying variables. This, not surprisingly, makes comparisons difficult. Similarly, the World Values Survey stems from individual-level survey data. While there are certain indicators of measuring what individuals think (or do not think) equate to a democratic government, it is not a direct measure of democracy within a country. What remains are the four measures. Polity, Freedom House (aggregate scores), and EIU have a single measure of democracy that allows for assessing similarities. While the V-Dem measure is not condensed into a single measure, it does include five "high-level" indices of democracy that are easily transferred into a dataset along with the other measures.[2] These five indices include an Electoral Democracy index, focusing on electoral-related freedoms and suffrage; a Liberal Democracy index, comprising measures of rights for individuals and minorities in protection against the state or majority; a Participatory Democracy index, addressing electoral and non-electoral participation in the political process; a Deliberative Democracy index, including measures concerning the political process and the level of respect for preferences involved; and finally, the Egalitarian Democracy index, that emphasizes the equal protection and access for individuals and groups in society as well as the equality in the distribution of resources to all societal groups[2]. Now that there is a clear understanding of the measures included in this chapter, we can dive deeper into the differences and similarities of each.

To compare the four measures, it makes most sense to start with displaying summary statistics for each variable. Table 11.1 displays the minimum/maximum values, mean, median, and standard deviation of each index included.

A few things can be taken from the summary statistics above. First, aside from the V-Dem indices, the bounds of the measures are quite distinct from one another. This can be attributed to the measurement and aggregation strategies of each individual democracy indicator. However, it is always useful to know the upper and lower bounds of scores as it helps conceptualize the location of countries on different scales. Second, these figures allow a little bit more information about the distribution of each measure. For instance, the mean values show the general average of the scores throughout the world. However, by looking at the median values, it is noticeable that all the V-Dem indices have medians lower than the average. This is a useful lesson as to why looking at the average, which takes into account the very high values and very low values of democracy across the globe may not always be the best value to analyze. Meaning, 50 percent of countries within the dataset fall below these median values. This is valuable for those interested in understanding the breakdown of each indicator and how an individual country score compares relative to the distribution of all others. Finally, the standard deviation allows for understanding the spread of the distribution. By taking the mean value and standard deviation, we get an understanding of how much variation there is within the measure. Higher-standard deviations indicate more

Table 11.1 Summary Statistics of Democracy Indices

Variable	Minimum	Maximum	Mean	Median	Std. Deviation
Polity	−10	10	4.12	6	6.16
EIU	1.08	9.87	5.43	5.68	2.17
Freedom House	1	100	55.79	59	29.74
V-Dem-Electoral Democracy	.023	.910	.535	.550	.252
V-Dem-Liberal Democracy	.012	.874	.412	.380	.259
V-Dem-Participatory Democracy	.010	.792	.342	.338	.198
V-Dem-Deliberative Democracy	.013	.884	.416	.393	.250
V-Dem-Egalitarian Democracy	.033		.400	.353	.234

spread around the mean, lower-standard deviations have a tighter spread. This relates to the 68, 95, 99 rule in statistics. If we move one standard deviation in either direction, it will cover 68 percent of all observations, move two standard deviations to cover 95 percent of all observations, and three standard deviations to cover over 99 percent of observations. This has applications elsewhere in statistics, but it is always good to know a bit more about the underlying distribution of a variable. It is also important to note that it is unwise to compare standard deviations from dissimilar scales. For example, comparing the Polity standard deviation of 6.16 to the EIU standard deviation of 2.17 makes little sense. However, since the V-Dem indices are on the same scale, we can get an idea that the most spread from the mean can be found in the Liberal Democracy index, and the least in the Participatory Democracy index.

In order to make direct comparisons across the existing measures, we can employ a simple correlation matrix. This matrix allows for understanding the strength and statistical significance of correlations between each measure of democracy. The correlation coefficients range from −1 to 1, indicating either a positive or inverse relationship.[3] It is essential to observe that correlation matrices only compare variables in a pair-wise manner, that is, two at a time. Table 11.2 displays the correlation coefficients for Polity, Freedom House, EIU, and the five indices from the V-Dem dataset. To interpret this table, one only needs to look across each variable to view how strongly they correlate with all others; dashes represent when the same two variables are correlated with one another, which would equate to perfect correlation.

The first thing of note with respect to the correlation matrix is that all democracy indicators significantly correlate with one another. They are all strong positive relationships, indicating there is much overlap in the measures of democracy. This is a positive as it offers a validity check—if each variable is intended to measure the level of democracy within a country and all correlate highly, it is a strong indication that the variables are performing as expected. However, they do not perfectly correlate, meaning that while some measures include particular characteristics of democracy, other measures include alternative factors. This is not to say that one is better than the other, rather, it is to reinforce the idea that measuring democracy is a difficult task, and some scholars emphasize certain aspects more than others within their measures. This variation can also be seen as a positive in that it allows scholars to adopt the variable most appropriate for a given analysis.

Not surprisingly, all the V-Dem indices correlate with one another above the .9 level and in many cases the .95 level, indicating near perfect correlation. Given that they all stem from the same dataset and do have some overlap even within particular indices, it makes sense these would share the strongest correlations. Still, these slight variations allow for scholars to highlight

Table 11.2 Correlations of Measures

Variable	Polity	EIU	Freedom House	E.D.	L.D.	P.D.	D.D.	E.D.
Polity	–	.810**	.855**	.866**	.812**	.844**	.803**	.747**
EIU	.810**	–	.952**	.900**	.918**	.908**	.896**	.886**
Freedom House	.855**	.952**	–	.950**	.946**	.940**	.926**	.919**
V-Dem Electoral Democracy	.866**	.900**	.950**	–	.973**	.970**	.965**	.939**
V-Dem Liberal Democracy	.812**	.918**	.946**	.973**	–	.970**	.975**	.966**
V-Dem Participatory Democracy	.844**	.908**	.940**	.970**	.970**	–	.957**	.943**
V-Dem Deliberative Democracy	.803**	.896**	.926**	.965**	.975**	.957**	–	.958**
V-Dem Egalitarian Democracy	.747**	.886**	.919**	.939**	.966**	.943**	.958**	–

$** = p < .01$

different factors central to the focus of their study. Aside from this, they do share strong relationships with other measures of democracy, especially the Freedom House measure.

Interestingly, the Polity variable shares the weakest correlations with all other measures of democracy. As Polity is one of the most frequently used variables in analyses related to democracy, this comes as somewhat of a surprise. It shares its highest correlation, .866, with the V-Dem Electoral Democracy Index, followed closely behind with Freedom House. It holds the weakest correlation with the V-Dem Egalitarian Democracy index, signaling these two measures are focusing on significantly different underlying factors. One could envision this as a negative in that one of the major indicators of democracy does not necessary align with other measures. However, one could also view this as a positive, noting that the Polity measure is the most unique view of democracy throughout the world relative to the other variables under consideration.

The EIU measure correlates strongly with all measures, but particularly with the Freedom House measure along with many of the V-Dem indices. This indicates that many of the factors that undergird the EIU measure are also captured in other measures. However, it is useful to understand that while these correlate at high levels, it may not be the exact same indicator that each measure is quantifying. It is also possible that different factors, such as individual electoral rules or level of participation in government by individuals, are picking up the same underlying outcomes. In the social sciences, these can be called proxy measures. They are not directly measuring something like the concept of "freedom" or "democracy," but there are real-world indicators that are nearly, if not perfectly, aligned with the same concepts.

With respect to the Freedom House aggregate measure, it shares the most consistent strength in correlation with all other democracy variables. It has one of the highest correlations with Polity at .855, only second to the V-Dem Electoral Democracy indicator. Aside from this, it shares correlations of above .9 with the EIU and all V-Dem measures. Again, this does not necessarily mean that each measure is taking into account the exact same underlying factors, but that they are including factors that are measuring the same types of outcomes.

Now that we have a clear view of each democracy indicator individually as well as how they compare with one another, we can move to discussing how these measures vary along the regional lines discussed throughout the previous chapters, including Sub-Saharan Africa, South Asia, East Asia and Pacific, Eastern Europe, Western Europe, Latin America, and Middle East and North Africa. This offers a view not only of how each measure performs individually, but also how each captures democracy across the globe.

DEMOCRATIC INDICATORS
THROUGHOUT WORLD REGIONS

Prior to delving into the many regions covered in the previous chapters, readers may want to review Table 11.1 of the current chapter to remind themselves of the upper and lower bounds of each measure. This will help conceptualize the variation across measures within each of the nine regions that will be the focal point of the remainder of the chapter. Also, there exists some overlap across some regions. For example, Afghanistan would be considered a part of both Eurasia and South Asia. Furthermore, while this chapter covers each region presented in the book, there will be some variations. For example, the analysis does not include a specific subcategory for Eurasia as the region spans over ninety countries, many of which that overlap with other regions that are discussed. In addition, I create a separate section that splits North America proper. I briefly discuss the differences between the United States and Canada with respect to democratic performance, then I include each country south of the United States in the Latin America category. My hope is these decisions create an intuitive way to compare and contrast across regions of the world.

One additional note is that while many of these variables capture the stringency of institutional arrangements as well as the rights guaranteed to citizens, they are not able to fluctuate with recent or ongoing political events. These measures take a heightened level of effort to compute and publish across all countries, so there is a natural lag to the democracy indicators. As we progress through the regions of the world, keep in mind that these measures will not reflect many recent changes in the political and cultural scene of a country.

Sub-Saharan Africa

The region of Sub-Saharan Africa is one that produces a wide variation with respect to the strength of democracy. Colonization, decolonization, and civil conflict related to religious, ethnic, and linguistic divisions all play a role in understanding this variation. The World Bank labels forty-three countries as being members of the Sub-Saharan region[4]. Table 11.3 displays the mean, median, minimum, and maximum values of each measure throughout Sub-Saharan Africa. Note that there are some measures that contain missing values that may slightly skew the figures. This is a common hurdle concerning data collection in less-developed regions of the world.

Prior to discussing specific indicators, there are a few things of interest by viewing the region-specific summary statistics. First, it is somewhat straightforward to see that across all indicators, the region has relatively

Table 11.3   Democracy Indicators within Sub-Saharan Africa

Variable	Mean	Median	Minimum	Maximum
Polity	2.95	5	−9	10
EIU	4.30	3.93	1.50	8.22
Freedom House	42.54	45.50	2	90
V-Dem-Electoral Democracy	.457	.463	.085	.840
V-Dem-Liberal Democracy	.314	.287	.013	.714
V-Dem-Participatory Democracy	.263	.260	.010	.542
V-Dem-Deliberative Democracy	.332	.318	.025	.736
V-Dem-Egalitarian Democracy	.306	.296	.034	.655

low democracy scores. Aside from the V-Dem Electoral Democracy Index, the mean levels of each indicator are on the lower half of their respective scales. Second, by taking a look at the median, minimum, and maximum values, we notice the variation between countries. On some of the indicators (Polity, Freedom House, and V-Dem Electoral Democracy), the median values are higher than the mean, indicating that outliers are driving the lower mean scores. Moreover, there is large disparity between the minimum and maximum values, indicating again that there is stark variation in strength of democracy throughout the region.

This variation becomes clearer when discussing specific indicators. In addition, we can begin to view the similarities and differences of each indicator by looking at the margins. For instance, the lowest score on the Polity scale within the region is −9, which can be attributed to Swaziland. Conversely, the highest score of 10, the maximum value on the Polity scale, is found in Mauritius. However, the EIU indicator labels Chad as the lowest performing country with a score of 1.5. The highest score, 8.22, is also in Mauritius, but does not reach the maximum score on the EIU scale. These differences continue in the Freedom House indicator, with South Sudan holding a score of 2 and Cape Verde holding the top score with a 90. Moving to the V-Dem indicators, there remains some level of deviation across indicators. For each index, aside from the Egalitarian Democracy index where South Sudan holds the lowest score, Eritrea holds the regional low score for the other four V-Dem indices. Furthermore, for all of the V-Dem indicators, Mauritius holds the top score. What this shows is that while these democracy indicators perform similarly in general, when dissecting individual measures, there is room to understand the nuance found in each measure, as they are picking up different low and high points. This is to be expected given the variation in measurement strategies across all democracy indicators as well as the distinct variation throughout Sub-Saharan Africa. This will be a continuing theme in many of the other regions, including our next region of interest, South Asia.

South Asia

South Asia is much smaller in terms of numbers of countries relative to Sub-Saharan Africa with only eight countries.[5] However, many of the indices included do not have data for Maldives, which again is a common occurrence in the data collection process but should be noted as Maldives tends to have high corruption,[6] indicating a relatively lower respect for democracy.

When comparing the summary statistics for South Asia with Sub-Saharan Africa, a few things stand out. First, on every indicator, both the mean levels and median values are higher in South Asia. Looking at Table 11.4, the minimum values are all higher in South Asia. Taken together, we can surmise that in general, South Asia is relatively more democratic relative to Sub-Saharan Africa. However, there are limitations to this view. First, keep in mind that the Maldives are not included in this analysis, which could slightly skew the numbers. Second, the maximum values are actually higher in Sub-Saharan Africa, indicating that at least one country in Sub-Saharan Africa is more democratic than any country in South Asia.

This variation shows the potential for outliers to drive these differences. Within the seven countries that remain, two can be considered significantly different from the others. Both Afghanistan and Bangladesh take up the lowest scores on each measure of democracy. Afghanistan is the lowest on the Polity, EIU, Freedom House, the V-Dem Participatory Democracy index, and the V-Dem Egalitarian Democracy index. Bangladesh holds the lowest scores on both the V-Dem Deliberative Democracy and Liberal Democracy indices.

There are additional interesting comparisons to be made within the region of South Asia. For instance, aside from the two outliers highlighted above,

Table 11.4 Democracy Indicators within South Asia

Variable	Mean	Median	Minimum	Maximum
Polity	4.71	6	−1	9
EIU	5.17	5.18	2.55	7.23
Freedom House	50.85	55	26	77
V-Dem-Electoral Democracy	.513	.527	.343	.669
V-Dem-Liberal Democracy	.360	.394	.137	.506
V-Dem-Participatory Democracy	.310	.314	.156	.422
V-Dem-Deliberative Democracy	.379	.403	.185	.534
V-Dem-Egalitarian Democracy	.311	.330	.147	.528

every remaining country does not fall below a five on the Polity scale, indicating less autocratic governments. However, there are interesting variations dependent upon the indicator chosen. Bhutan holds scores below median values on the Polity and EIU indices as well as being directly at the median value for Freedom House. However, in each of the V-Dem indices, Bhutan scores above the median value. Conversely, India holds the highest score out of any country in the region on the Polity, EIU, and Freedom House indices, but is only at the median position on each of the V-Dem indices. This is also similar to Nepal, which holds median scores for Polity, EIU, and Freedom House, but is below the median in all V-Dem indices. Pakistan and Sri Lanka are two interesting cases within the South Asian region. Pakistan scores above the median on Polity, yet is below the median on all other indices. Sri Lanka, however, holds a median score on the Polity and Freedom House scores, but is above the median on the EIU and all V-Dem indices. This again suggests that some of these measures are picking up on different underlying factors, hence this variation. It also reinforces the need to be wary of which democracy indicator is ideal for a given analysis. We will continue to see this variation in other regions of the world.

East Asia and Pacific

While chapter 4 focuses on China, it would be useful to extend the current analysis to the entire region. However, the issue of data availability again comes into play within the East Asia and Pacific region. The World Bank labels thirty-seven countries as being within the region;[7] however, many of these are tiny island states that are not included in many of the indices. We are left with twenty workable observations to analyze this region.[8] Also similar to other regions of the world, there are outliers on both sides of the continuum of autocratic to democratic. Table 11.5 displays the summary statistics for the region.

Both the means and medians are skewed downward because of some of the outliers included in this region. East Asia and Pacific nations have even larger disparities in democracy between minimum and maximum values than the Sub-Saharan Africa region. Much of this is driven by North Korea, which unsurprisingly holds the lowest position on all democracy indicators. However, North Korea is not the only country in the region that has issues maintaining a free and fair society. Other countries in the region score relatively low on all indicators, including Vietnam, China, Laos, Cambodia, Thailand, and Singapore. These countries hold scores at or below the median values on each democracy indicator. Conversely, the region also contains strong democracies. Three countries, Australia, Japan, and New Zealand, make up the most robust democracies. Australia and New Zealand

Table 11.5 Democracy Indicators within East Asia & Pacific

Variable	Mean	Median	Minimum	Maximum
Polity	3.05	6.5	−10	10
EIU	5.65	6.32	1.08	9.26
Freedom House	56.21	62	3	98
V-Dem-Electoral Democracy	.480	.481	.086	.878
V-Dem-Liberal Democracy	.373	.348	.012	.834
V-Dem-Participatory Democracy	.311	.266	.018	.705
V-Dem-Deliberative Democracy	.379	.373	.013	.804
V-Dem-Egalitarian Democracy	.359	.300	.091	.784

hold or share the top score on each indicator. Other relatively strong democracies in the region include Indonesia, South Korea, Myanmar, the Solomon Islands, and Timor Leste. This polarization is the dominant theme in the region, as there are few countries that are muddling in the middle between autocracy and democracy. This theme has been present in other regions already covered, but it is especially stark in East Asia and Pacific countries. It will be a continuous theme as we move through the remainder of world regions.

Eastern Europe

There is no clear definition of what constitutes Eastern Europe. However, the United Nations labels ten countries comprising the region.[9] To offer readers a more descriptive view of the region, I also include all countries to the east of the Baltic and Mediterranean Seas. This creates a dataset with twenty-three observations, many of which are solidly democratic, with a few outliers of note. Table 11.6 displays the summary statistics for Eastern Europe.

The first noticeable trait of the summary statistics of Eastern Europe is the generally high mean and median values on all measures of democracy. Sixteen of the twenty-three countries included are at a nine on the Polity scale and seven of those are at a ten, indicating a region where the norm is a strong democracy. This can be said for each democratic indicator. There are lower means in the V-Dem Participatory Democracy and Deliberative Democracy indicators, although these tend to be the lowest scores in other regions as well.

However, there are a few interesting outliers that should be covered prior to moving to the next region under consideration. First, two countries in the dataset, Russia and Ukraine, hold Polity scores of four, indicating a weak democracy or open autocracy. Russia holds the lowest regional score for Freedom House as well as the V-Dem Egalitarian Democracy index. Ukraine

Table 11.6 Democracy Indicators within Eastern Europe

Variable	Mean	Median	Minimum	Maximum
Polity	8	9	−7	10
EIU	6.45	6.63	3.13	9.03
Freedom House	72.86	80	20	100
V-Dem-Electoral Democracy	.641	.645	.270	.910
V-Dem-Liberal Democracy	.518	.509	.114	.842
V-Dem-Participatory Democracy	.437	.453	.118	.646
V-Dem-Deliberative Democracy	.483	.434	.092	.853
V-Dem-Egalitarian Democracy	.522	.507	.198	.831

is an interesting case as it holds a low score on Polity, it also holds a relatively higher Freedom House score of 62. Similarly, Ukraine holds a 5.69 on the EIU index, highlighting another instance where certain indicators cast different visions of democracy. Finally, Belarus is a clear outlier in the dataset. It holds the lowest score on the Polity and EIU indices as well as the V-Dem Electoral Democracy, Liberal Democracy, Participatory Democracy, and Deliberative Democracy indicators.

Taken together, the view of Eastern Europe is one where a large proportion of countries guarantee democratic liberties to their citizens, with only a few outliers that are less inclined to grant freedoms to the public. However, it is important to note that in recent years, there has been an increase in the number of far-right parties gaining power that may threaten this stability, especially in Hungary where far-right parties recently captured a combined 68 percent of the parliamentary vote.[10] Even with this potential threat, Eastern Europe is the first region covered where the modal outcome is a strong democracy, and aside from our next region, it is a region that holds some of the most robust democracies in the world.

Western Europe

Similar to Eastern Europe, there are not clear demarcations as to what constitutes Western Europe. The United Nations labels nine countries within the Western Europe region.[9] However, opposite to the approach adopted in Eastern Europe, I include all countries within Europe that are west of the Baltic and Mediterranean Seas. This allows for expansion of the analysis to fifteen countries. Table 11.7 displays the summary statistics for the region as a whole.

The first thing of note is the extraordinarily high means and medians for each democracy indicator. It is clear there is a culture of openness and freedom throughout the region, with the highest average levels on each indicator relative to all regions covered thus far.

Table 11.7 Democracy Indicators within Western Europe

Variable	Mean	Median	Minimum	Maximum
Polity	9.8	10	8	10
EIU	8.62	8.61	7.78	9.87
Freedom House	95.53	96	89	100
V-Dem-Electoral Democracy	.872	.879	.812	.910
V-Dem-Liberal Democracy	.808	.809	.739	.874
V-Dem-Participatory Democracy	.633	.632	.500	.792
V-Dem-Deliberative Democracy	.809	.810	.718	.884
V-Dem-Egalitarian Democracy	.791	.804	.679	.867

However, there are some interesting findings with respect to the minimum values on the indicators as multiple countries hold minimum values dependent on the index of interest. Belgium holds the lowest score on the Polity scale and EIU index. While still relatively high with a Polity score of eight and an EIU score of 7.78, it does indicate there are some problematic aspects within the institutional structure of Belgium that are picked up within these measures. Italy holds the lowest score on Freedom House, again indicating that varied measures produce varied results. Spain holds the lowest scores on three of the V-Dem indices, the Electoral Democracy, Deliberative Democracy, and Egalitarian Democracy indices. Austria is given the lowest score on the V-Dem Liberal Democracy index and Luxembourg holds the lowest position on the V-Dem Participatory Democracy index. This is important because while there has been some variation at the low and high ends of the indicators in other regions, it has not been as varied as it is in Western Europe.

However, Western Europe faces the same threats to democracy as Eastern Europe with the rise of far-right and nationalist parties. Most famous on the international scale is Marine Le Pen's National Rally Party (formerly the National Front), which captured 13 percent of recent parliamentary elections. However, other countries have seen such parties receive larger gains into the national legislature. For instance, Switzerland and Austria both have nationalist parties that have received 29 percent and 26 percent of the parliamentary vote, respectively.[10] Again, while Western Europe does face a potential regression in terms of democratic ideals, it still holds the strongest example of regional democracy in the world.

Latin America

The Latin American region comprises countries within North America, Central America, South America, and the Caribbean. As the region aligns more in cultural and historical similarities than simple geographic region, I believe this will be the most intuitive way to view the region. The dataset for this region includes twenty-three independent countries from the previously mentioned geographic regions. Similar to the Sub-Saharan Africa region, Latin America has a long history of colonization, civil strife, military coups, and other political events that cause general instability. However, there are some relatively open governments within the region. This is visible in the variation in the minimum and maximum values displayed in Table 11.8.

Delving deeper, there is clear variation in these figures across the region. Two countries stand out as the most open in the region, Uruguay and Costa Rica. Both of them hold the highest score on Polity, with Uruguay holding the highest position on the EIU, Freedom House, and V-Dem Participatory Democracy indices, while Costa Rica holding the highest position on the V-Dem Electoral Democracy, Liberal Democracy, Deliberative Democracy, and Egalitarian Democracy indices. Chile also holds high positions on each measure of democracy aside from the Participatory Democracy index, which is only slightly above the regional mean. In addition, there are other countries that possess relatively high scores, including Argentina, Panama, and Peru. All hold scores above the mean on each measure. Brazil also holds scores above the mean on each indicator, but it is crucial to know that this case offers an example of how these measures cannot adequately account for recent political events. Given the natural lag in producing these measures, it does not consider the election of Jair Messias Bolsonaro in 2018, a populist leader that could affect the long-term level of openness within the political system, similar to that of Donald J. Trump in the United States.

On the other end of the spectrum, not surprisingly, Cuba holds the lowest position on each democracy indicator as it operates on a one-party, communistic political system that guarantees few rights to the citizenry. Setting aside Cuba, Venezuela holds the lowest position on each indicator aside from the Egalitarian Democracy index, held by Nicaragua. Besides these extremes, there are many countries within the region, which are within the mid-points of each measure, indicating that for the most part, the region does not wholly guarantee freedoms nor possess adequate institutional arrangements to produce a stable political environment. One final note on the Latin American region is that it holds some significant differences between measures of democracy within the same country, indicating that there exists disagreement on the level of freedoms and strength of institutions in a given country. Guatemala and Paraguay offer good examples of this reality. Paraguay is scored a nine on the Polity scale, yet is below the mean levels of the Freedom House and all V-Dem indices. Guatemala is similar, holding an eight on the Polity scale, but is below the mean on the EIU, Freedom House, and Egalitarian Democracy indices. Remarkably, Guatemala scores relatively high on the remaining V-Dem indices, possessing scores above the mean on each.

Table 11.8   Democracy Indicators within Latin America

Variable	Mean	Median	Minimum	Maximum
Polity	6.34	7	−7	10
EIU	6.04	6.43	3.14	8.12
Freedom House	64.13	67	14	98
V-Dem-Electoral Democracy	.619	.650	.181	.887
V-Dem-Liberal Democracy	.451	.480	.084	.835
V-Dem-Participatory Democracy	.407	.429	.063	.719
V-Dem-Deliberative Democracy	.459	.472	.066	.830
V-Dem-Egalitarian Democracy	.400	.346	.175	.794

What we are left with is an interesting picture of the Latin American region. There exists wide variation with respect to institutional arrangements and freedoms to citizens, yet there are some countries that do create a relatively open society. This region also provided an example of how recent or ongoing fluctuations in the political environment are not captured by these measures. We complete our review of the world regions with one that is the least free and open, the Middle East and North Africa.

Middle East and North Africa

For much of the twentieth and twenty-first centuries, the Middle East and North Africa have been marred by international interventions, civil uprisings and war, as well as cultural and institutional barriers to openness. Not surprisingly, it is the least democratic region of the chapter. The World Bank labels twenty-one countries and territories within the region.[11] The dataset for the current chapter includes nineteen of these, as data are not available for Malta and the West Bank/Gaza. Table 11.9 provides the regional summary statistics.

The first characteristic of Table 11.9 is the astonishingly low mean and median values for each indicator of democracy relative to the other world regions. Therefore, the modal governmental structure within the region is far from free and open. Three countries hold the lowest score possible on the Polity scale: Bahrain, Qatar, and Saudi Arabia. Saudi Arabia also holds the lowest position on the V-Dem Electoral Democracy and Participatory Democracy indices. Syria possesses the lowest position on the EIU, Freedom House, and V-Dem Liberal Democracy indices. Finally, Yemen holds the lowest position on the Deliberative Democracy and Egalitarian Democracy indices. Other countries with generally low scores include the United Arab Emirates, Morocco, Oman, Kuwait, Jordan, Egypt, and Iran.

While many of the countries in the region hold low scores on the democracy indicators, there are a few bright spots worth mentioning. First, Tunisia

Table 11.9   Democracy Indicators within Middle East & North Africa

Variable	Mean	Median	Minimum	Maximum
Polity	−2.63	−4	−10	7
EIU	3.52	3.19	1.43	7.79
Freedom House	28.68	26	0	79
V-Dem-Electoral Democracy	.283	.267	.023	.763
V-Dem-Liberal Democracy	.202	.144	.033	.693
V-Dem-Participatory Democracy	.153	.110	.020	.432
V-Dem-Deliberative Democracy	.219	.188	.016	.704
V-Dem-Egalitarian Democracy	.217	.203	.033	.609

holds the highest score on the Polity scale as well as all V-Dem indices. The country went through a political upheaval during the Arab Spring (also called the Jasmine Revolution) in 2011, a series of political protests throughout the region calling for more political freedoms. While there has been difficulty transitioning to an open society, Tunisia serves as an example of the potential for countries in the region to shift to a more democratic form of government.

In addition to Tunisia, there are other countries that do produce a somewhat open society. Israel, holding the highest regional scores on the EIU and Freedom House indicators, is relatively open, which is not surprising given its Western orientation. However, the treatment and segregation of the Palestinian population within the borders of Israel as well as the occupied/disputed territories of East Jerusalem, the West Bank, Gaza Strip, and Golan Heights cannot be ignored when discussing the openness of Israel.

Iraq has also seen progress with respect to promoting a democratic form of government since the ousting of Saddam Hussein in 2003, possessing a six on the Polity scale and a score above the regional mean for the Electoral Democracy index. However, there is much work that remains for Iraq to be considered free and open as many of the other democracy indicators produce scores below the regional mean.

Finally, Lebanon scores above the regional mean on all democracy indicators. Lebanon serves as another example of how foreign intervention can contribute to internal strife. Furthermore, the Syrian Civil War has also affected internal stability within Lebanon. Aside from Turkey, Lebanon has taken on the most refugees fleeing the war. In addition to these factors, the general breakdown of Maronite Christians, Sunni Muslims, and Shia Muslims within the country and the power-sharing structure of the government tend to create political stagnation. For instance, it took nine months to form its most recent government in 2019 that at the time of writing this chapter, is on the brink of collapse. However, even with all the factors that affect the political environment within Lebanon, they still hold one of the most relatively open and free societies within the region.

Taken together, the Middle East and North Africa still struggles to create and maintain open societies that grant broad freedoms to all citizens and provide credible institutions for political outcomes. Having discussed the broad regions covered throughout the book, this chapter now offers a more concentrated view of the four countries that were included as case studies: India, China, Russia, and United States.

CASE STUDY COUNTRIES

The four case studies presented in previous chapters offer a way to view how democracy has worked (or not worked) within the borders of four world powers. Clearly, Table 11.10 shows a divergence between higher democratized countries, India and the United States., and less democratized countries, China and Russia. There are interesting themes that can be derived from the table. First, it is clear that China is the outlier in these cases as it holds the lowest scores on all measures. India has the highest score on Polity relative to the other countries, including the United States. However, the United States holds the highest score on every other measure included in the dataset. This is yet another instance of where different democracy measures are encapsulating slightly different aspects of democracy. Continuing with the comparisons of the United States and India, it seems they hold relatively similar scores on Polity and the EIU measure but begin to diverge with the Freedom House measures and separate more significantly in the V-Dem indicators. Aside from the Deliberative Democracy indicator, many of India's scores on the V-Dem measures are nearly half that of the United States, indicating these measures emphasize different facets of democracy within their measures.

Table 11.10 Democracy Indicators within Four World Powers

Variable	India	China	Russia	U.S.
Polity	9	−7	4	8
EIU	7.23	3.1	3.17	7.98
Freedom House	77	14	20	86
V-Dem-Electoral Democracy	.527	.090	.274	.822
V-Dem-Liberal Democracy	.394	.051	.116	.727
V-Dem-Participatory Democracy	.314	.044	.148	.582
V-Dem-Deliberative Democracy	.403	.116	.172	.563
V-Dem-Egalitarian Democracy	.330	.097	.198	.667

There are also some interesting differences between Russia and China. As stated previously, China holds the lowest score on Polity. However, Russia and China are somewhat similar on the EIU measure and only a six-point difference on the Freedom House score. The V-Dem scores for both countries are quite different, with Russia holding more than double the score of China on all measures aside from the Deliberative Democracy index.

This section has offered a more detailed view of the case study countries covered in previous chapters. Taken together, this chapter should allow students of democracy to understand how democracy varies across regions and four significant world powers.

In conclusion, the book as a whole provided a wide-ranging view of democracy. It began with a thorough examination of the underlying facets of democracy, allowing readers to understand the methodological strategies used to ascertain the extent of democracy in a country. From there, readers have enjoyed the opportunity to understand how democracy works across time and setting. The authors have analyzed democracy from a variety of scholarly approaches and perspectives in order to offer readers a comprehensive view of the concept. Finally, the current chapter offered an overarching view and breakdown of democracy across the world.

The expectation is that readers can walk away from the book with an extensive knowledge of the inner workings of democracy, factors that increase or decrease the extent of freedoms or legitimacy of institutions, as well as understanding of where democracy thrives and where democracy struggles to take hold. Furthermore, readers should be equipped to critically analyze the sometimes nebulous term of democracy. Adopting such a critical perspective is a fundamental quality of students and scholars. The hope is this book has assisted and motivated readers to do just that and, as warranted, to propel action toward protecting, strengthening, and celebrating democracy.

DISCUSSION QUESTIONS

1. Having read through this chapter, there is clear variation in the level of democracy around the globe. What are some factors that lead to this variation?
2. How can we view the variation in some of the measures of democracy within the same region? Why do you think some indicators give higher/lower scores in some cases? Can we think of this as a positive or a negative?
3. Given what you now know about democracy around the world, do you think there is a "better" way to measure it?

4. What does the future hold for the health of democracy? Given the rise of populism and right-wing party strength, does it indicate a downturn in democracy and freedoms?

NOTES

1. See chapter 1 for an overview of each measure.

2. Michael Coppedge, John Gerring, Carl Henrik Knutsen, Staffan I. Lindberg, Jan Teorell, et al., *V-Dem Codebook v9*. Varieties of Democracy (V-Dem) Project, 2019.

3. A positive relationship simply means two variables are moving the same direction. An inverse relationship means the variables are moving in the opposite direction.

4. *Sub-Saharan Africa*, The World Bank Data, 2019. https://data.worldbank.org/region/sub-saharan-africa.

5. *South Asia*, The World Bank Data, 2019. https://data.worldbank.org/region/south-asia.

6. *Corruption Perceptions Index*, Transparency International, 2018. https://www.transparency.org/cpi2018.

7. *East Asia & Pacific*, The World Bank Data, 2019. https://data.worldbank.org/region/east-asia-and-pacific.

8. In addition to the missing observations, both the Solomon Islands and Vietnam have a missing observation for the EIU and Freedom House indices, respectively.

9. *Methodology*, United Nations Statistics Division, 2019. https://unstats.un.org/unsd/methodology/m49/.

10. "Europe and Right-Wing Nationalism: A Country-by-Country Guide." *BBC News*, May 24, 2019. https://www.bbc.com/news/world-europe-36130006.

11. *Middle East & North Africa*, The World Bank Data, 2019. https://data.worldbank.org/region/middle-east-and-north-africa.

FURTHER READING

Coppedge, Michael. 2002. "Democracy and Dimensions: Comments on Munck and Verkuilen." *Comparative Political Studies*, 35(1): 35–39.

Munck, Gerardo L. & Jay Verkuilen. 2002. "Conceptualizing and Measuring Democracy: Evaluating Alternative Indices." *Comparative Political Studies*, 35(1): 5–34.

Skaaning, Svend-Erik. 2018. "Different Types of Data and the Validity of Democracy Measures." *Politics and Governance*, 6(1): 105–116.

Steiner, Nils D. 2016. "Comparing Freedom House Democracy Scores to Alternative Indices and Testing for Political Bias: Are US Allies Rated as More Democratic by Freedom House?" *Journal of Comparative Policy Analysis: Research and Practice*, 18(4): 329–349.

Epilogue

Saliba Sarsar

Democracy is in crisis around the world, appearing to be imperiled to varying degrees in many countries and most regions. While the absence of democracy is expected in authoritarian regimes, like the People's Republic of China (PRC), it is perplexing to find it weak or weakening in democratic settings, as in Europe and the United States. Perhaps democracy is more delicate and more vulnerable than previously thought. Unless we defend it with resoluteness and nurture it with resilience, it will wither and fade away.

As the contributing authors to this book completed their individual chapters in late 2019, the novel coronavirus (COVID-19) began spreading quickly from the city of Wuhan, China, to the rest of the world. This health catastrophe, the greatest challenge humanity has faced since World War II, has infected millions and killed hundreds of thousands. The loss of life, the lockdowns and resultant mental health issues, the subsequent socioeconomic problems, among others—all are testing our assumptions and what we have taken for granted for years and years, including the health of democracy.

In Sub-Saharan Africa, the coronavirus reached every country, with hotspots emerging especially in the South and West. Prevention and containment measures against its spread helped to keep the number of recoveries above that of fatalities. However, in Southern Africa, for example, "decades of government failures to effectively tackle endemic poverty and widening inequality, a lack of investment in public institutions, widespread corruption, flawed democratic systems, and impunity for rights abuses have eroded citizens' trust in governments and their ability to effectively respond to and mitigate the effects of a crisis such as COVID-19."[1]

In Central and Eastern Europe, several leaders in Hungary, Poland, Serbia, Montenegro, and elsewhere, have veered away from the principles of democracy.[2] When the pandemic hit Hungary, for instance, the parliament passed a controversial bill enabling Prime Minister Viktor Orbán to exercise broad emergency powers and rule by decree with no time limit. As Steven Feldstein argued, "Hungary became the first democracy to succumb to the coronavirus."[3]

In Western Europe, "[t]he pillars that were meant to hold the E.U.—the free movement of goods and people—crumpled, as borders went back up and panicked governments stockpiled medical supplies with little regard for their neighbors."[4] While citizens gave up some of their rights to fight the virus, the virus exposed several countries' lack of preparedness. It also revealed a lack of a common strategy to respond to the virus as well as to the external onslaught of disinformation, especially by China and Russia, whose governments exploited the emergency "to sow distrust, uncertainty, fear, and division across Europe."[5] This state of affairs has led Věra Jourová, vice president of the European Commission for Values and Transparency, to call for both watchfulness and a hands-on approach. "I always say that by killing the coronavirus, we should not also kill democracy and fundamental rights in Europe. We simply must not rely on democracy and a full system of fundamental rights automatically coming back. We have to be vigilant. We have to be proactive."[6]

In Latin America, while democratic governance had withstood major crises for a few decades, the pandemic tested governments' capabilities. Brazil, Chile, and Peru were among the worst hit. Brazil's President Jair Bolsonaro—with nationalist and populist views and with an antiscientific orientation—called the coronavirus a "little flu," and saw his country devastated by it. Moreover, some degrees of democratic retrenchment occurred. In Venezuela, authoritarian leader Nicolás Maduro resorted "to repression to enforce a quarantine."[7] In Argentina, while the government responded fast to the pandemic by imposing strict measures, the financial stability of the country worsened, leading to "economic contraction, runaway inflation, and a hard-currency squeeze."[8] It actually defaulted on its sovereign debt for the ninth time in its history amid the pandemic.

In the Middle East and North Africa, the pandemic reduced what was left of democracy and illuminated the stern face of authoritarianism. Severe measures that many leaders imposed included "executive overreach (even in Tunisia), ad hoc coronavirus task-forces, 'public [army] mobilization', states of emergency, lockdowns, and arrests."[9] The authoritarian, theocratic regime in Iran failed to act fast or responsibly. Both cynicism and ideology stood in the way.[10]

In India, the world's largest democracy, the pandemic gave national authorities the green light to force millions of citizens "to download the country's tracking technology if they want to keep their jobs or avoid reprisals."[11] In addition, accusations levied against Muslims blamed them for the pandemic.[12] Though these actions are disconcerting in themselves, they can be considered extensions of the Hindu nationalist agenda under Prime Minister Narendra Modi and his Bharatiya Janata Party (BJP).

In the PRC, the Chinese Communist Party, afraid to appear vulnerable, was sluggish in reporting on the virus, thus facilitating its quick spread. Its digital authoritarianism was enhanced to track and manage the virus. Though this approach worked to a certain degree, its success does not necessarily imply that authoritarian rule is superior to democracy or the answer to crises. "Some of the best performers in coronavirus are democracies—and some of the worst are authoritarian states."[13] Moreover, China's legislature, the National People's Congress, approved a national security law for Hong Kong that tightens control over this Special Administrative Region and facilitates the containment of antigovernment protests or democratic activity there.

In Russia, President Vladimir Putin wasted no time in taking advantage of the pandemic in order to augment his modern authoritarian rule and authority. For him, "Western liberal democracies are weak, globalism is fragile, and the Russian model of centralizing power in a strong leader is superior in times of crisis."[14] Ironically, instead of presenting a national response, he shifted the responsibility to regional authorities and "institutions that he himself dismantled over his decades-long rule."[15]

Last but not least, in the United States, there was a slow response to the pandemic. The Trump administration issued incomplete and inconsistent information about the necessary resources and timeline for fighting the disease and finding a cure. Like Putin, President Donald J. Trump shifted more responsibility to state governors in an effort to avoid blame. He criticized and even belittled those who disagreed with him, including the Congress, some federal agencies, and the media. Moreover, aside from slamming China for its handling of the coronavirus, he announced U.S. withdrawal from the World Health Organization (WHO). Although such actions enhanced his standing among his supporters, they neither communicated a positive expression of democracy and good governance nor represented the greater good for society. "To be strong in the face of foreign autocrats, the United States must be strong in its democracy at home."[16]

WHO chief Tedros Adhanom Ghebreyesus expressed concern over the response of governments to the pandemic, stating that "the level of political commitment does not match the threat level." He added further: "This is not a drill. This is not the time to give up. This is not a time for excuses. This is a time for pulling out all the stops. Countries have been planning for scenarios like this for decades. Now is the time to act on those plans . . . . This epidemic can be pushed back, but only with a collective, coordinated, and comprehensive approach that engages the entire machinery of government."[17]

This and similar approaches were pursued in several countries, including Taiwan, New Zealand, Germany, Iceland, Denmark, Norway, Finland, South Korea, Czech Republic, Vietnam, Greece, and Australia, where the fight against the coronavirus was more successful. Of note here is that women leaders headed the first seven countries on this list. Could it be that females are better prepared to address crises than males? While an answer to this question is far from easy, it is likely that men and women can succeed "if they are able to demonstrate a balance of strength and compassion—qualities that are easier said than done due to societal expectations placed on both genders."[18]

What is instructive about the behavior of authoritarian and nationalist populist leaders is that they often miss the mark, particularly when it comes to humane politics. Authoritarians, emphasizing strong central power and limited political freedoms, on the one hand, and populists, insisting on complete or increased state sovereignty and expressing antipathy toward pluralism, on the other, neither promote inclusive citizenship and equality nor efficiently and effectively practice responsible leadership to facilitate global coordination and collaboration. As Yuval Noah Harari writes, "Over the past few years, irresponsible politicians have deliberately undermined trust in science, in public authorities, and in international cooperation. As a result, we are now facing this crisis bereft of global leaders who can inspire, organize, and finance a coordinated global response."[19]

Contrary to authoritarians who disparage democracy and wish to break it down[20] and to populists who are "a real danger to democracy (and not just to 'liberalism'),"[21] democracy with all its shortcomings "is the most successful and most versatile political model humans have so far developed for dealing with the challenges of the modern world. While it might not be appropriate for every society in every stage of development, it has proven its worth in more societies and in more situations than any of its alternatives."[22]

As this and other pandemics and crises evolve, the fear is that democracy will continue to suffer, as will the world order of which democracies are a part. The necessity for democracies is to learn from their mistakes, to self-correct.[23] It is for them to be prepared to act expeditiously, competently, and effectually as well as to work cooperatively and collectively with others, including nondemocracies, in order to resolve critical problems related to disease, energy, climate, poverty, and so forth.

Equally urgent is the need for democracies to work in concert to stem the tide of authoritarianism and to advance human rights and humane politics around the world. Isolationism or disengagement from the world order *à la* populism is not the answer. The vacuum is usually filled by other great powers like China and Russia. "The danger we run by disengagement is that we enter a vicious cycle of withdrawal, authoritarian capture, and further distancing from the institution as its actions become more of an anathema to our interests."[24]

Maya Angelou once said, "Hope and fear cannot occupy the same space at the same time. Invite one to stay." While it is too early to tell, it can be said that the pandemic has become a marker distinguishing our past from our future. Let us learn from this tragic experience and move forward to dispel fear, invite hope, and strengthen democracy. That is our responsibility. Our collective wisdom, sustained action, diligence, and resilience will deliver us there.

NOTES

1. Tiseke Kasambala, *Heavy-Handed Pandemic Responses Could Fuel Unrest in Southern Africa*. Freedom House, May 11, 2020. https://freedomhouse.org/article/he avy-handed-pandemic-responses-could-fuel-unrest-southern-africa.

2. Zselyke Csaky, *Nations in Transit 2020: Dropping the Democratic Façade*. Freedom House, n.d. https://freedomhouse.org/report/nations-transit/2020/dropping -democratic-facade.

3. Steven Feldstein, "What Democracy Will Fall Next?" *Foreign Policy*, May 7, 2020. https://foreignpolicy.com/2020/05/07/democracy-pandemic-coronavirus-hu ngary-populism/.

4. Charlotte McDonald Gibson, "Europe in Crisis." *Time*, March 30, 2020, 24.

5. Judy Dempsey, *Europe's Missing Coronavirus Exit Strategy*. Carnegie Europe, April 14, 2020. https://carnegieeurope.eu/strategiceurope/81549.

6. Věra Jourová, in an interview with Sándor Zsíros of euronews, "Coronavirus: An Unprecedented Challenge to Democracy." *Euronews*, April 4, 2020. https ://www.euronews.com/2020/04/09/coronavirus-an-unprecedented-challenge-to-de mocracy.

7. Nicolás Saldías, "In Latin America, Coronavirus Threatens not Just Public Health, But Also Democracy." *The Washington Post*, April 16, 2020. https://ww w.washingtonpost.com/politics/2020/04/16/latin-america-coronavirus-threatens-not -just-public-health-also-democracy/.

8. Ryan Dube and Santiago Pérez, "Argentina Defaults on Sovereign Debt Amid Coronavirus Crisis." *The Wall Street Journal*, May 22, 2020. https://www.wsj.com/ articles/argentina-moves-closer-to-sovereign-debt-default-amid-coronavirus-crisis -11590160035.

9. Layla Saleh and Larbi Sadiki, "The Arab World between a Formidable Virus and a Repressive State." *openDemocracy*, April 6, 2020. https://www.opendemo cracy.net/en/north-africa-west-asia/arab-world-between-formidable-virus-and-repr essive-state/.

10. Maysam Behravesh, "The Untold Story of How Iran Botched the Coronavirus Pandemic." *Foreign Policy*, March 24, 2020. https://foreignpolicy.com/2020/03/24/ how-iran-botched-coronavirus-pandemic-response/.

11. Patrick Howell O'Neill, "India is Forcing People to Use its Covid App, Unlike Any Other Democracy." *MIT Technology Review*, May 7, 2020. https://www.tec hnologyreview.com/2020/05/07/1001360/india-aarogya-setu-covid-app-mandatory/.

12. Amy Slipowitz, *Why We Should Be Worried about India's Response to Coronavirus*. Freedom House, April 13, 2020. https://freedomhouse.org/article/why -we-should-be-worried-about-indias-response-coronavirus.

13. Zack Beauchamp, "The Myth of Authoritarian Coronavirus Supremacy." *Vox*, March 26, 2020. https://www.vox.com/2020/3/26/21184238/coronavirus-china-aut horitarian-system-democracy.

14. Ann M. Simmons, "Putin Exploits Coronavirus to Justify Centralized Russian Power." *The Wall Street Journal*, March 27, 2020. https://www.wsj.com/articles/p utin-exploits-coronavirus-to-justify-centralized-russian-power-11585306801.

15. Mike Smeltzer, *As Coronavirus Cases Surge Across Russia, Putin Retreats*. Freedom House, May 11, 2020. https://freedomhouse.org/article/coronavirus-cases -surge-across-russia-putin-retreats.

16. Brian Katulis and Trevor Sutton, *Don't Let the U.S. Response to the Coronavirus Crisis Do More Damage to Democracy*. Center for American Progress, April 6, 2020. https://www.americanprogress.org/issues/security/news/2020/04/06/ 482717/dont-let-u-s-response-coronavirus-crisis-damage-democracy/.

17. As quoted by Joshua Berlinger, *CNN*, March 6, 2020. https://www.cnn.com/ 2020/03/06/asia/coronavirus-covid-19-update-who-intl-hnk/index.html.

18. Austa Somvichian-Clausen, "Countries Led by Women Have Fared Better Against Coronavirus. Why?" *The Hill*, April 18, 2020. https://thehill.com/chang ing-america/respect/equality/493434-countries-led-by-women-have-fared-better-aga inst. See also, Anne North, "Are Women Leaders Better at Fighting Coronavirus? It's Complicated." *Vox*, May 21, 2020. https://www.vox.com/2020/5/21/21263766/c oronavirus-women-leaders-germany-new-zealand-taiwan-merkel.

19. Yuval Noah Harari, "Disease in a World Without a Leader." *Time*, March 30, 2020, 47.

20. Arch Puddington, *Special Report 2017 – Breaking Down Democracy: Goals, Strategies, and Methods of Modern Authoritarians*. Freedom House, n.d. https://fr eedomhouse.org/report/special-report/2017/breaking-down-democracy.

21. Jan-Werner Müller, *What is Populism* (Philadelphia, PA: University of Pennsylvania Press, 2016), 103.

22. Yuval Noah Harari, *21 Lessons for the 21st Century* (New York, NY: Spiegel & Grau, 2018), xviii–xix.

23. Roland Rich, *Democracy in Crisis: Why, Where, How to Respond* (Boulder, CO/London: Lynne Rienner Publishers, 2017), 211.

24. Andrew Wilson, as quoted in William McKenzie, Lindsay Lloyd, and Christopher Walsh, *Democracy Talks: COVID-19, Authoritarianism, and Democracy*. George W. Bush Presidential Center, April 14, 2020. https://www.bushcenter.org/pub lications/articles/2020/04/democracy-talks--covid-19--authoritarianism--and-demo cracy.

Index

About the Contributors

Dr. **Julius O. Adekunle** is a professor of African history at Monmouth University. He was educated in Nigeria and Canada. He is the author and editor of several books including *Culture and Customs of Rwanda* (Greenwood Press, 2007); editor of *Religion in Politics: Secularism and national Integration in Modern Nigeria* (Africa World Press, 2009); coeditor of *Democracy in Africa: Political Changes and Challenges* (Carolina Academic Press, 2012); and coeditor of *Converging Identities: Blackness in the Modern African Diaspora* (Carolina Academic Press, 2013). His research interests include culture, politics, religion, and leadership.

Dr. **Kenneth L. Campbell** is a professor of history at Monmouth University, where he has taught Western Civilization in world perspective and a variety of upper-level and graduate courses in British and European history for over thirty years. He received his doctorate in British and European History from the University of Delaware. In addition to other administrative posts at Monmouth, he spent seven years as associate dean of the School of Humanities and Social Sciences and another seven as Chair of the Department of History and Anthropology. He has presented scholarly papers at numerous academic conferences and received the Monmouth University Distinguished Teacher Award in 1995. Dr. Campbell is the author of eight books, including *Western Civilization: A Global and Comparative Approach* (two vols.) (2012), *Ireland's History: Prehistory to the Present* (2014), and most recently, *A History of the British Isles: Prehistory to the Present* (2017).

Dr. **Stephen J. Chapman** is an associate professor of political science at Monmouth University. He received his Ph.D. from Binghamton University (SUNY). His research focuses on both state and local politics in the United

States as well as pedagogical analyses. While his expertise and research emphasize the American setting, he is trained in quantitative research methods and regularly teaches course on research design and methodology. Some of Dr. Chapman's publications include "Human Costs in Cleavage-Based Politics in the United States," appearing in the *Journal of Transdisciplinary Peace Praxis* (2019), "What's in a Website? E-government Scores and Municipal Characteristics," appearing in *Public Administration Quarterly* (2017), and his forthcoming article titled, "The Dark Side of Responsiveness: State-level Responsiveness to Climate Change," appearing in *The Forum*.

Dr. **Rekha Datta** is interim provost/senior vice president for academic affairs and professor of political science at Monmouth University. In 2017–2018, she was Senior Fulbright Scholar. She is author of *Contemporary India* (Routledge: 2017), *Beyond Realism: Human Security in India and Pakistan* (Lexington Books, Rowman Littlefield: 2008, 2010), *Why Alliances Endure: The U.S.-Pakistan Alliance, 1954-1971* (South Asian Publishers: 1994), and co-editor, with Judith Kornberg, *Women in Developing Countries: Assessing Strategies of Empowerment* (Lynne Rienner: 2002).

Dr. **Kevin L. Dooley** is an associate professor of political science at Monmouth University where he teaches courses in political theory, ethics in international relations, and comparative European politics. His research is focused on two main areas. While the first examines the role of globalization in the revival of certain Central and Eastern national minorities, the second studies the role that allegories have played in the development of political philosophy. Among his publications are *Politics Still Matters: Globalization, Governance, and the Revival of Regional Minorities* (2008) and *Allegories and Metaphors in Early Political Thought: From Plato to Machiavelli* (2018). He is coauthor of *Why Politics Matters: An Introduction to Political Science* (2013, 2015, 2020).

Justin M. Liu is a junior at Massachusetts Institute of Technology. Although he is majoring in biological engineering and loving the challenges of science research, he is also interested in studying humanities and the social sciences. He is fascinated by how science and technology affect the development of human society.

Dr. **Peter W. Liu** is a professor of criminal justice at Monmouth University. He teaches multiple courses at the undergraduate and graduate levels, including criminology; juvenile justice; research methods; senior seminar; crime control in Japan, China, and the United States; advanced data analysis; and comparative justice. His research interests focus on juvenile delinquency, comparative justice, issues in policing, and crime prevention. He has authored and coauthored three books and texts, and published a number of journal articles.

Sam Maynard is a DPhil candidate at the University of Oxford. His research specializes in political party adaptation in Latin America with a special focus on Argentina. He received his MA, with distinction, from Georgetown University in 2016. He is also a lecturer in political science at Monmouth University.

Dr. **Kenneth Mitchell** is a professor and Chair of the Department of Political Science and Sociology at Monmouth University. His publications include *Pesos or Plastic? Financial Inclusion, Taxation, and Development in South America* (Palgrave/MacMillan, 2019; co-written with Robert H. Scott), *State-Society Relations in Mexico* (Ashgate, 2001), "Will that be Cash or Credit? Payment Preferences and Rising VAT in Argentina," *Journal of Post Keynesian Economics* (2017), "Old Malbec in New Bottles, The Return of Neoliberalism in Argentina," *Monthly Review* (2017) (cowritten with Robert H. Scott), "Don't Cry for Argentina—It Is Not 2001 Again," *Challenge* (2014) (cowritten with Robert H. Scott), "Models of clientelism and policy change: The case of conditional cash transfer programs in Mexico and Brazil," *Bulletin of Latin American Research* (2011) (cowritten with Aaron Ansell), and "An institutional anomaly, longevity, and competition in the Dominican party system," *The Latin Americanist* (2010).

Dr. **Joseph Patten** is an associate professor and former Chair of the Department of Political Science and Sociology at Monmouth University. He earned his doctorate from West Virginia University. His specializations are in public policy; political campaigns at the national, state, and local levels; the United States Congress; the American Presidency; and media law. He serves as the adviser to Monmouth University's Debate Team and as the University Liaison to the Washington Center Internship Program. His primary research interests include the United States Congress and American Politics. He is coauthor of *Why Politics Matters: An Introduction to Political Science* (2013, 2015, 2020).

Dr. **Thomas S. Pearson**, former provost and vice president of academic affairs at Monmouth University, is professor of history at Monmouth and a specialist in modern Russian history. He is the author of *Russian Officialdom in Crisis: Autocracy and Local Self-Government, 1861–1900* (Cambridge University Press 1989/2004), coauthor (with Roxanne Easley and Mark Davis Kuss) of *Modern Russian History: The Search for National Identity* *and Global Power* (Cognella Academic Publishing, 2020), and numerous articles and book chapters on state-peasant relations, the role of the law and judicial institutions in pre-revolutionary Russia, the politics of Russia's leadership, and the development of civil society in Russia in the imperial, Soviet and post-Soviet eras. His current research focuses on the life and career of Count M.T. Loris-Melikov and the significance of his political reforms for the Russian empire and on the control of the Russian land captains over the peasant villages from 1890 to 1917.

Dr. **Saliba Sarsar** is a professor of political science at Monmouth University where he teaches courses on the Middle East and International Relations. He earned the BA in political science and history interdisciplinary, *summa cum laude*, from Monmouth College, and the doctoral degree in political science from Rutgers University. He is author of *Jerusalem: The Home in Our Hearts* (2018) and Peacebuilding in Palestinian-Israeli Relations (2020); coauthor of *Ideology, Values, and Technology in Political Life* (1994) and *World Politics: An Interdisciplinary Approach* (1995); editor of *Education for Leadership and Social Responsibility* (1996), *Palestine and the Quest for Peace* (2009), and *What Jerusalem Means to Us: Christian Perspectives and Reflections* (2018); and coeditor of *Patriarch Michel Sabbah—Faithful Witness: On Reconciliation and Peace in the Holy Land* (2009); *Principles and Pragmatism—Key Documents from the American Task Force on Palestine* (2006); and *Democracy in Africa: Political Changes and Challenges* (2012). He guest edited a special issue of the *International Journal of Politics, Culture, and Society* in 2004, focusing on Palestinian-Israeli relations, and a special issue of the *Journal of South Asian and Middle Eastern Studies* in 2020, focusing on Israel, Palestine, and the challenge of peace.